Sometimes One Bag of Potato Chips is just not Enough

Praise for

Potato Chips for the Soul: A Second Bag.

"Whimsical, humorous, prophetic, just a few of the adjectives that describe Cunningham's second swipe at turning his observations on life into lessons about life. Not only are his 103 chapters brief and readable, they're sermons minus the preaching."—*Lee Coppola, dean of St. Bonaventure's journalism school (1996 to 2011), Honoree into the Buffalo Broadcasters Association Hall of Fame*

"You know what they say about potato chips…it's hard to eat just one. The same goes for this book. More slices of life and learning make this collection another must-read for everyone."—*Brian Higgins, U.S. Representative for New York's 26th congressional district*

"Brendan has that unique ability to take the smallest detail, the seemingly most insignificant element and weave a tale that entertains and enlightens. His stories go down easily like a cold margarita on a sun-blasted day at the beach."—*Monish Bhattacharyya, Actor, Director, Fellow Bon Vivant*

"…. impressive with the gifted uniqueness of making a lasting Impression…A fantastically witty and meaningful book!"—*Gary Occhino, PGA Director of Instruction & Certified Performance Coach*

"…a pleasure to read. Sometimes tricky, sometimes cavalier, always with lots of truth showing a great love for writing and in one word: BRILLIANT."—*William F. Higgins, U.S. Marine, Realtor Associate of the Year (2015), Buffalo Niagara Association of Realtors*

. "…a fabulously entertaining read! Cheers to Brendan Cunningham on capturing real life moments with incredible humor, warmth and honesty. The diverse stories keep one eagerly anticipating the next and wishing there were more!"—**Catherine Burkhart, Board of Directors member American Repertory Theater of WNY (2018)**

"Brendan always reminds us, through stories and journeys, that life is simple and to enjoy each day, every song and all the gifts—*especially potato chips.*"—*Tom McDonnell, owner of Dog Ears Bookstore*

"An amazing storyteller shares his life's wisdom, brimming with humor through another bag of an addictive snack…. You might agree or passionately disagree, but you *will* crave for more."—*Nonna Gerikh, author of MAGIC IN MAUVE*

POTATO CHIPS FOR THE SOUL
A SECOND BAG

Brendan J. Cunningham

Moonshine Cove Publishing, LLC
Abbeville, South Carolina U.S.A.
FIRST MOONSHINE COVE EDITION May 2019

ISBN: 978-1-945181-58-0
Library of Congress Control Number: 2019939382
Copyright 2019 by Brendan J. Cunningham

Cover design and photograph by Moonshine Cove staff.

Dedication

To my Marilynn, who taught me to laugh all over again.

Acknowledgment

Once again, I have to thank Gene Robinson and all the folks over at Moonshine Cove Publishing for partnering up with this, the sequel to POTATO CHIPS FOR THE SOUL... in this, my SECOND BAG. Hopefully, you the reader will find a few more slices of life to enjoy after working in the salt mines all day. Perhaps this book will simply serve to rile you up even further. Either way, it's all good. Something to remember as you read through each of these super short stories is that many of them are more like snapshots. They pop up like photographs in time and capture a particular moment. You will note this particularly when I discuss Donald Trump and or Hillary Clinton. Time moves very quickly and the outcome of some of the events I have discussed needs to be appreciated in the moment I wrote about them.

I want to extend a special thanks, too, to my good friend Michael Breen for his assistance in some of the early edits. He helped to crystalize my thoughts and reminded me of the importance of the Oxford comma. My sweetheart, Marilynn DiGiulio additionally provided me with some special insights after I completed the first draft and afforded me serious moral support through the entire endeavor.

It would be remiss if I did not mention my former mother in law, Mrs. Jean Seibert, who passed at the ripe old age of 102 during the writing of this book. She inspired me with her observations and her special appreciation of one of the chips from my last volume which was entitled: *On Using the Good China.* More than any other story, I think that was the one that epitomized the totality of both of these books. As you read through this volume you will get a sense of what I am always conveying and that is, that it all counts, so make sure you do what you can do each day to make sure you make it count as well.

To those friends and colleagues who offered some early reviews, I would like to additionally extend a hearty thank you. They include: Lee Coppola, Dean of St. Bonaventure's School of Journalism (1996 to 2011), Honoree into the Buffalo Broadcaster's Association Hall of Fame. Thank you to Brian Higgins, U.S. Representative for New York's 26th congressional district, for not just recognizing a good book when he read it, but for being one of the best darned congressmen anywhere. You're the guy that truly knows how to get things done. To Monish Bhattacharyya, Actor, Director, and Fellow Bon Vivant, thanks for the kind words and reminding me what a ROUGH CROSSING really is (a play by Tom Stoppard we both starred in during much of the writing of this book.). To my golf coach and life guru, Gary Occhino, PGA Director of Instruction & Certified Performance Coach, you taught me more than you will ever know and some of it actually had to do with golf. Your inspiration was a big part of this book. To Catherine Burkhart, Actor, Director and former member of the Board of Directors of the American Repertory Theater, your kind words are duly noted .I would also like to extend a special "Sempre Fie" and thank you to William F. Higgins, U.S. Marine, Realtor Associate of the Year (2015), Buffalo Niagara Association of Realtors; your feedback offered me some special grounding which I think the book needed. And lastly, I wanted to give a special accolade to Tom McDonnell, owner of Dog Ears Bookstore, located in the heart of beautiful downtown South Buffalo, NY. His review was heartfelt. His support and his ability to supply me with a proper venue at book signings was and is significant, but more importantly his dedication to getting children and young people in general, to develop a special fondness and appreciation for reading, is beyond measure. For his efforts in this department alone, I can state for the record that this is truly the best way to "Make America Great Again."

Contents

Introduction

For those of you who were not able to read the original *Potato Chips for the Soul*, you guessed it; this is the sequel. Perhaps the word sequel is a bit lofty, so let's say it is a second book in the series of snippets, observations, rants, life suggestions, ramblings, and stories from my very sordid life as a "Shanachie." That's an Irish term for a *story teller* in general, and if I am anything at all, I am that. The balance of who I am and how I reveal myself through my writing was fully detailed in the first *Potato Chips* book, and if you read it, you would have learned that many of the stories you will read in this work as well the original, are derived from my life as a professional actor, a business coach, a Real Estate Broker, a motivational speaker, a political activist, an ordained minister, a father, a husband several times over, and ultimately an irrepressible and all-around *bon vivant and raconteur*. I noted the first time I set pen to paper, or fingers to keyboard, that if you were thinking that this format was reminiscent of the *Chicken Soup for the Soul* series, that would be truly splendid. My take on this was, of course, BUT, how much chicken soup can one guy eat? Can we all say BORING? No! Quite to the contrary, I say screw the chicken soup and throw me a bag of potato chips any time. They are so much more fun and you can eat a few or gobble down the whole bag. That's what this book is all about, so enjoy. There will be times when you smile to yourself and recognize some of what I am suggesting as being very familiar territory for you. There will be other times when you definitely do the LOL thing. There might be still other times when one of these chips gives you a belly ache and you find it seriously disagreeable and difficult for you to digest. That's all by design. Just reach a little further into the bag and eat another one. You'll be feeling fine in no time at all.

One of the things you should glean after a few, is that each little chapter, or story, or chip, is orchestrated not in any particular order. They are all designed to be stand-alone essays but at times they might make reference to a previous episode. Something else you will quickly discern is that each of them is also quite short and rarely will you find one cresting the 750-word mark. Because of this, as one of the readers of the first *Potato Chips* book pointed out, this book makes for perfect reading on the *John*. I take no umbrage at this, as some of my best reading takes place on *the throne* while I am taking care of business. Some of you who are equally unpretentious might find yourselves admitting to that, too. For the rest of you, who do you think you are fooling? So, sit back and enjoy. Read one, or read them all at a single sitting. Your proctologist would probably give you a stern admonishment to this last suggestion and he should. So just read one, or maybe two at the outside, that is, if you are otherwise engaged as we have described in this instance. If on the other hand, you are snug in your pajamas and nestling down to *beddy byes*, you might want to read a whole bunch of them until you decide to fold yourself completely into the arms of Morpheus. Either way, I am sure you will have a fun time delving into this, the second bagful of *Potato Chips for the Soul.*

1. Don't take the last one…

If you are like me, you were probably raised with this same stern admonishment,

"And whatever you do, don't take the last chip, or the last donut, or the last slice of turkey, or…" well, you get the drill.

I suppose it was our parent's way of instilling in us the subtleties of the concept of sharing. Perhaps it was one of their initial attempts at introducing some of the basics of table etiquette and courtesy, and frankly, it was probably not a bad thing at all. Manners have become seriously lax over the last two generations and don't even get me started about people wearing hats in the house and baseball hats turned around at the dinner table. It reminds me of the dialogue between the two producers.

"All actors are animals!"

"Well, don't you think, perhaps that is a bit harsh?"

"Ever eat with one?"

But having said all this, I have to share something with you that really had me perplexed. So, let me tell you about Louie.

Louie is this 18½ lb. little nugget of a rescue dog that I got recently to supply my high approval needs and to act like a sort of mascot in my office. He is beyond the beyond of adorable, and is a 5-year-old mix of dachshund and poodle; he's a "doxapoo." He looks like Benjie with *jerry curls*. I would be remiss if I did not tell you that I had some very specific requirements when I went out to get a dog. First of all, if possible, I wanted to do the right thing and get a rescue dog. That proved to be a lot bigger challenge than I had anticipated, but more on that later.

Here were my additional requirements. He had to be able to travel in the car, and be a model citizen at an office. I wasn't going to leave him at home all day because that would have been cruel on too many counts. He had to be friendly and non-threatening. I could have gone with a chimp, but that presented other issues. OK, so here is the short form on how Louie is working out. This little guy is an "out of the park" home run. Everybody loves Louie. People genuinely look forward to coming in to see him. He is the best good-will ambassador one could have ever hired. I am already anticipating that at some point he is going to storm into my office and insist on renegotiating his contract. No matter, it was a veritable stroke of genius getting this guy and now we go everywhere together. It is almost like having a very well-behaved child that happens to be irrepressibly cute at the same time.

Of course, as you would have guessed, he isn't perfect. On a few rare occasions, there are some guys that come in who he just doesn't like, and he barks at them. Well, it really isn't cool having a dog barking at people. Yet, oddly enough, he never barks at customers. So, customer service, being clearly ingrained in his genetic code was an added bonus. He does, however, as I have mentioned, bark at some (of the agents) that come in periodically. (If, you read the first book of "Potato Chips for the Soul," you would have learned that I run a real estate office when I am not writing, or acting, or speaking around the country on various topics.) So, I hit upon an idea. I noticed there was this one guy. I will call him Ron. He particularly set Louie off every time he came into the office. This forced me to act quickly. I would go out immediately and assure the dog that everything was cool and Ron wasn't a bad guy. Now Ron is this crazy Scotsman who stands about 6'5", and because he is so tall, he tends to slouch, like a lot of tall guys do. Perhaps they do this in a bizarre effort to make the rest of us think they are not that much taller than we are. It's not a good plan and it doesn't work all that well for them. He still looks pretty tall to most of the 7 billion people on the planet. It is an especially ineffective strategy in most of Asia where Ron looks like Goliath no matter what he does. This slouching, unfortunately, gives him an odd appearance. It looks like he is trying to sneak up on you. And that's exactly what, I think, Louie was thinking. I started giving Ron some dog biscuits. I told him:

"Ron, he just thinks you are trying to sneak up on him. Give him a biscuit right away and he will be fine."

The only issue is that it worked out better than expected, and now, Louie has got Ron's number and knows he is going to be taken care of whenever he sees this giant leprechaun coming in the door. I decided to take my brilliance one step further. I took a little bucket and placed a whole bunch of biscuits in it and left them at the front desk. This was just in case I had to be further armed for other approaching hostiles.

OK, so the other day, in strolls Ron. Right on cue, Louie begins his momentary tirade. I waltz over to the front desk to hand Ron his biscuit so we can complete our newly established Pavlovian ritual and he can give it to Louie; and, what do you think I noticed. There was only one single dog biscuit remaining. OK, I have to ask myself, is this coincidence? Has Louie somehow figured a way to get on top of the desk and steal the biscuits? My first suspicion was that the agents were eating the biscuits themselves. Maybe they were demonstrating that they were aware that there is an expectation, if not a requirement, to leave one of *anything and not eat the last one*? If this was in fact not the case, what does this say about instinct? Was Louie being a true gentleman or was this his instinct kicking in…telling him to leave the last biscuit for another dog? I don't know, but I have to tell you, it really is making me scratch my head. I just don't get it. Perhaps, Louie is more highly evolved than even we are? Hmm…?

Note to Self: There are many people (and dogs, too) who would take the last biscuit but who would not take the last lifeboat.

2. Stop and Smell the Roses

How many times have we been reminded to do just that, especially by older people who forgot to do this and now live in a sea of regrets for not doing this? Do roses really smell all that good? Let me share a little something that truly makes me feel privileged. I am, in addition to being a writer, an actor who periodically appears in one of the two summer productions of Shakespeare in Delaware Park. Now, for those of you that are not denizens of Buffalo, New York, Delaware Park is one of the more magnificent parks that Frederick Law Olmsted designed before his most famous opus, that anyone who has ever visited NYC would tell you is, Central Park. This monstrously large stage that hosts the second largest FREE Shakespeare Festival in the United States each year (entertaining nearly 40,000 fans) is nestled between the beautiful Hoyt Lake and the world-famous Albrecht Knox Art Gallery. To get to the seating area (or the lawn where you take your folding chair) directly in front of the Stage, you have to walk through the *Rose Garden.*

Now let me tell you, this is not your average run of the mill rose garden that your grandmother had in her backyard. No sir, our boy Frederick, in keeping with his knock your socks off park designs, really had a great day when he laid out this very special piece of paradise. Located in the *Rumsey Forest* area of Delaware Park, it is a 33 bed rose garden. It is serenely surrounded by stone columns reminiscent of a Greek temple. Even if you hated roses, in late June, the month the first production of Shakespeare gets underway, the rose garden is glorious. All year long I look forward to walking down the hill and strolling through the *Rose Garden* on my way to the show. Every once in a while, I actually stop and lean over and stick my big honker of a nose right in one of those little horticultural masterpieces. I breathe in deeply. Then I go down and get ready to suit up and perform one of the bard's plays to a hill filled with theater aficionados from all over the country. Three hours later, BAM, I reverse my route and just as I crest the hill, the balmy summer breezes caress my nostrils, and my soul is enriched, with the fragrance of roses; thousands of them. A lot of people don't understand why I give up half my summer and bust my ass for 6 nights a week and say words that most people will tell you they understand when they really don't. Truth be told, in most cases, most of the audience gets about half of it and the rest are simply bluffing or too drunk to care. Suffice it to say, however, I do it for a lot of reasons. I love the process of showing up for the first read through, when most of the actors don't even have a clue as to what is happening. I love how you gradually see the play move from page to stage, and each of the characters quietly emerges as a living entity right before your eyes. I love when we have our first round of rehearsing in a flea-bitten rehearsal space somewhere downtown in the bowels of the theater district and we all get restless waiting to mount the actual show on the real stage. But one thing I just adore, the one moment I actually savor in my mind, is that stroll through the park, twice a night, when the show starts rehearsing on the actual performance space.

So why do people tell us to stop and smell these blasted flowers. Perhaps it is simply a metaphorical way to say slow down and take some time to enjoy the more innocent facets of life. For me, it is a much more literal interpretation. Smelling the roses in the *Rose Garden* becomes almost a sacramental cleansing for me. I know that if I am conscious on my death bed, much like Hemingway's fisherman in the *Old Man of the Sea* who was "dreaming of the lions," I will be thinking of the *Rose Garden* and smelling the roses in my mind.

Note to Self: Find your Rose Garden, and savor it.

3. Opening Doors

"Après vous." After you" was one of the first phrases I learned in my high school French class. To this day, whenever I get on an elevator, enter or leave an office building, or frankly, get anywhere near a door and there is someone near me, I extend this courtesy in French, regardless of where I am. I guess I need to simply chalk this one up to one of my myriad of eccentricities. You should know, by the way, that, bizarrely, nobody ever even bats an eye at me. No one ever comments that they don't speak French. I never get asked what it means or if I am from France. People just move ahead of me and graciously or ungraciously accept that I am letting them go ahead of me. Is it wrong? Who knows? But there's something else that I have noticed that has nothing to do with my feeble attempt to be a Francophile. We all get to *open doors,* and every once in a while, someone opens one for us, too.

I am not referring to the literal, physical act of opening or grabbing the door and pushing where it says *pull.* I am talking about the situation that occurs when we open a door for another person and help them advance in their career. I am considering those times when we were a good friend, a mentor, or perhaps even a spiritual guide and we helped people move on, or up, or through, a difficult situation, or helped them to bridge a transition. We have all heard the expression, "It's not *what* you know; it is *who* you know." "*Ain't* that the truth?" How many times have you been *the person* that someone knew? Think of the last time someone dropped your name in an effort to get to the right person who could help them. The entire basis of referral marketing centers on this concept of "who do you know who?" "Boy, *so and so* must really have friends in high places." I mentioned earlier that I just automatically say "*Après vous*"to anyone within a thousand leagues of a door. I also have consciously gone out of my way whenever I could, to figuratively *open doors* for young people who are trying to climb the corporate ladder. I have consistently made introductions to friends of mine that might have a product or service that others might want or need, so that they in turn, can possibly grow their respective businesses. It is as natural to me as breathing. As an entrepreneur who has learned to build a good business based on word of *mouth advertising.* It is essential that I work with people that I know, like, and trust. The reciprocal of this is also true.

Those individuals in my network hopefully feel the same way (about me) and they in turn might want to refer me. They might want to *open doors* for me as I have for them. It's all good.

Here's another reason why I o*pen doors*. From the earliest of my memories, I have been aware of those people in my life that have helped me become who I am today. They may have taken the guise of friends, teachers, supervisors, brothers, parents, co-workers, cab drivers and whomever. I would be a totally different person and in a totally different place in my personal journey if it wasn't for the thousands of people that helped open some of those many doors. I am grateful to them all. Now clearly, some of the doors that were opened revealed greater and more important realities than others. All of them, however, were important. That's why I take it as an almost sacred charge to *open doors* for others. It's what I do. Should I dare say, it is what you might consider doing, too? Why? The simple answer is because life is hard. And this footrace that we are all in for 70-80 years is not without its difficulties.

So now, having said all this, here's is the big "aha" moment for you. Please continue to follow my metaphor life is a race. But no one and I mean NO ONE gets to come in first. We are all running along at our own pace, and we all end our race when we do. At that point, we move on to the next incarnation, go to heaven, or hell, or maybe just Detroit, and we are done. How much better is the race for all of us if we look around and help some of the slower runners keep up? How much better would you feel if along the way, some of the on lookers, popped up periodically and offered you a swig of water and hurled a bit of encouragement your way? We all need that. No one gets to the finish line by themselves. There are always people in our lives that we hopefully are conscious of who are helping us through this portal and that. The next time you see yourself pushing your brains out trying to gain entrance to some place that is important to you… stop. Acknowledge that it says *pull* on the door, and look around and see who you might extend a courtesy to and let them enter before you.

Note to self: It is not always about you. "Après vous."

4. Coffee

Don't you just love a good cup of coffee first thing in the morning? I know I do. I am amazed at how many different ways, and how many different varieties of coffee concoctions there are and how a veritable industry has developed around this dark and bitter brew. The city of Seattle should officially be declared the Vatican City of Coffee drinkers in the Western World. If you ever go there, the first thing that will strike you is, it seems that there is a *Starbucks* or a *smarbucks* or *coffee buck's* emporium just about every 50 ft. I was amazed to see that if you drive down some of the roads outside the city, you will see some of those little sheds that you can buy at Lowe's or Home Depot for about $1500.00 and how the locals take them and convert them into coffee houses. Now they are not like the *coffee houses* of the beat generation, with hipsters sitting around smoking God knows what, and reading bad poetry and all. They are actually more like coffee dispensaries. Either way, you see them along both sides of the road, and you can literally stop your car and leap out kicking and screaming and get your next mocha fix. I can remember when I first went up to visit my brother Tom who lives in Port Townsend, just to the north of the city. Upon seeing all these coffee shacks. I thought to myself, *how much coffee can these frigging people drink?* It's insane.

Let's talk about making coffee. When I grew up, most people's homes smelled of freshly brewed coffee (and cigarettes). More than likely, it was *perking* on the stove. Enter *Jolting Joe (DiMaggio)* a few years later, and we have the next evolution of coffee making: *Mr. Coffee.* For the more sophisticated and well-travelled foodies out there, who objected to this commoditizing of their favorite beverage, we also see the emergence of the *French Press.* OK, get your mind out of the gutter. This is not a new sexual position. If you are unfamiliar with this method of making super strong and flavorful coffee, suffice it to say, making coffee in the *French Press* is not for the wimpy. You take freshly ground coffee and place it at the bottom of a cylindrical shaped pot and pour boiling water over it and let it sit for a few minutes. Then you take this device that is similar to a plunger and you press the grounds out of the solution, and in essence, you have an inch or two of coffee silt at the bottom. You are left with super high-octane coffee. I would take *French*

Roast coffee, which is a very dark roasted variety, and pretty strong to begin with, and grind it up extra fine (which makes it even stronger and make it in the *French Press* (which continues to intensify the flavor.) I was literally left with nitro methane fuel. I would go on to drink the entire pot by myself and wonder why I was talking like a cokehead on steroids. I eventually had to stop, because I was bordering on bursting into a different dimension on an entirely new time line. But *man, oh man* that was one helluva cup of coffee.

Today, we have witnessed a total renaissance in the making of coffee with the emergence of the *Keurig* machine. With so many people willing to drop 5 bucks for a cup at *Starbucks*, this seems to be the new alternative to getting "fresh brewed coffee" at a reasonably affordable price. We simply cannot escape seeing this wonderful brown nectar delivered to us through those ubiquitous *pods*. In this new millennium, the *Keurig* device has taken on an almost sacramental reverence. I recently heard a Real Estate competitor of mine talking about an office that she opened and she told me, "it has everything, a great location, a core group of good agents, it even has a *Keurig*." I remember thinking to myself: well, *you've got to have a Keurig. What would be the point of living if you didn't have a Keurig?* Unfortunately, she had to close that office in little over two years. I guess in business sometimes you need to have a lot more than a *Keurig*.

Don't even get me started on flavored coffee. I think that is truly a world that has earned the right to be called abominable. Throw in some flavors, a pint of whipped cream, and 1800 calories later and *BAM* you have whatever kind of atomic Frappuccino's you can imagine. If I wanted a thick shake, I would have gone to *McDonald's.* It's not cool and it is a far cry from my mother's perked coffee.

Note to self: Hey, who do I have to kill to get a decent cup of coffee around here?

5. Find your Happiness

Last Friday night, I had the good fortune to attend a Black Tie (optional) gala for one of the Associations at which I hold membership. It was being held at one of the posher country clubs in my area. There were a number of friendly faces at my table of 10 and I was smart enough to position myself between two people that I knew would supply just the proper audience for my relentless need to be a raconteur. I also made a point to be facing the dais so I wouldn't wind up with a sore neck by the end of the night, since I knew there was going to be a sea of speeches being made. They were installing the incoming President and her support team.

One of the guests at my table did not fare as well in the seat selection department that evening and later told me he was sandwiched between a woman who had thoroughly douched herself in "Eau D'Old Lady" and someone who talked "at" him all night. Hey, if you are going to one of these affairs, and so many of us are obligated to do so from time to time, do a little early research beforehand and position yourself ahead of time. (I got there 15 minutes early and scoped out the entire seating arrangement to tilt the odds in my favor. I've learned, after many painful events, to do so and it makes for a more tolerable evening. Frequently, I have even enjoyed myself like I did this night.

OK, now for the big surprise. At the penultimate end to the complete body of speech making, the Master of Ceremonies, who happened to be the gentleman who was keeping company with the newly installed President, turned to the audience. (*Keeping company:* how's that for a bit of a nostalgic reference?) Let's get back to Mr. MC. He continues and requests 5 minutes more of everyone's time to make an announcement. He asked for silence. He asked for their attention. He then got down on his knee and proposed to the President. I thought it was one of the sweetest and most sincerely spontaneous moments I have ever seen. He then stopped her, before she could respond, and said:

"Since all of our closest friends are here and I don't have to return the Tux until morning, and since there just happens to be a judge with us about 5 feet away from the podium, I am going to ask that we get married right here, right now: tonight."

Well, as you can imagine, that's one big enchilada to leave hanging out there. There were a few gulps in the audience. Luckily for Mr. Bold and Beautiful, the lady in question not only said yes, but the genuine affection that the entire room felt for both of these singularly special and blessed people was palpable. What a great ending to an important evening. It was fabulous. Everyone joined the bride and groom at the bar and hoisted several drinks to wish them both well. But of course, by now you know, there is one more chapter to this story.

As I was leaving the event, I ran into a business acquaintance who happened to be at the bar and who did not attend the event. She asked if I was coming from the installation dinner and I said yes and then I asked her, "Did you hear what happened?" She showed some concern and responded with a staccato "No." I proceeded to tell her with a high level of glee in my voice about what I thought was a truly special moment, and I was flabbergasted at her reaction.

"That's ridiculous and probably one of the most selfish things I have ever heard. I would have thrown a drink in his face. **It's all about the man, isn't it**? What a terrible and rude way to propose to someone!"

I tried to head her ravings off at the pass by saying, "No, No, No, you don't understand, they are really happy. It was magical for them. It's all good."

She snorted back, "WELL, IT WOULDN'T HAVE BEEN GOOD FOR *ME*!"

I remember thinking to myself, in spite of the fact that this was a very attractive and upscale lady, *that's why you are alone at the bar, honey.*

 It's tough being so miserable.

Where does all that misery come from and why is it so necessary to share it? I generally tend to be happy for other peoples' happiness. Am I going about this thing called life all wrong? I don't think so.

Note to self: Find your happiness. Be happy for others in their happiness, and keep your misery to yourself.

6. "I'm kind of a big shot…"

Every one of us has something in common; at least that's what Oprah Winfrey asserted once when she was talking about all of the 10,000 plus interviews she has done throughout her career. She said every person asked her when the interview was concluded:

"So how did I do," or

"How was I," or,

"Was that all right?"

Every guest she had ever had, wanted some sort of validation. This was true, regardless of whether it was the Dalai Lama, a current or past President, an increasingly popular, up and coming actor, or a Hollywood megastar. Obviously, as we make our journeys through this life, some require a little more validation and some are truly vexed in that they cannot get enough, ever.

From time to time, I do speaking engagements. Frequently, and prior to my taking the floor, the M.C. or the producer of the event, will ask me to supply them with a short bio so they can properly introduce me when the time comes for me to do my thing. When I first started out, my bio was pretty long since nobody knew who I was, and I had to expand on that. As I proceed in my career and schedule more speaking events, my bio gets shorter and shorter. The hope is that after a while, the host speaker can simply say "Here's a gentleman who needs no introduction, Brendan Cunningham." At which point, there is riotous and thunderous applause as the audience gets ready for an out of body, life altering presentation. I'm kind of a long way from that point, but it's something worth striving for, at least. Oddly enough, I do not have nearly as big an ego as most people would think. I would be less than truthful if I didn't tell you, however, that I have a healthy enough supply of what I call "moxie" to get the job done. You can't be shy and reserved and get up and speak in front of hundreds of people and expect to be interesting. That's what I think, unless you are like the comedian, Steven Wright, who has made a career out of being a pathological introvert on stage. One of my favorite lines of his is:

"I like to put the plug in the bathtub when I am taking a shower. I pretend I am in a submarine that has been hit by a depth charge." Another is:

"If you put instant coffee in the microwave, does it go back in time?"

OK, so I am at an event and this guy saunters over to the table next to me and I overhear him ask one of the ladies, if this was in fact table 22 and if the seat he was standing in front of was taken. She assured him that he was correct as to the table number, and yes, the seat was available. He sat down and proceeded to introduce himself to the young lady, and she gave him a perplexed look. This must have been based on *the fact* that he presumed that the mere mentioning of his name should have been followed by choirs of angels from on high heralding his arrival. Clearly, she had no idea who the heck he was. He very deprecatingly looked at what he was now deeming to be some poor, little, unobtrusive waif and instructed her, leeringly saying, "I'm kind of a Big Shot."

I definitely did a spit take. If I was texting, I would have had to write, LMFAO. Are you kidding me: Big Shot in your own mind, perhaps? I couldn't believe the sheer unadulterated smarminess or this guy's level of conceit.

This reminds me of another story my daughter Alice shared with me that made me chuckle, as well. She was in her early to mid-20s, and she was in one of the local hot spots on Chippewa Street in downtown Buffalo, NY on a Friday night. Now for those of you who know nothing about the Queen City, that's where a lot of young people go to let loose and there are scores of upscale bars, draping both sides of the street. Some of them even cater to older dudes like me and what they call a mixed crowd, whatever that is. One night she is out with a group of her friends sitting at a bar. She is all dolled up, and a not so unattractive young gentleman approaches her and offers to buy her a drink. She says thank you and starts up the conversation and tells him her name and assertively asks:

"What do you do? He sheepishly and incredulously looks at her and tells her very matter of factly, "I play hockey!"

"Oh," she responds, not really impressed because at the time she was just about to enter law school and was not particularly sports minded. She innocently continued and inquired further, "So do you play for some town team, or league, or something like that?"

Now an essential part of this story hinges on one of the unfortunate handicaps my daughter received from me. She has a total disregard and lack of interest in hockey. Neither of us could care less about hockey. When I went to my first *Sabers* game at what was known as *the Aud back* in the late 80s (it has since been torn down and replaced by a state-of-the-art arena that has the name changed every year), I asked, "What time is the puck off?"

This is in a town that eats, drinks, and breaths HOCKEY. You can only imagine the lambasting I had to withstand that night.

Let's get back to Alice. The hockey player in question was none other than the Number 1 goalie in the entire NHL that year. He literally had just gotten back from winning the gold medal at the Olympics. His picture was probably on the front page of the Buffalo Evening News that day. He couldn't believe there was actually someone in this sports obsessed town who didn't know who he was. It was inconceivable.

No Score!

When Alice told me the story, we both laughed our asses off.

Note to self: You are only a big shot in your own mind.

7. The Chrysler Building

There is a triptych of the Chrysler Building conspicuously fixed on the wall behind my desk at my Real Estate office in Tonawanda, NY. The Chrysler Building is, in my opinion, one of most beautiful skyscrapers in NYC and one of the finest examples of Art Deco architecture anywhere. Periodically, I interview candidates who are considering entering the business and I explain that once they become licensed, they can sell Real Estate anywhere in New York State. I then ask them if they can tell me what building is represented in the expertly framed, matted, black and white photos behind me. Some of the natives of the Big Apple get the answer correct but even there; we are talking only 50%. Most will either say:

"I don't know," or they will take a stab at it or say:

"Oh yeah, that's the Empire State Building."

If they take the stab at it, I will make a big fuss as if they have gotten it correct. I ask them to stand and take a bow. They usually resist, and I prompt them until they stand, and just as they stand, I make a buzzer sound and say:

"Wrong! Wanna take another stab at it?"

I eventually put them out of their misery and tell them the correct answer. I go through this charade every time to make a point. It lightens the mood and gets their attention. I ask them, "OK, you are at a cocktail party and someone tells you they are interested in buying some serious commercial Real Estate in Manhattan. They tell you they have their eyes on a building that perhaps one might have heard of; it's called, the *Chrysler Building*. What do you do?"

Most of the interviewees tell me that since they can sell anywhere in NY state, they would take the guy down there and sell it to him. Once again, I ask them to stand and take a bow. No, I insist they take a bow. I smile and give them applause. They light up because they know that I know that they have been listening to me. They finally got one right. After a few seconds, I make my buzzer sound one more time and tell them

"Wrong Again!"

"Just a few minutes ago, you didn't even know what building it was. Can you tell me what street it's on? Is it Midtown, Uptown, Downtown,

Eastside, Westside...where is it located exactly? How many floors does it have? What is the total usable square footage? You don't know!"

It is at this point, I soften my position and explain that since doing a transaction like this is so beyond the level of their expertise and so not anywhere near their primary market, all they can hope to do is spin their wheels and waste an inordinate amount of time, money and energy. This holds true for both themselves and their *would-be* clients. They should simply refer it to an agent in NYC who specializes in large buildings of that type. That's right; you pick up the phone and call someone who can handle it properly. Sure, you cut yourself in for a referral fee, but you don't try to run with this ball because you can only screw it up. The best professionals never hesitate to refer things to others in their fields who are more adept at specific situations. Real Estate attorneys refer divorces to Divorce attorneys. Patent attorneys refer gangsters to Criminal Attorneys. All attorneys can legally handle all aspects of law within their given states, but the smart ones specialize. They do not hesitate to refer clients to specialists when needed. It is more than just common sense. It is part of the fiduciary relationship that places the clients need above the attorneys. (Real Estate agents function as fiduciaries, too.) Doctors do something similar. They do this not because they are fiduciaries, but because it is sound medical practice. If you have a blemish on your face that is concerning you, your GP can and will look at it, but invariably he or she will refer you to a good Dermatologist. If you go in for your annual checkup and you are over 50, you can bet the good doctor will refer you to a Proctologist for your colonoscopy screening. All of the best professionals stay within the area of the expertise. You should too. Things get totally screwed up for everyone when people forget this little truth.

Note to self: Stay with what you know. Stay within the area of your specialty.

8. Dog Supplies

God knows, in America, we love our dogs. This is especially true today. When I was a kid, we always had a dog. They were always well taken care of, and were very well fed. Heck, they ate what we ate. I'm half Italian, so a lot of times *Skipper* would eat left-over spaghetti. If he was really lucky, he would get some lasagna. I can even remember him eating an occasional side salad. I didn't eat mine; that was for sure. "*Chipmunk,* this must be your lucky day." What's that you say, "Hold the onions?" Yeah. I'm not big on onions either. (Actually, all kidding aside, onions are toxic for dogs.) OK, perhaps it was all wrong, but they all lived healthy and long lives. Today, we would probably be arrested for cruelty to animals.

Fast forward: have you been to a pet supply place recently? I recently picked up a bag of kibble for my dog, *Louie,* and it was called *Surf and Turf.* Specially designed for dogs only, it *contained no grains* or fillers, and had actual steak and lobster in it. I was only half kidding at the checkout counter, when I said, "Heck, I'm going to eat this myself, screw the dog....and what about the grains? Weren't we all raised on *Wheaties* and *Cheerios,* and their *whole grain* goodness? My Dog is eating BETTER than I am. *Louie* is one lucky son of a bitch," and I mean that literally.

Let's kick this up a notch. Do you know what his favorite treats are made of: duck tenderloins. All right, they are dried and look like pieces of jerky but I still had to ask the lady who owned the store,

"Could I eat *these?*" She responded guardedly, probably because of liability implications.

"Well, you could, but they're really designed for non-human consumption."

I'm thinking, come the zombie apocalypse, these little nuggets might do really well in a pinch.

What about all those toys that the stores feature for our canine pals? Are we not seriously way out of control with all this stuff? What ever happened to a ball, or a stick? Those things worked pretty well when both I and every other kid in America were appearing in our own film version of *A Boy and His Dog.* I would be hard pressed to think that that the dogs of today have somehow amazingly evolved that much more so that they are only placated by video games and the like. Then there is the clothing. It seems, these days, people have gotten obsessed with *dressing up* Fido, too. I have to confess: I saw a special on a jacket from *Eddie Bauer* and bought it for Louie. After I made my purchase, I realized, *I* didn't even have an Eddie Bauer jacket. What the hell was that all about?

Now let's talk about cats. Oh, God, please let's not. That's where we truly dip into the world of total insanity. Do we really need all this stuff to have a better pet?

Note to Self: Sit Rover, sit.

9. Having a Woman President

As I write this story, I have to place the telling of the tale in a context. It is just two weeks after one of the more controversial elections in our nation's history and Hillary Clinton surprised many by not winning the White House. It would have been the first time a woman would have gotten to sit in the big chair in the Oval office. I have a feeling that over the next 20 years or so, many of the pundits who predicted that she was a shoe-in, will have written their books and will have offered many a theory as to why the results were what they were. There has been, at this point, many a left-wing backlash, that insists that their candidate lost because of some gender bias or because of some considerable right-wing blarney that states that a woman is simply not biologically fit to sit in the White House. Conversely, there were many of her constituents that insisted that they were voting for her simply because she was a woman. To this last group, I take the most serious amount of umbrage. Hillary Clinton lost not *because* she was a woman. Hillary Clinton lost because she was the wrong woman. The word *woman* should never have ever even entered into the equation.

It would be just as wrong to say that I voted for Obama because he *was* a Black Man. To say you *wouldn't* vote for him *because* he was Black would be worse. Let's really create a justifiable furor and tell people in some other election, *I am voting because he is a white man.* The notion of color or gender should never enter the conversation because by now if we are considering ourselves to be anything less than an enlightened country, we should be voting for the candidate that best represents our interest and that of the American people. Suffice it to say that both of the candidates in this race were conspicuously and unusually flawed. It would be remiss not to say that. I can remember being asked when her husband Bill was running some 20 years earlier:

"Do you think America is ready for a woman in the White House?" I was less than warm in my response, when I shot back:

"I am embarrassed that anyone in this day and age would even ask a question like that."

What does having a vagina have to do with whether you are a good leader? We have seen many remarkable female monarchs throughout history and some of them did a lot better than their male counterparts.

ONE'S ABILITY HAS NOTHING TO DO WITH GENDER! Golda Meir, Indira Gandhi, Queen Elizabeth I and II are just a few of the female luminaries that have graced the world stage. They were all superlative in their own rights and none of it had anything to do with the way they went to the bathroom. The Clinton thing was a fiasco from day one and the fact that the DNC anointed her without even the remotest consideration of anyone else is where the seeds of her own defeat were sown. The entire Bernie Sanders debacle was the ultimate nail in the coffin to ensure that everyone had to recognize just how flawed she actually was. Some of her most resolute supporters will tell you the election was rigged; she got the popular vote, etc. Here's the deal: SHE LOST. It is over. Stop the music. But let's underscore this for the sake of the conscience of history; it had nothing to do with her vagina.

We will have a woman in the White House one day soon. When we do, it will be great. When will that happen? It will happen on the day when the best person for the job steps up and runs. It will happen when she is able to fend off all the attacks that come with the ridiculous campaigning process and she wins. At that point, all of us will notice something. We will mutter to ourselves, "Huh, and she just happened to be a woman" ....and that it had nothing to do with it.

Let me share a more personal story that better explains my position. In the early 1990's, I happened to be president of the local Lion's club. Like many service organizations, they were facing diminishing membership and relentless absenteeism at meetings. I suggested, to the sheer horror of some of the group, that we should seriously consider allowing women to join our chapter. I proposed this when I was running for an unprecedented third term and I was totally amazed at the push back I got on what seemed like a long overdue move and one that could do nothing but build our core base and add a much-needed breath of fresh air. I made the front page of the local newspaper and was asked about my *bold* decision and why I would think this was a good idea. I responded with, "...because, this is 1992, not 1792."

So how did it play out? We virtually doubled our size in the first year, and there was a woman president at the end of the subsequent third year. Today, the group is doing better than ever. There was one gentleman in the group who was adamant that even though he was a member for what was approaching 30 years, if we let women in, he would quit immediately. Prior to the approval of the resolution, I informed him, "We will miss you."

I must confess: I was merely being polite, because I knew that we wouldn't. Oh, and I lost the election, but I was able to get the resolution passed, so I figured we all won in the long run. It was the right thing to do.

Note to Self: Race and Gender have no place in a conversation regarding performance. To suggest either of these is limiting. It is embarrassing for all of us.

10. "We'll always have Paris."

Serious movie buffs will recognize this as one of the signature great lines from the classic 1942 film *Casablanca*. It featured two of Hollywood's icons in the making, Humphrey Bogart and Ingrid Berman. It tells the tale of two star crossed lovers and how they find each other in Paris during the height of the German occupation of France in WW2. It proceeds to show their romance blossom, before they lose each other as the world becomes mired in the relentless churning sea of Nazi aggression. The plot thickens when it is revealed that Ingrid Bergman's character, Elsa, has returned to her husband (who has recently escaped from a POW camp after fighting for the Resistance). Of course, the tortured married couple meets up several years later with Humphrey Bogart's character, Rick, in the mysterious and exotic French Moroccan city of Casablanca. This is where he says the immortal line, upon seeing her sitting at the bar in his own *Café American* (called *Rick's* by the locals), "In all of the crazy gin joints in the world, she has to walk into mine."

As you can imagine, things get a bit tense, and in one of the great climaxes in cinema history, having found her true love Rick again, he convinces her to get on the last out-bound plane for Lisbon so she can be safe from the Nazis who are in hot pursuit. Unfortunately for them, they now have to resign themselves to their terrible fate; this time, they will probably lose each other for good. Rick kisses her goodbye, holds her tightly knowing it is the last time, he tells her:

"We'll always have Paris."

Sometimes that's all we have. Many of us are dealt a bad hand in life. Some of us choose really bad cards ourselves and make our lives much worse than we should. Either way, there are good times, bad times, happy times, and tragic times. Life is a series of events and there are many things and people that each of us would choose to forget. Regrettably at times, these instances are followed up with the thought, *if only we could (forget) somehow?* On the other hand, every one of us has a *Paris* in us. We all somehow get to have that one singular time or event that seems to give our life meaning, or hope, or remind us that we had a special someone in our life that made us feel so much more than just special. We felt loved. We can never forget those precious moments because sometimes it is the only thing that gives us the will to go on, the power to persist, and the motivation to get up and face the demons one more time. *Casablanca* is one of those classic films, not just because it had a star-studded cast. It is great not just because of the amazingly skilled direction of Oscar winning director Michael Curtiz. It isn't even memorable simply because of the few familiar lines I have mentioned already. It is important because it underscores one of most important things that give meaning to all of our lives. It reminds us of what is truly important. Sadly, sometimes we only get to have it once, and we must cherish it, if only in our memories.

Note to self: When it comes to our most important memories, let's all take the time to tell ourselves to "Play it again, Sam."

11. Soft Shelled Crabs

I have often joked that if I was on death row and had to make a request for a last meal, I would order the *soft-shelled crab*. Why? Because you can only get them when they are in season and the season runs from April to September. If I am to be executed in October, they would simply *have to wait* to pull the switch on me; pretty smooth, huh? Actually, I think they would insist I order something else, like a hot dog and fries, but in this case, this unique bill of fare gets to give me another chance at a bit of levity. Surprisingly, there are many who are unfamiliar with this scrumptious seafood delicacy. For the uninitiated, let me go directly to Wikipedia: "Soft-shell crab is a culinary term for crabs that have recently molted their old exoskeleton and are still soft. [1] Soft-shells are removed from the water as soon as they molt to prevent any hardening of their shell. [2] This means that almost the entire animal can be eaten, rather than having to shell the animal to reach the meat."

So here is the deal: you get to eat the whole dang crab. Many gourmands will tell you that crab is a million times more flavorful than lobster. Unfortunately, the crab is a lot smaller. It is also a billion times bigger pain in the buttocks to eat. That's because there isn't all that much meat in a blooming crab. In fact, if you buy a pound of lump crab meat, it takes about 32 crabs to complete your order. I laugh when I go down to Maryland. If you drive along the coast there and you stop at some of the restaurants along the Chesapeake you will see signs telling you "all the crabs you can eat" for like 3 bucks. What a deal! The only thing is that it would take you about an hour to eat one even if you had the correct surgical instruments, and these guys are only going to give you a wooden mallet. That's one hell of a lot of banging, and by the time you finish eating your first crab, you are ready to hit the waiter in the head with that same wooden mallet. No, the soft-shelled crab is the only way to go. You can even eat one on a bun and have a soft-shelled crab sandwich. It's divine with a little dollop of tartar sauce. My personal preference is to have a pair of them sautéed in a *beurre blanc* sauce. A lot of people insist that they are turned off by the thought of eating the legs of the crab in their entirety.

"I just picture them wiggling around in my mouth."

I feel a similar concern when I eat a *French fry*. I can hear the poor *fry* screaming in my mouth as I bite into it, "Stop, YOU'RE KILLING ME!"

Come on, man, get over yourself here.

Any way you eat them, when it comes to Soft Shelled Crabs, you cannot miss. What other delectable dishes are you missing? If you are one of those confirmed meat and potatoes people, come on, and live a little. Get out of your comfort zone. I recall the time when I went to a *dim sum* bar in Chinatown in NYC. My brother Denny pointed to one of the dishes that were racing past him. Trays of these tasty little morsels were propelled past us by the wait staff who were pushing their carts through tight little aisles. In places like this, you simply point and they drop a hot plate of some sort of dumpling in front of you and, "Voila, Chinese heaven." In this case, she very quietly responded:

"Yes, you want the chicken feet?"

I concede, that was a little too adventuresome, even for me.

Note to self: Soft shelled crabs for everyone.

12. Peanut Butter and Jelly

Remember when you were a kid and your mom would make you a peanut butter and jelly sandwich for lunch. Actually, if you do, you were a pretty lucky kid. A lot of kids didn't get to have a mom and some others didn't get to have one that could take the time to make them one of these gooey delectables. I have to admit, I had both and I was blessed with an incredibly special mom. She made me *peanut butter* sandwiches because I just wasn't big on the jelly. My brother Denny would eat any kind of jelly, grape, strawberry, and peach, whatever. I think he would have eaten a plain jelly sandwich without the peanut butter. He was kind of weird that way. We always suspected he was either adopted or a Russian spy undercover. He used to do something that would actually put me into another dimension. Every once in a while, someone would buy a box of *Entenman's* Chocolate donuts. You know the ones that would have 8 perfectly glazed chocolate donuts lined up all in a row. They came is a box a little bit bigger than a box of Aluminum foil. He would take one single bite out of each of them and put them back in the box, bite side down. The unsuspecting donut consumer who came along next, would reach in and grab a donut and just as they were about to sink their teeth into one of those beauties, they would say:

"WTF!"

I was only about 6 when I was groping for just the right words of frustration, but I knew there had to be a more impactful way of indicating my anguish other than just bursting into tears and yelling:

"MOM!"

But let's get back to the peanut butter.

My mom would actually take the time to cut the crust off my peanut butter sandwich, too. Years later, after she was gone, I remember thinking what a wonderful gesture of love and affection that was. It is the tiny gestures like these that conveys the greatest feeling. I have to admit, till this day I love peanut butter. I have learned to use it in a lot in many of the dishes I prepare. This is largely because of my appreciation of Thai cuisine where they use peanuts and peanut glazes in many of their dishes which tend to be on the spicier side.

I can remember one day when I was helping do the shopping with my mom and I grabbed a jar of *Skippy* off the shelf and threw it in the cart, only to be horrified to learn the next day that it was *Crunchy*, not *Smooth*. It was almost as bizarre as reaching in and grabbing one of those donuts with a bite out of them,

"MOM!"

These days, so many kids are allergic to peanut butter. YIKES! To me that is almost like being allergic to love. It is inconceivable. OK, perhaps I am being a bit melodramatic. But "a life without peanut butter is not worth living." Who said that? Wasn't that a famous philosopher like Nietzsche or Rene Descartes? It could have been. It should have been. I feel sorry for all those poor little guys who will have to go through their entire lives never having the sensation of having that fragrant, gooey, nectar, stuck to the roof of their mouths so they can hardly speak. It's one of the things that just makes life worth living. Peanut butter and jelly, they go to together like a horse and carriage. I'll just take the peanut butter myself. I tend to be a bit of a purest and I don't have a horse any way.

Note to self: Life is better with peanut butter (and jelly, if you have to have it.)

13. Go to the Wake

If you are Irish, you know that wakes are kind of a big deal. Needless to say, different ethnic groups celebrate death, or perhaps a more appropriate way to say this is that they "address" death according to their religious or cultural predilections. With the Irish, there is usually a lot of drinking and joke telling and laughter, and frequently, much of it is at the dearly departed one's expense. There is almost a party-like or festive atmosphere. Of course, it is not all tom foolery. There is certainly a sufficient amount of hand wringing as well. This is performed by a cadre of sallow faced older women with lipstick applied hurriedly, so that they look their best as they proceed to accompany the revelry. But never you mind, let's hoist a glass to dear old Paddy anyway. It is said that the Irish drink too much. Why do they drink so much? In most cases they will tell you that they drink too much to forget their problems. What's their biggest problem? They drink too much.

Now I am blessed in that I am half Irish and half Italian. It is a great mixture. It gives me the ultimate in yin and yang. (If you come to my house, you will be assured of plenty to eat and plenty to drink.) So based on this preamble, it is no great secret that I have gone to my share of *Italian* wakes over the years and they are very different affairs. (My mother was one of 12 children and they each had a mess of children to boot!) Italian wakes are quiet and somber affairs and usually very respectful and serious. Fortunately, there is one thing you can expect for sure: there is a big meal waiting for you at one of the relative's houses. Someone is sure to be fretting about, "Is there enough Lasagna to go around, who is going to pick up the cookies, oh s---, I shouldn't have added nuts to the salad, so and so has colitis, etc."

The Italians, unlike the Irish who like to drown their sorrows in alcohol, express their grief through the sharing of food. Neither is incorrect; it is just a part of their respective cultures. The Jamaicans, conversely, really have a rousing good time. They literally *celebrate* the fact that they had the person that left them in their lives for as long as they did, and what a blessing it was to have them with them at all. I love that. I had the uncanny good fortune to see this for myself when I went to one of the saddest wakes I will ever recall. It was for a 7-year-old little boy who was one of the most beautiful souls I had ever seen. His family showed the most incredible amount of joy for how God had blessed them for giving them this special gift, *if for only 7 years*. I have to tell you that this is a faith that was beyond anything I have ever witnessed. I was a puddle. As much as I would like to think that I have a deep conviction in my beliefs, these wonderfully joyous people shamed me with their piety and faith. I felt truly humbled to be a witness to their convictions.

Here's the real reason you should go to the Wake. You go out of respect for the living. The dead guy is probably not going to care that much. Death is a part of life. When I hear people say, "I don't do wakes," I want to bitch slap them like Don Corleone did to Johnny Fontaine in *The Godfather.* Show some respect. Sometimes you may have had differences with the deceased and you may have continuing existing difficulties with the family. Suck it up and show up at the Wake.

I personally think the *Funeral* is mostly for the immediate family and is not for friends and acquaintances, but that might be my own personal bias. Funerals tend to be especially sad and in the case of the Italians, my brothers and I would disrespectfully take bets on who was going to jump in the grave first after the body. It was never a pretty sight and it is more than understandable, too. The more modern custom of going to the mausoleum first and then having the guests disperse from there has lessened the impact of the weeping and gnashing of teeth, and I think this is a little healthier for all parties concerned.

Here's another reason why you should always go to the Wake. The way most of us have evolved in our respective lives, we frequently seem to only make a connection with most of our family and friends at weddings and funerals (wakes.) Don't think your absence is not going to be noticed if you are a *no show*. When I buried my father nearly 45 years ago, I can tell you who was there, but more specifically, I can tell you who surprised me with their conspicuous absence. I can remember thinking, *that's odd, after all, my dad did, for so and so, and they didn't even have the decency to stop by and to say their farewells.* I was equally and pleasantly surprised by those who broke their asses to get there. There are many subtle things that go into building and maintaining relationships. Sometimes the way you terminate one is as important as the way you initiate it. *Going to the Wake* tells people you are a person who had some worth because you are taking the time to show that the person, who has left, that their life had *value. It had meaning.* The best thing you can ever do to a bereaving family is to show up at the Wake and share a pleasant story of how you first met. You might share a tale about something that person did for you that no one knows, or tell a funny story that you will always associate with them. Blessed are they who mourn, for they shall be comforted. You just have to do your part and show up, so you can do the comforting. Got it?

 Note to Self: Show up for the Wake.

14. Bookstores

Regrettably, bookstores are going the way of the Dodo Bird. Don't get me wrong; there are still a few of the giants like *Barnes & Noble* out there who seem to be thriving, but the little neighborhood store around the corner is a rarity these days. *Amazon* has gone a long way to kill off most of them, and don't get me wrong, again, I really, really, love Amazon. I love the free shipping and the fact that I can expect delivery almost before I hit the click button to make my purchase. If it helps get people to read, I am all for it. One of the things I will miss is wandering through the shelves and reading an actual hard bound book before I buy it. I love to sit and peruse the pages. Book stores used to make great first date places because it gave you the opportunity to discuss what was your favorite book, the different genres that intrigued you, and it gave you a more substantive conversation than, "So how about that Kim Kardasian's butt, it's pretty big isn't it?"

No, I suspect, our children will talk about what bookstores used to be like the same way the older generation speaks about home delivery of milk. It will become meaningless, and sometimes annoying, nostalgia.

I had an interesting conversation recently with a guy who I would consider to be a borderline computer genius about how smart phones have made us all dumb since we no longer have to remember numbers or read maps or know anything about geography (because they all have a GPS on them.) His response took me back a bit. Essentially, he argued that we no longer needed to use those parts of our brains, since RAM was much better and faster than our own abilities to summon up information that we should just know. At some point, I argued in return, that eventually we will be so dumb that we really won't be able to perform simple functions without the assistance of machines. His conclusion was that I was correct. It was a natural part of evolution and he looked forward to the time when *artificial intelligence* ruled. I gotta tell you, I intoned a huge sighing and depressing *wow*. That should give us something to look forward to, or perhaps not? I recognize the need for progress. I want you to think about that for a moment and the price you have to pay. Here's a quote from the great courtroom drama, *Inherit the Wind.* Here we see Clarence Darrow (in the guise of Henry Drummond) making the point so much better than I could.

> Gentlemen, progress has never been a bargain. You have to pay for it. Sometimes I think there's a man who sits behind a counter and says, "All right, you can have a telephone, but you lose the right to privacy and the charm of distance. Madam, you may vote, but at a price. You lose the right to retreat behind the powder-puff or your petticoat. Mr., you may conquer the air, but the birds will lose their wonder and the clouds will smell of gasoline.

When the bookstores are gone, I will feel like a veritable marshmallow when I get all shmaltzy over how quaint they were. I am blessed to have a wonderful bookstore in my little neighborhood in South Buffalo called the *Dog Ear's Book Store.* It is more than just a super cozy bookstore; it has a café where you can get a quick bite to eat and talk about the book for which you just paid slightly under retail. Hey, they have to stay competitive, don't they? I have done several book signings there; together with a number of other local authors. They do something else there that makes it pure magic. It is a reading haven. Several nights a week, the parents take their kids there and the owner reads books to the little tikes. He reads from big books, and little books, books with pictures and books that have lots of words in them that not everyone in his young audience will understand. They're all real honest to goodness books, too. He isn't reading the words from a *Nook* or an E-book. Those things have their place. But there is nothing like the smell of the page and the feel of a book in your hands. It is a great way of instilling the importance of reading to those who will come after us. Book stores: try to visit one today, before it is too late.

Note to self: Go to a book store. Buy a book and read it.

15. Hanging Pictures

"So, how's it hanging?"

When it comes to hanging pictures, there are several schools of thought on the subject and I am going to suggest that none of them are right and none of them are wrong. Suffice it to say, however, if you are in the opposing camp of either, you will be convinced that the other side is not just wrong; they are idiots.

Let's consider how the first group hangs a picture in their house. This is the group that takes a somewhat scientific approach. There will be lots of measuring. There may be multiple yardsticks in use for any number of days, with several people involved during all steps in the process. For more serious projects, several weeks of planning and conferring might be appropriate. On occasion, there might be an electron microscope or two. There may be sketches laying out how each of the pictures will be positioned. They might be arranged this way or that, and of course, each of them needs to be placed correctly at *Optical Center.* This is serious business. Please, be warned, this is not simply hanging a picture. It is an all-consuming process of predetermining the re-ordering of the cosmos and how it will affect all other bodies within the gravitational field within a minimum of 2-3 parsecs. A degree in celestial mechanics would be desirable, but an engineering degree is required, and, at the very least, a consultation with someone who is properly accredited in a related life science or who has similar certifications in either architecture or interior design. Come on, you didn't just think you were going to throw it up on the wall, did you? Practitioners in this camp will additionally never even consider starting the process if all of the necessary hardware hasn't been purchased and properly laid out on various tables well before hand. Trying to accomplish proper distancing without Laser sighting is not even possible. That would be too ludicrous. It would be almost like thinking that Donald Trump could actually get elected to be president. Now how far-fetched would that be? How ridiculous?

Then there is the camp that does the exact opposite. They would have developed a near fatal case of hives, if they even read the paragraph above. No, these are the folks who *just hang it.* There is no measuring. There are no sketches, or plans, or blueprints. Hell, you don't need any fancy hanging equipment. All you need is a nail and a brad and a pair of eyeballs. Bang, bang, bang and the picture is hanging. How hard was that? What the hell was all the fuss about with you guys? There; it looks perfect.

Here's the crazy thing. If you didn't watch either group go through their various machinations and you just came along to see the finished product, I will hazard the guess, that the results wouldn't be all that different. How can that be, you ask? I don't know the answer, but I can only suggest it is yet another great mystery in this thing that we call life. As you might suspect, I am in the latter camp and believe that there are two rules. Rule number one: don't sweat the small stuff. Rule number two: see rule number one.

Note to self: Where the hell is my hammer? I gotta hang some stinking pictures! NO, NO, NO.... ruler; why would I need a ruler?

16. The Courage to Write

I had a curious thing happen to me at a book signing for my last book. Whenever possible, I try to make these events a little more interesting by reading a few excerpts from the book and sometimes I include some of the back stories; and, based on my history of doing stand-up, my exchanges with the audience tend to be pretty lively. Heck, I'm a story teller, so there is nothing like giving me a bit of encouragement so I can go off on a relentless tangent or two. I really enjoy fielding the various and sundry questions, and smile when I get asked the never to be missed "how long did it take you to write it question."

This one time, however, I was given pause, when a good friend of mine asked in a very nonchalant, non-hostile way, "So how do you get the courage to write what you do?" Now depending on the tone of the speaker, this could almost be like she was saying:

"WHERE DO YOU GET THE BALLS, to say the things that you do?"

But it wasn't like that at all, thankfully. No, it was almost like she was asking me, "*How could **she** muster the strength to write?*"

I smiled at her and accepted her question in the tone that I thought was appropriate. I offered her my sincerest encouragement. One of the greatest things one can do in this life for a fellow traveler on this spaceship called Earth is to give them encouragement. I love that word, *encouragement*. It literally means, to give one courage. Heck, who doesn't need a little courage from time to time? I know I do. More times than not, we have the courage, but we simply forget that we do. Remember the story of the Cowardly Lion in *the Wizard of Oz*. The Wizard had to remind him that he had the courage all along. It was he who was the one that spearheaded the assault on the Wicked Witch of the West when it came time to rescue Dorothy. The Wizard told him that it wasn't that he lacked the courage; he merely needed a medal to prove that he had it. I went on to tell the nice lady in the audience, as I had explained in my last book: one should write about things that they know. Each of us has a book or two in them. Some of us will actually get to write one. Does it take courage? Sure it does. But we all have courage, most of the time; we simply need to be reminded.

Then I asked her, "What's the worst thing that can *happen?*" She writes something, and somebody doesn't like what she wrote. Big deal! I guarantee someone won't like it. You know up front that you cannot please everyone and besides: who cares? Katherine Hepburn once said, and I am paraphrasing, "Forget about the critics. Someone will always have something bad to say about your performance. Just make sure you are happy with it."

I was thinking, as an extension of her question, that she might have also been asking me, "How do you get started?"

I told her about how I stole an idea from John Madden, the colorful football commentator. He sat down one day and started writing about something he knew something about, namely football. He wrote a page a day and after 365 days he looked down and exclaimed!

"Hey I wrote a book!"

What did he call it: *Hey, I wrote a book!* I thought that was a great formula and it is pretty much the same one I follow now. It puts me in the habit of writing. *If you want to be a writer, you have to write.* I expanded on my previous response to her and added this to the mix, thinking that that would be additionally helpful to her. Of course, I followed up with the expected question and asked her warmly and supportively, "So does that help, did I answer your question?"

She smiled and said, that no actually I hadn't, and then elaborated on her previous question.

"WHERE DO YOU GET THE BALLS...?"

Note to self. You write your book and I'll write mine.

17. Wednesday

You have all heard it before: *Wednesday is hump day.* Now some of you gutter minds out there are probably thinking that this is where the book loses the P.G. rating. To you I say: *Shame on you.* No, to most of us, we will simply think that this is the middle of the week and that we have gotten *over the hump.* You know, like the hump on the camel. When did this get to be a BYOC (bring your own camel) world? And what kind of a camel is it? Is it a Bactrian or a Dromedary camel? Gotcha there, didn't I? For those of you who are less informed about the world of camels, it is the Dromedary that has two humps. The single humped Bactrian is much more suited for transporting people, is larger, and is truly the beast that warrants being called *the ship of the desert.* But let's get back to those crazy humps.

We talk about getting over the hump in the middle of the week almost as if to say, TGIW (thank God it's Wednesday.) Have our lives become so insanely arduous that we are struggling to make it to…Wednesday? Three days into the week and we are looking to take the gas pipe? Man, you might need to consider a different line of work if that's the way you find yourself thinking. I know most of us work pretty hard and some of us don't love our jobs as much as others profess to love theirs. But here's the deal. How many years do you think you have coming to you? There is a wonderful song in the musical *Rent* that talks about the 525,600 minutes each of us has in a year. It is called *The Season of Love.* It is a great song from one of my least favorite musicals, but it has a more important message. We each get approximately 525,600 minutes to use as we see fit. Now, lop off a third of them, if you are lucky, and you get a good 8 hours sleep every night. Cut another 20% if you have a long commute and you live anywhere near L.A. or NYC or Boston. Now you are down to about half the original number. If you want to go to the bathroom every once in a while, and if you are prone to eating spicy Mexican food, you might have to cut that number in half again. If you are a woman who takes an inordinate amount of time getting ready for dinner and you go out more than 3 nights in a week, you might actually be in the red at this point. So just so that we are clear: That original number of over a half a million minutes is not a heck of a lot of time. So, what are you going to do? Be miserable for the rest of your increasingly short life thinking about how you are going to bring your camel to work and maybe get over one of his humps? It's pretty silly when you think about it, isn't it?

I say: go out and act boldly! Take your life by the ass and say: *hang on; it's going to be a wild ride.* Regrettably, for all of us, life is just too damned short. This is true regardless of how long you live. Don't spend it cheering that you simply made it to Wednesday. Wow, what an accomplishment that is. Kick that camel in the rump. (Well, don't really, because I hate people that are cruel to animals, and besides, the camel will spit at you.) No, kick him in the rump and tell that dirty old camel, *heck, I wish it was Monday and I had a whole 7 days MORE ahead of me so I can get the most out of this life.* The camel won't know what the heck you are talking about, and if it is a Bactrian, it will be too depressed over its lack of a second hump to even want to respond.

Note to self: Love Mondays because you get to start all over doing something that hopefully you enjoy.

18. Gym Etiquette

For those of you who are *Seinfeld* fans, you might remember that as George Costanza discovered, peeing in the shower is generally considered to be unacceptable behavior at the gym. Then, too, you will be reminded that in the same episode, Elaine Benes was seriously offended when some lug at the gym rejected her initial flirtations and then went on to not wipe off the rivers of molten sweat, he had left behind him after using one of the machines. These are serious and obviously common-sense infractions in the social order in the world of the gym. For some of you, who are among the uninitiated, there are other more subtle rules and mores that need to be observed.

My daughter Alice, as a sign of her deep affection for me, is constantly urging me to go to the gym more often. I suspect she does this because, as I get older, she thinks the old man is not as sharp and swashbuckling as he used to be, and I'd like to keep him around a little longer, if for no other reason because he makes me laugh. It is always quite touching when she urges me to go. I know I probably try her patience a bit when I make an excuse, like I'm busy this morning, or I have to wash the car, or I have to slop the hogs today, or Venus is in retrograde, or some other similar tripe of an excuse like that. (As a side note: I live in a city and I don't actually own hogs.) I had an additional chuckle when she first shamed me into joining the local gym, and she ran me through some of the more subtle rules of the road that I had not even begun to consider.

First, there was the dress code. Now as some of you may have gleaned from a few of the previous "chips" in the last book, I tend to be always conspicuously overdressed. I don't even own jeans. If I did, I would call them dungarees. So, if no one gave me the heads up, I would show up at the gym, and I might be wearing a nice pastel colored, Ralph Lauren, golf shirt and khakis. Why is this? I have to tell you, it's pretty simple. I really am not looking to break a sweat; I just want to stay toned a little. For the fashion conscious at the gym, this would be wrong, wrong, wrong. She explained that I needed to wear a tee shirt (preferably with some logos or pictures relating to a gym or with guys pumping iron on them.) If the tee shirt was torn or if it looked like I was wearing it after I was ejected from a speeding car, that would be even better. I should wear shorts, too. Longer shorts were good, daisy dukes were not. No long pants were allowed under any circumstances. That would just be stupid. I could not wear regular shoes. I had to wear what I would call sneakers or, as she would call them, athletic shoes. Boy, she was killing me here. OK, check, I've got the outfit down; what else did I need to know?

Well, this was a big one for me. *I was not allowed to talk to anyone at the gym.* A friendly nod of acknowledgement was more than sufficient. For most people, that was no big deal. But I am a guy who likes to talk to everyone. I'm a real jabber jock.

"Hey, how's it going? Bet you're busting a gut on that machine there? So how long have you been coming here? You know, I don't think this regimen is working for you; you still look pretty fat to me. I mean we're not talking Hindenburg fat, but maybe you should try something else."

I don't know, I thought that was a pretty good icebreaker.

Alice doubled down on me, and insisted that whatever I did, I wasn't even remotely to consider *flirting* with any of the woman there. That was a major no, no. The women were there to exercise. That was all.

"Don't be bothering them," she told me in very lawyer-like terms.

No attempt at idle chatter was acceptable. Now I have to admit, I was somewhat taken back by the implication that I would be as bold and inappropriate as that, to force my affections on these poor unsuspecting behemoths who were conspicuously slathered in perspiration. How could I not flirt with them? What could be more attractive than a wriggling, overweight woman, wearing headphones, pounding out a war path on a *Stairmaster*, who was obsessed with dropping 20 lbs. that day? Now don't get me wrong. I am no prize either. Years earlier when I probably was in my prime, my daughter reminded me then, that I was no longer "where it was at." At best, I was "where it had been." OUCH!

All of that being said, I'm wearing my tee shirt and shorts, with my required athletic shoes and I'm talking to no one when I go the gym. I am a model citizen, a veritable mummy. It does pain me to tell you that I now I feel like the Maytag repairman when I go to the gym. You remember him. He was the loneliest guy in town. *Don't even think of starting a conversation with me, you brazen hussy, you!*

Note to self: For God's sake, just leave me alone, I am getting my athletic togs on and going to the gym. (Who wears togs anymore?)

19. It's Organic

"You have to try this. It's *organic.*"

For the record, when most people demand this of me, I am tempted to say, "Manure is too, and you should eat that."

Too many of us in the developing countries have become obsessed with eating better and eating healthier and eating things that are *organic.* For the most part, I typically think, *what a scam.* I was in a supermarket the other day and I saw bananas on display and they were marked at 49 cents a lb. It seemed like a fair price to me. Just as I was about to grab a hand full, I noticed that two counters over they had more bananas and they were marked 69 cents a lb. I quickly put the bananas down and went over to the other counter. I looked at the more expensive bananas and tried to ascertain what made them better. Oh, I see it now, they were marked *organic.* Now I know some of those *greeny vegetarian types* out there, you know, the ones that look like death warmed over, would easily step up and prove to me, if even at only the microscopic level, that the organic bananas were a world apart. They would chastise me and tell me about all of the toxins the Monsanto group was responsible for and how the agriculture industry has done more to pollute the earth than all of the coal miners in the world and that by buying the regular banana, I was one of the biggest parts of the problem. I can accept that. And, as I imagine one of these tree hugging sons of bitches accosting me in the produce section, I'm thinking of simply flipping my banana around and pretending it is a pistol and telling them to, "Go ahead, make my day."

Dirty Harry aside, I gotta tell you, just as a lark, I decided to buy one of those *20 cent extra* bananas. I bought a bunch of the less expensive ones, too. You know the ones that were obviously loaded with unimaginable toxic waste. They looked identical. The next day, I ran the all-important taste test. Please note, they looked identical on the inside as well. Finally, the moment of truth arrived. This was a special day. I felt like, for the first time, I was acting as a *banana sommelier.* I have eaten thousands of bananas in my life time. I slowly ingested the soft yellow flesh and savored it, being careful to provide the maximum and equal number of chews to each. I made sure I sniffed each one before proceeding. And then it was time for the judges to step forward

(Oh, that's me, I was the only judge. I guess I was getting carried away for a moment.) Are you ready for the great reveal?

They were identical. For a hundred bucks, I couldn't tell you the difference. And I would like to think that I am one smart banana. *One banana, two bananas, three bananas more, if you could tell the difference here, you should buy the store.* Then you could go out and scam all those idiots who think they are adding 10 years to their lives by paying 20 cents a lb. extra for those stinking bananas. Organic? I'll give you organic.

Note to self: and you can stick your banana in your……ear.

20. The Final Farewell

All right, what's it gonna be? Are you going to be buried or do you want to be cremated? You could opt for just donating your body to medical science and calling it a day. Most people tend to go with doors number one or two here, but that's OK either way. I was thinking that I would like to donate some of my organs but I am not sure I would like to have my skeleton hanging around somewhere. I can only imagine some of those sophomores in anatomy class tickling my ribs or doing God knows what to me. Come on, you know how some of these geeks are? No, I'm thinking the cremation route is the way to go. In fact, I am thinking of planning ahead and going in to see my local funeral director and telling him what I have decided to do. It would go something like this.

"So, I have decided on cremation."

"Good, that's what many of our clients are electing to do these days. It's is certainly more affordable than traditional internment."

"Yeah, that's what I was thinking, so to lock in the best rate, I would like to do it today, you know before the prices go up. I can only imagine what it will be like 20 years from now."

"What do you mean, today?"

"I would like to get cremated today."

"But you're not dead yet."

"Oh, you see, I knew there was going to be a catch, it's always like this, there is always an angle here. If I can't get cremated today, the deal is off."

What do you think? Should I try it to see what happens? OK, all kidding aside, I have to share something with you that really made me laugh out loud. As I was sitting in church the other day, I was reviewing, in the bulletin, the actual policy on cremation for Catholics. As of 1963, the Church officially declared that cremation was acceptable. There were a myriad of reasons prior to this declaration as to why this was previously *verboten* but it was all good now. Of course, as you would expect, however, there were a couple of caveats. The *cremains* had to be interned in a Catholic cemetery. I really laughed out loud this time and said to myself: *Hey, business is business.* The church might be willing to roll over on a 2000-year-old dogma, but they weren't going to take it on the chin and lose money. It's bad enough that bingo was gone. But wait! There were a few other practices that were frowned upon, too. Obviously, you couldn't simply get left in an urn on the mantle. That goes without saying, since they lose the opportunity to sell you the little plot in the officially blessed hallowed ground. You couldn't get scattered, either. That practice, by the way, is actually discouraged and virtually illegal in every town and city in the USA. Have you ever seen the YouTube where the guy is attempting to scatter his father's ashes at sea and he tosses them directly into the wind and gets a face full of the *ashen old man*? I love that. What a mess. But here is the rule that I loved the most. You were not allowed to divide the ashes up. You know, you couldn't give half to one sibling and a quarter to the wife and the rest to whomever. Now that was something that never dawned on me.

"Listen, I think I got a leg here? Anyone want a leg? Oh man, this has got to be the head. I mean we didn't call him an old bone head for nothing. No, I don't want that part, how about a thigh. No, I'm a white meat fan, no dark meat for me."

I cannot tell you how pleased I am that someone would have even had the forethought to consider this. Who would divide up the ashes? Is it me?

Let me tell you a story. (Many) years ago, when I was in my early 20s, I happened to go to funeral memorial where the dearly departed had elected to be cremated. The service was at the house and it was kind of like a cocktail party without the cocktails. You know, they had coffee and finger sandwiches and some somber conversation. It was very pleasant. It was no Irish wake, that's for sure. I had never been to one of these things before; everyone that I knew got buried. At one point, I noticed a small urn on the mantle. When no one was looking, I decided to take a peek inside. I opened it up and saw all this crumbly stuff and nearly freaked out and practically spilled it as I raced to put the cover back on and get it back on to the mantle. My heart was pounding, I had a giant bead of sweat running down my brow, and the wife of the recently bereaved having glimpsed this near debacle came over to me. She leaned over and whispered in my ear with the gentlest of smiles on her face and told me in a reassuring and soothing voice. "It's potpourri."

Note to self: OK, let's go get cremated.

21. It's the Wizard...

These days, with all the Harry Potter hoopla out there, there seems to be an awful lot of fascination about wizards and wizardry and magic and all sorts of falderal along these lines. Is anyone asking, like I am: *what's that all about?* It is almost like people seemed to be obsessing after an easy solution to everything and anything, and somehow, they are hoping to simply snap their fingers, or wave their magic wands, and *poof,* results. Wouldn't it be great if we could all have a magic wand? Wouldn't it be awesome if we didn't have to do the work and actually have to surrender to the discipline? Years ago, I was given some advice that I took to heart and it seemed to offer me a metaphor about life, and oddly enough, it came from my golf teacher. I was blessed because, although I am a seriously less than average golf player, my teacher gave me what I needed to know from a skill perspective, so I could enjoy the game based on my limitations of age and time commitment. In truth, he gave me so much more than that. He gave me sound advice for a better life. I will share two of the things he passed on to me. Are you ready? Good, now sit down and listen.

First of all, let me give him his first homage by telling you his name. He is Gary Occhino and he is not just a teaching golf pro; he is a great guy, a wonderful family man, and a great ambassador for the planet. Sometimes you have people cross your path who truly make the world a better place and Gary is just such a guy. Here's one of his golf lessons. I always screw it up by misnaming it, but essentially it is what he calls the 5-pace-rule or the 5-step-rule. It states quite simply that we get 5 steps (or paces) to *get over* a bad shot. The same is true for a good shot. If you are stewing in your juices about hitting the ball into the woods or into the lake, or you simply take a duff, it will screw up you next shot and the one after that and so on through the remaining 18 holes or so. You blew it. Get over it. Then the next shot is an entirely new experience with none of the bad karma or feelings from its predecessor. Golf is so much like life in this very specific regard. We all screw things up. GET OVER IT! Some of us really screw things up so much that everyone turns and points a finger and says, "Did you see what that guy just did; what a moron!"

You've got a lot of shots left in you to make up the entire game. Conversely, you have to get over your great shots as well. Yeah, you just keep thinking how you just looked like Arnold Palmer on that great shot you just made and you can bet your partner in your foursome a beer at the 19th hole, you will have a better than average *stinker* on the next shot. Good or bad, GET OVER IT! The next shot is a stand-alone shot. It is in its own universe. Treat it as such. I quote this story often to my sales associates when they blow a deal or fail to close on a prospect. Let's kick things up a notch here. What's that you say; you had a bad marriage? GET OVER IT! I always like to say that *hell, the first marriage is like the first waffle, and it should be thrown away.* (Does that make me sound a bit jaded? I'm not sure; just checking.) Regardless, of when I tell this story, it always seems to put things in the proper perspective. I think there is a special magic in this advice and life (golf) lesson. Thank you, Gary.

Now to the story that is more germane to the topic. I was telling Gary about some clubs I was thinking of purchasing and a particular set of *Callaway* irons that I thought would be good for me. He gave me some good info and sound advice again, and as you would suspect this great *sage of the links* did it again. He gave me a brief note of admonishment and told me:

"Remember, it is the wizard, not the wand."

The greatest set of clubs in the world wouldn't do you much good if you didn't have the fundamentals of a good swing under your belt. If the wizard had great skill, he could make any old wand do his bidding and probably with results that weren't that surprising. Want proof? Take a look at some of the clubs people were using fifty or a hundred years ago. They were incredibly primitive, and yet really skillful players could play a helluva round of golf with them. I have a good friend who is a terrific golfer. He was on a golf scholarship to Niagara University years ago. He told me he was shooting in the 80s the first year he started playing as a junior in high school. He was 17 or so and a gifted athlete, so he had youth and strength on his side. Today he is in his 60s. He doesn't have youthful prowess going for him anymore but the equipment has evolved very dramatically and perhaps it has offset that a bit. The drivers are 10x the size. We have fiberglass shafts. Even the balls have changed. Guess what? Yes, no surprise: he still shoots in the 80s today.

What's more to the point, I would have to say he is still a pretty good golfer. He's probably a pretty good wizard, too, I would have to reckon.

Note to self: It's the wizard, not the wand.

22. Cheaters...

...No, not as in bad husbands who have broads on the side, or women that are messing around with guys named Sven the pool guy. I am talking about reading glasses, you know, *cheaters*. I always prided myself as having eyes like an eagle. I never needed glasses, and then one day, pretty much on my 45th birthday, I got up, picked up a newspaper, and screamed:

"Aaah, I'm blind."

I couldn't believe it. Everything was a blur. This couldn't be happening to me. I rushed off to see the eye doctor and have my eyes looked at and the doctor reassured me that blindness was not a serious concern and that my eyes were changing slightly and I would need a very mild prescription for reading. This was not possible. Nobody wore glasses in my family. My father was pushing 50 and he didn't wear glasses, but then again, I do recall that he used to read with a large magnifying glass in his hand. I always thought he was just doing a bad imitation of Sherlock Holmes and never considered that he might just be too vain to break down and face the reality that he needed glasses. OK, back to my situation.

The doctor informed me that this was a natural part of the aging process and he would write a script. He told me that there was nothing to be concerned about and that in fact, I was merely suffering from a weakness in one eye and the other one was pretty good. I thought about this and had a Eureka moment and exclaimed. "Wait a minute, are you saying I could wear a monocle?"

I was thinking, how cool would this be, a monocle. Who the hell is wearing a monocle these days? I would be unique. *Hey, look honey, there's that dapper guy over there with a monocle.* Excellent Smithers!

The doctor said, "Well you could, I suppose. I'm not sure how many guys are wearing a monocle these days. I mean, you would kind of look like Mr. Peanut a bit, wouldn't you?"

I was not dissuaded. "And your point is?"

I was this close to being the guy with the monocle and then in a tiresome moment of practicality, I relinquished and dejectedly told him, "No, just write the script."

At this point, being an actor, I considered how I could take my new prop, the glasses, and point it at people as I was making emphasis. I envisioned how I might have one of the arms in my mouth as I was appearing to be deeply involved in thought. I could jab it at people in an accusatory gesture. This was going to be a whole new world for me. *Glasses*: how awesome was this going to be? It would be worth it to forego the uniqueness of the monocle to work on new ways to enhance my characters with yet another prop.

Now the key was to get the right frames. I went to the optometrist store, and after about an hour perusing through about 200,000 different frames, I selected the classic Clark Kent look in a tortoise shell color. I thought this new, studious look would open up lots of possibilities for me. I opted for blended bifocals, and they ran me about $350. I collected them when they were ready and for the first hour or so I practiced my various gestures and was really getting into my new found toy. I think I might have made it to about the 4th hour of ownership when I realized that I had lost them. *OH, THIS WAS JUST GREAT!*

OK, so I am on the way back to the optometrist to go get a replacement pair. I begin to think about the new policy of deficit spending I was about to initiate if I was going to keep myself in glasses. Then I remembered the rest of the conversation I had with the doctor.

He told me that not only weren't my eyes all that bad but if I wanted to, although he didn't actually recommend it, I could just go to the *Dollar Store* and get a pair of *cheaters*. I was appalled. *Dollar Store* glasses; what kind of a cheesy prop would that be for me? OK, $350.00 versus a buck? I, at least, needed to consider it. I go the *Dollar Store* and what do I see: the mother lode. They have dozens of different frame designs, and then I discover that not only are my eyes not that bad, I can get away with using the lightest magnification they offer: 1.00. (15 years later I am up to a whopping 1.50.) I leave that day with about 10 different styles, big ones, little ones, round ones, square ones, black frames, brown frames, metal, and today I have them all over the house. Now when I lose them, who cares? What other options did I have? It would have been unimaginable for me to wear the string around my neck like secretaries did in the olden days. No way, that wasn't going to happen to me. As Mick Jaeger said, "You can't always get what you want, but if you try sometimes, you get what you need."

I may not have a monocle, but now people know me as the guy who always attempts to stab them with his glasses when he is talking. It's just great.

Note to self: Now where the hell did I put my glasses?

23. Gas...next exit.

I love taking long car trips. You know, the kind of jaunts that you take where you know you will have to stop for gas at some point. Of course, it would make a lot of sense if you thought about it for a bit beforehand, and mapped out precisely where you would need to stop for gas, based on your fuel tank capacity. No, that would be too much like planning ahead and would rob me of the spontaneity of seeing the warning light on my dash board that tells me I have 5 miles left. I love that light. And you know what, that light is never going to come on unless you are in either a rain storm that is reminiscent of the Great Deluge or on some deserted highway that is as dark as a cow's stomach. But there it is, right on cue. That crafty little warning light is practically blinding you now. It's time to start dropping your standard series of F-bombs. Now let's move on and progress to demanding: *COME ON, WHERE THE HELL IS A F****** GAS STATION?*

You're in luck. Finally, the *highway gods* smile on you. They actually take pity on you, you poor pathetic traveler. Finally you see a sign. It indicates that there is food and gas at the next exit. You're going to make it. It is just 2 miles ahead. Now here's where those same gods have their first series of chuckles at your expense. You are thinking that you will be able to see a gas station and maybe some sort of fast-food restaurant *from the highway* before you slide onto the off ramp, right? No way, now what fun would that be? You must take the ramp and drive at least a half a mile and make another left or a right. It isn't till you get to that intersection that you will receive the next bread crumb clue. And, there it is. At last, you read the next sign in your treasure hunt that shows a series of icons that translate as *Service: 2 miles.* Wow, how lucky can one guy be? You probably see a picture of a fork as well, which translates as food. Tiny beads of sweat begin running down your forehead. It is almost like you have malaria. Your jalopy is literally running on fumes and your spirit of adventure isn't what it used to be. You really don't feel like getting stuck on some back road at night. Wait a minute! Isn't this one of the locations from one of the big dance numbers in the movie *Deliverance?* You think to yourself: *Uh, oh, was that a banjo I just heard?* Oh, stop it. Just stop it!

Come on, man. How overdue for a miracle are you? Guess what? You get one. You deserve it. There it is way off in the distance. You see it. It's a light. It is more than a beacon of hope. Is it? It is! It looks like a service station; thank you God, thank you. You think, *maybe this is where you see one of those funny billboards that say,* **Eat Here, Get Gas.** You roll to a stop totally out of gas, and gleefully anticipate hopping out of the car to reach for the pump and you finally realize; they are closed. *SON OF A BITCH!* Those highway gods are sure mean, aren't they?

OK, I will admit this has never actually happened to me. I would be remiss; however, if I didn't tell you I have gotten really, really close on one occasion or another. So, based on this, I really and truly make an effort to *never,* and I mean *never,* get off a highway for gas, or a bathroom or whatever, *unless I can see it from the highway* before I make the exit. Every time, I have attempted to go on the great quest for the traveler's holy grails, in hopes that there will be a service station, etc., it always turns out to be the wrong kind of adventure. Why ruin a fun trip by neglecting to do a minimum of planning. It's kind of dumb if you think about it. But who said I was smart anyway?

Note to self: Is that a gas station up ahead? Please God, tell me it is!

24. The Greatest Books

At this point, based on the title here, I could do the predictable listing and categorizing of a series of books. OK, where would I begin? I suppose I could start with *the Bible*. It's a pretty nifty book, or should I say, series of books, because depending on the translation you use, it might have 45 books in the Old Testament and 27 in the new one. Together they make up a (total) book that has affected most of Western civilization's development and at least three of its major religions. If nothing else, it has an incredible impact on our history. Additionally, I might include some others from my personal list. I would definitely include Marcus Aurelius' *Meditations.* It is not one that comes to mind for most, but here this philosopher king (emperor) offers us some wonderful advice for leading a good and proper Stoic life. I love how he proclaims that "even in a palace a man might live well." Yes, I think I would definitely include that one. How about some fun picks? I like the *Count of Monty Christo* a lot. It's a page turner and the characters are so well developed that it makes this tale of love and revenge an absolute essential for me. Thank you, Alexander Dumas; *they don't call it a classic for nuttin.* What else should make the list?

Here's an interesting exercise. You can google *top 10 books* and see what some algorithm will tell you are the books that should be on your must-read list. One of the lists has 50 greatest books, and the list includes books like, *Madame Bovary* (Flaubert), One Hundred Years of Solitude (Marquez), *In Search of Lost Time* (Proust), *To the Lighthouse* (Virginia Wolf), *The Red and Black* (Stendhal), and *Dead Souls* (Gogol).Now, if you looked at this list of books, and if you are like me, you are probably feeling like a bit of a barbarian and saying to yourself, *S***, I haven't read any of those.* Heck, I would venture to say that no one I know has read them either, so does that mean that I'm the president of the *Barbarians are Us Club*? If I accept that accolade, I have to confess, at least, that I *have heard* of two of them. Does that get me a pass? If we are really going to be honest here, I would have to tell you that if I lived to be 1000, my life would be more than complete if I never read anything by Proust. What a flipping bore that guy was. Now I would have to step in and add some equal time and tell you, some of the other books on that top 50 list included, *Huckleberry Finn* (Twain),

Gulliver's Travels (Swift), the *Odyssey* and the *Iliad* (Homer) and yes, I have read them and loved each one of them. If I had continued rambling on, I might have added each one of these to my personal list, but one list might really be as good any other, so here's where I finally get to the point of this little tale.

The Greatest Books are the books that you have read or that you are reading. They increase in their overall magnitude of greatness if you are reading them *right now*. Churchill said it best, "You are what you read."

Now, if all you read is the *Enquirer* or *People Magazine*, not to get judgmental, you are living on fast food for the mind. Most fast food is junk and at best you will get a bellyache and not look healthy. You cannot be a health nut and eat that crap all the time and look or be healthy. Likewise, if you are reading crap, you have crap for brains. This is why one needs to cultivate their reading habits just like they would their eating and drinking habits, or their work habits, or their sleep habits, and so on and so forth. The Greatest Books that you are reading right now, or re-reading because they meant something to you way back when you read them the first time, shape your thoughts in the present and contribute to your continuing quest for becoming great and becoming the best person you can be. So, put down that dime store novel and pick up something worthy of your time. You only have so much of that left and you have to let it count. Want to read a truly great book? Pick up a copy of *Potato Chips for the Soul.* I hear the sequel is even better: *Potato Chips for the Soul: A Second Bag.*

Note to self: This is a really great book. I am glad I'm reading it.

25. Spontaneity

There's much to be said about spontaneity. Now bear in mind, I tend to be really big on spontaneity, but sometimes it has its limitations, and frequently, it is downright inappropriate. In a relationship, more times than not it is like spring time, and it literally can be like the proverbial breath of fresh air. It can be redemption. There are few things more tragic than seeing what was once one of those definitive beautiful loving relationships and watching it turn sour. We see it all the time. The vicissitudes of life and the surrendering to the mundane seems to beat them down every time. Can anyone join Peggy Lee and me in a chorus of *Is That All There Is*? Boredom is like cyanide in any relationship. Spontaneity is essential to keep it fresh and alive. The great Hindu work, the *Kama Sutra,* professes to be able to keep intimacy alive by categorizing hundreds of different sexual positions in an effort to keep the partners from resorting to the same old same old routine. Some of the positions have lovely names like the lotus blossom, or the Sultan. Some can only be mastered if you have a minimum of 4 Olympic gold medals in gymnastics. Either way, it's a nifty little how-to book, especially for guys like me that have only mastered the age-old *bull in the china shop* position. Seriously though, it is certainly a worthy read and *George Costanza* would have fared a lot better if he could only have remembered if it was "a counter clockwise swirl at the end, or simply an intermittent stroke

As I have indicated, however, sometimes spontaneity in a relationship can be a bad thing. Let's presume you have to go to a funeral at 9 a.m. tomorrow. You start the following conversation:

"Oh, what the heck, let's go get breakfast at Denny's instead and have a few grand slams and take in a good, solid, power walk at the mall first. Why start the day all depressed? We can catch up with the family sometime in the afternoon. Heck, your mother's dead anyway. She won't miss us, that's for sure."

Now, you could try that play with your wife and or your significant other. Believe me; I would love to see that. How can you not admire people who act boldly and aren't owned by society's conventions? I would think in your case, the swelling should go down in about a month, maybe two. Try to keep a little ice on it, in the meantime. How big should the ice pack be? About the size of one of those glaciers in Greenland should be about right. Generally speaking, spontaneity doesn't work all that well in business or professional circles either. You are on trial for murder and your attorney literally has your life in his hands and he decides to show up in his gym cloths because he wanted to get in a good intensive work out before starting his deliberations. He's all sweated up, but boy he's convinced the words will be flowing like honey and it will be hard to tell if Johnny Cochran hasn't just come back from dead. OK, maybe it's your turn to sweat? How about you're going in for your colonoscopy, and just before you fade off into LA LA Land with that super drug the nurse just administered, and you see the doctor approach with some giant hose in his hand, and he turns his baseball hat around and yells out to everyone right at black out time:

"OK, let's see what this baby can do, YEEHA!"

No, consistency of procedure would probably win out over spontaneity in this situation.

Spontaneity usually is best applied when we have smaller decisions to make. A good rule of thumb might be the lower the consequence the more acceptable the use of spontaneity becomes.

"What should we do tonight, honey? I know, why we don't we…?"

"Hey, instead of simply just going on the boat tomorrow, how would you feel about parasailing instead?"

"Instead of a movie tonight, let's go dining and dancing."

"How would you feel about my taking on two new sister wives?"

You might want to get ready to duck on that last one, even if you are a Mormon.

Note to self: I've got an idea. How about I stick this whipped cream in your eye, instead?

26. Fossils

A lot of people are superstitious and carry *lucky charms* in their pockets (no, not the magically delicious cereal. You can only imagine what a mess that would make after a while. Sometimes, they may carry amulets with varying degrees of mojos ascribed to them and still others will carry some sort of religious objects, like crosses or rosaries. A lot of Greeks and Muslims carry different types of *worry beads* and these days everyone seems to want to quietly, in their own ways, tap into something that might provide them with a bit of centering. Hey whatever, nobody is being hurt here and if some little *object* helps you out in any way, I say, *bully for you.* I carry a tiny fossil.

I have been fascinated by fossils since I first discovered what they were as a child. It probably isn't all that unusual, since most little boys have a similar obsession with dinosaurs and all things prehistoric. I can first recall learning how they seemed to almost be frozen in time, having gotten swallowed up by some mud bog somewhere and literally petrified (turned to stone) over the millions of years that they lay there until someone was fortunate enough to unearth them. There are few things more enjoyable than to walk a creek bed with a little child and discover fossils together. A similar kick can be derived by planting potatoes. The tubers grow under the soil and when the green tops above the soil tip you off that they are ready to harvest, all you need to do is get an eager kid and tell him to start digging gently and it becomes the ultimate treasure hunt. They practically lose their minds in glee. Who knew digging for potatoes could be such fun... but, back to me and my fossil.

I don't carry a fossil because of any magical properties I think it might possess. If I did, I suspect I would have to attend the church of the *Immaculate Fossil* on a regular basis and I don't remember seeing one of those in my travels. If I do find a church like that, I will wager they will have some incredibly weird dogma and ritualistic practices. No, it is nothing like that, really. I carry a little fossil that is nothing more than the petrified remains of a tiny sea scallop. Maybe it is a bay scallop because it is hard to tell. The sea scallop today has a smooth shell and the much smaller cousin, the bay scallop, has ridged edges like the shell of *Shell Oil.* It's hard to know who was who back then, because over the course of thousands of millennia, they may have switched dress codes. Either way, my fossilized favorite has ridges. I carry it as a gentle homage to my father who made his fortune in the shellfish business and I carry it to remind me of the fact that you are dead a long time. In the grand scheme of things, this creature in my pocket has been around for hundreds of millions of years and I have been around for little less than three score and ten. In the great wheel of creation, I am a pipsqueak. I sometimes find myself stroking it in my pocket when I am on line at the checkout counter. Perhaps it centers me a bit and subtly reminds me that I'm not going to be on the line for hundreds of millions of years and maybe I should simply take a giant non-fossilized chill pill. It is not a religious thing at all, it is a reminder thing.

How many of us carry photographs in our wallets (and now on our smart phones) to remind us of our loved ones. We might have pictures of our wives or our sweethearts. We might have various pictures of our children or our dogs. We might even have pictures of a sailboat we have been scheming about or images of anything that take us to a place for a fleeting moment and guide us to either our dreams or our memories. I carry a fossil. It doesn't make me a bad person. It simply provides me with a bit of perspective.

Note to self: What's in your wallet, or your pocket? (Gee, that almost sounds like a commercial.)

27. Selfies at Auschwitz

James Olsen, Paul J. Pansini, and Jeffrey Mathew Palazzo: these were the first three names my eyes caught inscribed on the edge of the *Reflecting Pool* at *the World Trade Center memorial.* These were just a few of the bravest of the brave; the first responders who ran into the trade center on 9/11 in the fleeting chance that some could be saved. Their names are permanently on display together with the names of the other 2982 that met their fates that day. If you are a native New Yorker, it is difficult not to be particularly moved by a visit to the memorial. For many of us, it is more personal. Each of us has their story of where we were that day. But regardless of where you were, in spite of the personal investment or loss you might have experienced, September 11th, 2001 divides history. We have gotten used to speaking about our world in terms of B.C and A. D. but today we speak of America and the world as we know it, as post and pre 9/11. We live in a different world today.

In March of 2017, I made my first sojourn back to what became known as *ground zero*. It was my first glimpse up close. I finally got to view the memorial. I saw the imprints where towers *One and Two* stood. I saw the reflecting pool that was constructed there, and considered what a fitting architectural tribute it seemed to make. I witnessed the onlookers and became conscious of the sense of loss many of them seemed to be reliving in their respective silences. And then I became painfully aware of something else which made me very angry. It made me bitter and brought me close to lashing out at the offenders. I don't understand how anyone could treat this as anything less than hallowed ground. Yet there they were. There were scores of what I will disparagingly refer to as *tourists* that seemed to be having quite the good time of it. They were laughing and horsing around and some were even taking *selfies*. There were several teenagers throwing coins into the pool, I guess, in some bizarre tradition of making a wish. What the hell was this all about and how could this be happening? Where was the respect for the sacrifice? I have no wish to get all biblical on you here but I can recall the story of Jesus literally *losing it* in the temple when the money changes were having a grand old time and he began turning their tables upside down and he berated them proclaiming, "My house is a house of God, but you have made it a den of thieves."

71

He had every right to be outraged as did I. Anyone that lived through the horrors of that day in September, little less than a generation ago, should have been equally offended. I was quite distraught and I shared my outrage with Jay, an artist friend, who I happen to be visiting. Artists sometimes have an extra unusual take on things and he said to me, "It's really quite awful when you think about it. It's like when you see people taking selfies at Auschwitz."

We both concluded at the same time speaking in unison, "*What the hell could these people be thinking?*"

It is only wrong in about 6 million ways.

I don't know if things were very different a hundred years ago or not. I really doubt however, that there was this same craven lack of sense and sensibility back then. One thing I must assuredly suspect is that this newly evolved lack of respect that we as a society seem to have whole heartedly embraced does little to make us a better people. It does less to improve the lofty core values that we espouse as a free society. So, for the record, I am just going to tell you up front, I am not going to have an ironic twist in this monologue. Neither will you hear me going for the cheap laugh. I just can't do that this time because that would only further contribute to the disillusionment I experienced that day. I am simply going to say that I was embarrassed and ashamed by people's reactions.

Note to self: none.

28. IHOP

Let's run an experiment. Ask the first 3 people you run into under the age of 20 what the initials IHOP mean. Don't be surprised if 2 out of the 3 don't have a clue. They could even come back with *I Heart only pancakes.* It's close, but no cigar. OK, for those of you *youngins* that might fall into that 2 out of 3 category I alluded to, IHOP stands for *the International House of Pancakes.* I always thought it was a funny name for a firm that specializes in flap jacks. I mean, it sounds kind of lofty, and at the bare minimum, a bit pretentious, doesn't it? Don't get me wrong: I love pancakes. I especially like buckwheat pancakes. The problem is they're really hard to find but I know you can definitely get them at the good old IHOP.

I have to tell you though, the last time I went there, I ran into some problems when I was midway through my short stack. I was forced to ask myself: when did we come up with a million different kinds of pancakes? I can remember blueberry and buttermilk, silver dollar and pecan, but I was literally overwhelmed at the selection and the depth of toppings I could subsequently order to improve upon an already great invention. There were mountain ranges of cream cheese and sundry confections swirling on some of those Johnny Cakes. You could have strawberries, and peaches, and whipped cream, and chocolate, macadamia nuts, and walnuts. You could build a veritable *Everest* of pancakes if you were so inclined. Just take your time; you can wait for the paramedics to arrive with the clamps. I am not sure how you can recover after you devoured one of those 2000 calorie *snacks.* I know I would absolutely have met my match here. I couldn't do it. After eating one of those meals, I would personally have little choice but to simply just place my face right down in the plate with all the maple syrup in it, and be forced to take a giant-sized siesta. OK, it wouldn't be a nap at all. It would be a full-fledged coma. Boy, we sure do like to take things to extremes in this country, don't we?

How about KFC? What does that stand for, what do those letters mean? OK, if you answered *Kentucky Fried Chicken,* we have a bell ringer. But here comes the big question. Have we become so obsessed with getting our food delivered to us so much faster that we have to use abbreviations? It is almost like we have to sneak up on it. (OK and for the record, IHOP is by no means considered fast food. Don't get me wrong. You actually have to sit down and eat it at a table, after you are served by a real live person.) But wait a minute. Maybe we should have KGB food that is strictly for Russian spies. We could have NSA, or FBI food for those that are sworn to protect and defend our country. Can you see where this is going? Don't you think we are a little out of control, here?

Note to self: Can I just get a corned beef on Rye? Is it that difficult? Do I have to send it UPS?

29. Guilt

Let's take a survey. Guilt: is it a good thing or a bad thing? It's your call. OK, before we get into one of those humanistic arguments that claim, "That there is neither good nor evil but thinking makes it so." Let's consider a few things. I grew up in a Brooklyn neighborhood that sported just as many Menorahs as Santa Clauses around holiday time. You want to talk about some serious guilt? Because I was the product of a parochial education, if you didn't walk away with your genetically coded supply of guilt from the nuns, you were either dead or they made sure that you were. The best part is, they really didn't feel guilty about that either. Everyone knew that on Friday, if you ate a tomato sauce on your macaroni that even had the suggestion of meat in it, you were sure to be one of the many logs that got tossed onto the hell fire after you were gone. It was all good. I am certainly no worse for the wear for it, and frankly, I harbor no ill feelings for the poor old nuns. Regrettably, many of my classmates would argue differently. Heck, I guess I was just smarter than they were and knew you were supposed to take things like that with a little grain of salt. My Jewish friends might not have fared as well, I suspect. They used to tell a joke. (Hint: try reading the following with a Yiddish accent. It's a lot funnier.)

"How many Jewish mothers does it take to change a light bulb?" Answer: just one.

"All right, be that way, I'll just sit here in the dark."

Guilt: it's all about guilt. But here's my question. Is it all bad to have a little guilt? Now I am not suggesting that all the mothers of the world, Jewish or not, should go around spreading guilt like peanut butter on bread. (The Italian mothers are pretty adept at this too, by the way.) I'm not even a mother, but I delight in answering the phone and after I have said hello, I love to throw in, "So what's happening, you don't call, you don't write?"

Today it seems no one is accountable and no one is required to be guilty about anything. Husbands (and wives) are given a veritable *carte blanche* to go out and cheat on their wives today. They are not getting a pass for being unfaithful. They beat the rap because they have a *sexual addiction.* If you get in an accident with your car, regardless if you were driving like a maniac you will still have the protection of No-Fault insurance coverage, right? I don't know but maybe a little guilt would be a good thing in these cases. I can remember learning about the basics of Freudian Psychology and the theory of the Id, the Ego and the Super Ego. The Super Ego developed last in healthy adults and was the seat of the conscience. In the case of psychopaths, no such development occurred and they simply had no conscience at all, ergo, they suffered from no guilt. Let's make a decision here. No conscience is probably a bad thing, right. If it was acceptable to run around with no conscience, we would have a totally anarchistic society. Most of us would find that to be a repugnant way of living. It would be what Thomas Hobbes described in his book the *Leviathan* as "life in the natural state; which was crude brutish and short." No, I say, *bring on the guilt.*

The problem with our society today is we just don't have enough guilt. What's that you say? "Screw the old lady. Let her sit in the dark."

Well, if that's how you feel. I won't feel guilty at all for not inviting you over to my house for Sunday dinner this weekend. So there!

Note to self: I am OK with a little guilt. We would all be better off if we felt that way.

30. Braces

Few things identify the socio-economic group you belong to more than the quality of your teeth. Persons of lower socio-economics, generally have teeth that have either not been attended to at all, or appear to show evidence of a lack of good dental care. There is no implied judgment here. It is just the way it is. I can remember chatting with a friend of mine who was frequently condescending and she referred to someone as a *loser with jacked up teeth*. Now granted, she might have been a loser but the jacking up of the teeth might not have had very much to do with her at all. This might have been her reality more due to either an accident of birth (bad genes) or her parents not being able to afford braces. When you see a beautiful young lady and she is in her 20s and she has a mouth full of spectacular, pearly whites, that are perfectly in line, it is reasonable to presume that she endured several years of torture at the hands of some sadistic orthodontist. One can also presume that her parents could have been driving a Mercedes for what they spent on those braces. The third thing that you can presume is that, for a great portion of her adolescence, she was hopelessly relegated to the geek of the week club together with scores of other metal mouths. For upwardly mobile folks, or for those that are really well off financially, it just won't do to have crooked teeth. An overbite is only acceptable if your first name is Kukla.

Many years ago, when I was in my mid 20's, I happened to be having a somewhat torrid affair with a young lady who I will call, Mary Jo. After several weeks of intimacy, I recall her sitting on the foot of the bed and she looked toward me with the oddest expression. She had a small pink, plastic case in her hand that appeared to be very precious to her. She began to speak. I didn't know what was in the case. I remember thinking in a brief moment of panic, "Oh My God, she is going to take out her dentures?"

I regrouped. I composed myself and began to suspect that perhaps she was simply taking her diaphragm out; in which case, no big deal, but why the odd expression? Then she began ever so cautiously to speak. Finally, Mary Jo made the big reveal. I took a deep breath. I swallowed even deeper, making sure she didn't notice my trepidation.

"I feel we have gotten to know each other pretty well by this time, (she paused), so I just need to tell you, (she paused again), but, but…. *OK, damn it,* I am supposed to wear *a retainer* at night. I have been really bad lately and I have to start wearing it, or my teeth are going to start moving around all over my head and I don't want to have to start wearing braces again at my age."

Do you have any idea how relieved I was? I had visions of her popping those choppers out of her mouth and chasing me around the room with them. Yikes! Talk about giving me the *heebie jeebies.*

"Oh, a retainer?" I yelled to her in ecstasy and delight.

Here's the reality: many people who have been fortunate enough to have had their parents pay for their braces, are frequently urged to wear *a retainer* for years afterwards. What can I tell you? Teeth move. Too many of these closeted, ungrateful, offspring simply choose to ignore their dentist's reprimands and 10 years later they are urged to wear braces, *again.* So now we have a new group to add to the previous socio-economic chain. These are the goofy people, who really regret not doing what my 4-year old daughter Alice used to tell me:

"You're not *wistening…*"

Note to self: If you were fortunate to have parents who cared enough to go broke to buy you braces so your teeth would be straight: wear your F****** *retainer*.

31. Coupons

Fasten your seatbelts; when it comes to coupons, you are moving into a whole new world. First of all, let's start with the basics. How do you pronounce this word? Depending on the part of the country you are from, you might call them coupons (as in, *coo* pons.) Other people might call them (*Cue* pons, with what linguists call a *milky oo* sound.) I once asked a friend of mine and he immediately responded and told me he had always called them (*Cwah* pons.) He really didn't, but it is always nice to know that there is more than one *Smart Alek* in the group. Because it is becoming more and more expensive to navigate through a family budget in 21St Century America, many people have resorted to using coupons to stretch their hard-earned dollars. It's not necessarily a bad thing; however, how one goes about using them is the key to creating value for fun and frivolity.

Here's a suggestion of how one might *not* want to use the infamous coupon. I have a competitor in my market who was actively trying to recruit one of my agents to go and work for his company. This guy was a legendary great *schmoozer.* He invited the agent to lunch at one of the nicer eateries in town and just as the bill came to him, he whipped out his trusty *10% off* coupon. Now I am just going to take a stab at this and say I am not sure he made the most positive impression with my agent. I am fairly confident that this is the case because my agent came to me and told me the entire story. She told me how flattered she was that someone took notice of her *book of business* and wanted to work with her. She explained to me what a knowledgeable business person her host seemed to be. She then proceeded to tell me she couldn't believe what a cheap skate he looked like when he produced the whopping 10% discount coupon.

"What the hell was that all about?" She asked.

"Boy, they really must be counting their *shekels* over there."

One can use restaurant coupons with close friends. I find it is usually best to use some disclosure when you use one, even with them. Senior citizens might get an added pass, but again they should be used among friends and not if it is going to become a major issue or a production the way we saw Jerry Seinfeld's parents attempting to use the tip calculator. Incidentally, and as it should always go without saying, the tip should be determined as if you were paying the price before the discount was applied. More times than not, this can cut deeply into the face value of the coupon and you might discover it wasn't such a good deal after all.

Here's an interesting spin on the idea of the coupon. It is called the *Groupon.* I have found that *Groupons* can be a wonderful thing and I make no bones about using them (again with discretion.) They do several things. They provide a relatively serious discount for the product or service you might be using and I find that, particularly with restaurants, they get me to try new places that I might not have thought of using, if I wasn't introduced to the special deal. That's a good thing for everyone.

On the other hand, I have seen several people take the whole coupon thing to ridiculous extremes. Now I am not talking about those people you have seen on shows that are actually called *extreme couponers.* Those people make it a full-time job to get the best bargain, and yes, you can save so much money that they actually give you money back at the super market checkout. That's more couponing than I want to do. I have, however, seen people who will actually take the Sunday paper and sit with it all day. They cut out what seems like hundreds of coupons and all too often they do so for products they will never use. They will cut out coupons that offer a tremendous discount for cat food. What's wrong with that? THEY DON'T OWN A CAT!

So, here's the deal. Coupons can be a cool way to save a few bucks. Just don't go over board and keep them in perspective, and recognize that there *is* always a time and a place. Remember what we said about cremations a few stories ago? Just because you have a coupon doesn't mean you have to use it to get *cremated today.* I know you can save 15%, but you should at least wait to die.

Note to self: Wanna get married this weekend? I've got a 20 % off, coupon at the Cracker Barrel.

32. Real Men

Real men change diapers. Suffice it to say that the roles assigned specifically to men and women have changed over the years. These days, in the earliest part of the 21st Century, when it comes to parenting, there is an increased expectation of job sharing. This is certainly true in most of the industrialized countries in the modern world. In the undeveloped countries, and in cultures that still are heavily invested in the machismo notion of gender expectations, it is still business as usual. In this world, it is still the woman who carries water from the river and takes care of 100% of the childrearing. Not so, for the so-called modern man. And that's a good thing. At least, I think it is.

I will be the first to tell you that changing diapers was not my favorite thing to do. I could go on to tell you, and any young man who is expecting to be a father, that I'm not going to race to the head of the line to change just any baby's diaper. It is totally different with your own child. My daughter still gets upset when I introduce her to people as *the fruit of my loins.* I suppose I might object to it, too, if I was like her: a young attorney who expected to get taken seriously. I chalk it up to father's privilege (it's like when the President claims Executive Privilege). Perhaps it is just a case of early onset goofiness, but either way, I simply expect to get a pass for being glib. But regardless, when it is your kid, the diaper thing isn't all that upsetting and I am convinced that real men simply deal with it. It certainly gives you a lot of clout in years to come, when those same adorable little cherubs begin to get mouthy in the early teen years and beyond. You just sit back, declare to the masses of their friends, "Hey, knock it off, I changed your diapers!"

All of their friends will grunt a giant "OOO" in unison and the offending child simply knocks it off and responds:

"DAD!"

Let me speak to those manly men who just don't get it. You become a better husband by sharing the more unpleasant tasks of childrearing. Regardless of what your wife tells you, she is absolutely exhausted. You could be suave and debonair and go out and buy her flowers, but it is a helluva lot more powerful if you to deal with one of those poopy diapers and give your beloved a break. Listen, I don't care if you are super dad or just think you are. The Mrs. is going to have you beat on the diaper routine by a minimum of 50 to 1. She is the one that will get up in the middle of the night, beating you 10 to 1 on that. I know; you need your rest. You have to go out and work in the jungle tomorrow to bring back the buffalo. The difference is this: I'll bet she probably is going to a full-time job as well, plus she is assuming 90 % of the babying chores as part of her first job. I realize I am making sweeping generalizations here, but there is more truth in my shotgun statistics than not.

Let me go one step further. I kind of lose respect for a guy who doesn't step up and do what he needs to do in this department. Here's the deal. Any dope can be a father. It takes a special guy to be a dad. Being a dad is a serious job. A great dad should be totally secure in their masculinity and as such they should understand their role as a loving husband. That includes changing diapers, and sporting those trendy, papoose carrying devices. They will be totally committed to doing what needs to get done. Getting your hands dirty is simply part of the gig. And just for the record, nobody is buying that thing about the buffalo anymore and all that toiling in the jungle. There are no buffalo out there. We don't want buffalo for dinner.

Note to self: Let me shake your hand. You're a real man. On second thought; perhaps, we will just fist pump.

33. Big Lips

OK, stop the presses! I am all for taking care of yourself. There is nothing wrong with going to the gym and eating right and doing whatever you can to keep father time from making you look like his grandmother. You might even consider having a little *nip and tuck* here and there. If it makes you feel better about yourself, if it gives you an extra lift in your step, it's all good. But, let's think about this for a second. Have you seen some of those people that seem to have taken things a bit too far when it comes to the plastic surgery department? I was going to say that, after a while, some of them look like mannequins, but in all too many cases that would be insulting to the mannequins. And what the hell is going on with those lips?

There seems to be a trend in the modern world of plastic surgery for women to make their lips look fuller. My question is this: fuller than what, a supertanker? I am loath to single out any one particular celebrity, but let's take a look at former soap star and current reality queen, Lisa Renna. This was a very attractive lady. I'm not sure who advised her, though, because she elected to go out and have injections in her lips that now make them comparable in size to the Presidents that sit on top of Mount Rushmore. They are *gynormous.* I know that's not a real word, but in this case, it perfectly describes them. Let me kick it up a notch, and this might sound a little cruel, too. They are the exact same size as those red wax candy lips we would get at the candy store when we were kids. Is there anyone out there that really thinks this is an attractive look? I cannot imagine that there is. Now I'm really going to feel awful if it was an accident on the surgeon's part and he was intending to make them just slightly larger and something went wrong. Perhaps there was some undue swelling or something? Somehow, I don't think this is the case. I think she wanted the *gynormous* look and she got it, and now tens of thousands of other women around 50 seem to be lining up for that big lip look too. It's crazy.

Now a lot of you might defensively chastise me and say "*that beauty is in the eye of the beholder."* There is no argument here on that point. You might persist and tell me that fashions change with the times and again I would agree with you. What some people deemed beautiful in the 17ᵗʰ century, when men preferred a more *Rubenesque* shape, was very different with the leaner look in our weight conscious world today. And now, even that seems to be shifting with the proliferation of plus sized models and the reaction to the normally higher caloric intake of most people in Western civilization. The fashion thing is what it is. I get it. It changes. But come on, I still have to ask you: what's with those giant lips? I don't know, maybe it's me. It just isn't making it for me. They might even be dangerous. If somebody ever gets the lips laid on them with a pair of those behemoths, you could find yourself in traction for a week.

Note to self: Back off, big lips.

34. D'em Butter Lambs

If you are from the Buffalo, NY area, you know all about *d'em butter lambs*. They seem to be everywhere around Easter time. It is hard to know exactly how the tradition started but it probably had something to do with many of the ethnic immigrant groups (Polish, German, Irish, and Italian) that included these festive little guys as part of celebrating this most solemn of Christian (Catholic) holidays. At the time of this printing, the original purveyor of these lambs, based on their own invoices, will make about 80,000 of these little guys to sit on the tables as a standard accompaniment to Easter Dinner. Additionally, if you are in Buffalo at that time of the year, you might have to go on your annual visit to the *Broadway Market* to get your lamb. While you are there, you will pick up a myriad of other ethnic foods to help you build your perfect meal for that special day. Something I cannot figure out is how cooking a ham that day is also part of the tradition. I know about the Easter bunny, but the Easter pig, not so much? Maybe it is just a coincidence and it has something to do with the large Irish population that the Queen City has amassed. No matter, I like a good ham dinner. But let's get back to the lamb.

The *butter lamb* is supposed to be symbolic of Jesus, the *Lamb of God*. And the red ribbon around its neck is to pay respect to the blood He shed for us. The little red flag that sits on top of the collar is to remind us of His victory over sin, and the two peppercorn eyes are to show us that He is the *light of the world*. It is a deeply religious symbol and a nice one at that. The *butter lamb* at the Easter table has been a Buffalo family tradition for many generations but I suspect that few people will remember what it is all about and most will treat it like a fabled version of the Easter bunny, or as a tradition as silly as an Easter egg hunt. I suppose I shouldn't be too disappointed because all traditions seem to lose something over time. Traditions are wonderful things and they can bind us as a culture and a civilization. The Jews really stand out on this concept and literally would have been lost to the sands of time if it wasn't for the constant reinforcement of their (sacred) traditions. I love the entire scene of the Seder meal celebrating Passover when the first question is asked:

"Why is this night different from all other nights?"

During the course of the communal meal, there is a further admonishment, after there has been a review of many of the passages describing the 10 plagues, and the flight of the Israelites out of Egypt as described in the book of Deuteronomy (26: 5-8). We are told to:

"Go and learn."

It is an annual commitment to knowing the history of a people. Musically, it is best commemorated in the words of Tevye from *Fiddler on the Roof*: it is a tradition. The why was less important and it was sufficient to simply proclaim:

"...Because it is a tradition."

No other explanation was necessary.

Few Christians would be able to connect the tradition of the *butter lamb* back to that night of the first Passover. The *butter lamb* is a modern-day manifestation of the *Paschal Lamb*. For most of us, however, it is a merely a cute novelty. America is a giant melting pot. Today, we seem to be constantly reminded that we are a nation of immigrants. How sad is it that as the many cultures come here, they tend to lose so many of the traditions they brought with them from wherever, and replace them with new American traditions, which to me seem to be frequently watered down and with so much less meaning. Wolfing down your *Starbucks* coffee on the way to work every day is not all that important a tradition. It deserves little fanfare. I should also clarify here that not all traditions are good. I would be remiss if didn't demand the elimination of the tradition of wife beating in all of its forms. Yeah, we can live without that tradition for sure. But perhaps I am being inappropriately nostalgic when I say; we would all be a lot better off if we kept a little closer to some of the family traditions that made us who we are as a people. I would like that.

Note to self: So why do we do this, because it is a tradition. Maybe we should talk about it. Maybe we should consider going to church too while we're at it?

35. Bumper Stickers

OK, suffice it to say that here are two kinds of people that have bumper stickers. You have your general, all-purpose, variety of meat heads, and then you have your freedom of speech advocates that want to force you to accept their opinions or their political endorsements (because, obviously, they are right and you are wrong.) So, let's initially consider this second group. Sporting a bumper sticker 60 years ago that simply said "I like Ike" did not mean to imply that, if you supported the other candidate, you were at a minimum hopelessly confused. It simply stated that I like this guy, and I'll bet you have a bumper sticker on your car that says you like your guy. So, let's go have a drink and discuss it.

Back then, one could be reasonably certain that no one was going to come to blows over a decision to place a sticker on the outside of one's car. Today, political stickers like these almost seem to threaten people. They dare the onlooker to make an opposing comment with a high degree. This is then met with serious hostility. Bumper stickers have become inherently confrontational. Whether this was intentional or not is arguable. Suffice it to say that if you drive around with a *Trump* sticker or a *Hillary* sticker, more than one person will step up and want to kick your ass. If you get off with someone merely flipping you the bird, you should say *thank you,* because things could have gotten so much worse. In our society's quest to flaunt its freedom of speech, now more than ever, if you decide to feature that particular freedom on your own personal billboard, the bumper sticker, you are electing to live life dangerously. I still like "Ike," but then again, I have always lived life on the edge.

And there's that first group. Is it wrong to refer to them as meatheads? I don't think so. I willingly state this based on what they seem so obsessed with posting these days. Here's an actual sticker I saw the other day:

"If you are riding my ass, could you at least pull my hair?"

What the hell is that all about; come on, really? I know that you have probably seen some equally stupid or offensive stickers out there, haven't you? Here's another one:

"I stop to poop."

You cannot make this stuff up. I'll bet you are in for some seriously scintillating conversation with the person that is driving a car with that on their bumper. Then there is the sticker that tells you how proud the bearers are of their children going to this school or having them graduated from that one. Now, I am not suggesting that they shouldn't be proud. I am only questioning the venue. What if I'm stuck in traffic for an hour or so? Think about it. I have nothing to look at but your lousy bumper sticker as you are obnoxiously declaring to the entire world that you are so stinking proud of Johnny or Jenny. Why? Because they have been privileged to go to some incredibly, economically upwardly mobile, super cool, suburban, private school. Perhaps it irks me a little, and I might frustratingly mutter, well, *bully for you.* But at some point, in 96-degree heat, after two hours or so, even me, Mr. Nice guy may want to simply get out of the car and open your door and punch Johnny or Jenny, or Muffy or Scooter, right in the nose. Oh, they're not in the car with you, you say. I suppose that's because they are at lacrosse practice? *Then how about if I just take a piece out of you?*

How about the one that says *I brake for squirrels.* What are you suggesting? Are you telling me that I'm that barbarian, son of a bitch, that bastard, who speeds up when I see one of those lovely, bushy tailed, little rodents? Oh, so you think you are better than I am, don't you? Again, you are forcing me to get out at the next intersection and grab you by the throat.

WANT A BUMPER STICKER: I'LL GIVE YOU A STINKIN BUMPER STICKER!

Note to self: I don't care what you say; I still like IKE! I like squirrels too.

36. Segues

In this 21st century world we live in, we are frequently required, if we are to have effective communication, to use something that is called a *segue.* So that we are clear as to the usage of this quasi-technological sounding word, let's look to our dear friend Merriam-Webster. Actually, that's not a person. That refers to the Merriam and Webster Publishing Company, who started selling dictionaries in Springfield, MA back in 1834 or so. Here's how they define the usage of the word segue.

1. To proceed without pause from one musical number or theme to another.
2. To make a transition without interruption from one activity, topic, scene, or part to another, segued smoothly into the next story.

It is this second usage I wish to explore with you, with the key referring to transitioning into the next story. Some people are great when it comes to segueing appropriately and others will leave you considering that one of you needs to be in a mental institution. We will be having a conversation and talking about politics and one party might be of the opinion that Donald Trump is a meathead. HOLD THAT THOUGHT. They don't actually say that he is and then the discussion drifts to talking about the pope. Now bear in mind, 20 minutes have elapsed since Trump monopolized the conversation. We have discussed kids and soccer, what we are having for Sunday dinner, and now we are on to the pope, and we get a really bad *segue.* The more liberal minded of the two, says:

"Speaking of meatheads…"

"Wait, why is the pope a meathead? What makes you say that?"

"I didn't say the pope was a meathead. I like the pope. Why would I say that?

"You just did. We were talking about the pope, and I said I thought he was doing a good job, and you said, speaking of meatheads?"

"No, I didn't…Oh; I was talking about Donald Trump!"

WTF, you think to yourself (Wow, that's fantastic!)

"THAT WAS 2O MINUTES AGO!"

I mean, help a fellow out here. Stick with the conversation. That's how arguments start. I had another situation pop up just the other night. My closest friend Marilynn and I were talking about the Oscar awards (for 2016) and how we really like the movie *Lion* and how it didn't win. Neither of us could remember the actual winner. Half an hour later, we are discussing something that might have been a solution to the secrets of the universe and, all of a sudden, she yells out, almost as if it was a cry for help after being washed overboard on the high seas, *"Moonlight!"*

I didn't know what to say, not realizing that that was the name of the film that won the Oscar that year, the film title that neither of us could remember.

I said, "What?"

She shouted it out again in her usual dulcet tone.

"Moonlight!"

I thought we were playing some bizarre new word game where the idea was to shout out any word that popped into your head. I didn't fully understand the rules of this new game but I thought it would be fun. I love games, so I shouted back, *"Chicken heads!"*

I thought for sure that it was a better word and maybe it would actually put me way ahead on points. I am very competitive when it comes to games. Again, I wasn't really clear on how the scoring went. No matter; she was resolute. She fired back, with a twinge of hostility this time, almost as if to ask, *what are you stupid or something?*

"Moonlight!"

I was momentarily shaken. Should I double down? Was she just bluffing? What were we actually playing for? How high were the actual stakes? This could be big. It could change everything. Without knowing what the hell we were actually talking about, I reasoned that maybe I should just play it safe and concede.

"OK, you win, *moonlight.*"

I continued, even more sheepishly, "I gotta admit, I thought I had you with *chicken head.*"

I was dejected, thinking, *wait a minute, there was no way I could have lost with chicken head.* But then I more pensively considered that perhaps what they say is true and sometimes, *Discretion **is** the better part of valor.*

"OK, I'll go with *Moonlight.*"

"No, you big silly, that's the name of the movie."

Twenty years from now, I still will be convinced; I had her with *Chicken head*. I mean, come on, who are we kidding here? I can hear a lot of the men out there saying, "OK, OK, sometimes being smart is better than being right."

You know what I think? I think all politicians should run on a platform that guarantees us a better *segue.*

"...and so my fellow Americans, ask not what your country can do for you, ask what you can do for a better *segue.*"

Note to self: Please give me a better segue.

37.   The Wedding

There was a time when *the wedding* was a special time, a solemn event that commemorated the uniting of two humans in a bond of love and matrimony for the rest of their natural lifetimes. These days, virtually all of the solemnity has been driven from the ritual and we are left very frequently with a very strange occurrence, indeed. It runs from a perverse sort of endurance test to a badly orchestrated fashion show, with scores of onlookers who sit about and tally up their lists of complaints. This should be a happy day for everyone, right? Why would there be any complaints?

Complaint number 1 almost always has to do with the food.

"My food was too hot."

"My food wasn't hot enough."

"My steak was too tough."

"The portions were too small."

"The portions were too big." (Yeah, they complain even if there was too much; go figure.) "The sauce was too greasy."

"The sauce was too spicy."

"You know, I am not supposed to eat nuts. I have diverticulitis." (Maybe they decided to put nuts in the dish just to knock you off; ever think about that?)

"I didn't like the tomato sauce. I *like* a sweet sauce."

I didn't like the tomato sauce. I *don't like* a sweet sauce."

We could go on from here, but I think you have the idea. The next complaint has to do the site selection, and or the music.

"The room was too big; the room was too small."

"The room was too crowded.

"I couldn't find the bathrooms; and yada, yada…"

"I hated the music. Who listens to this crap that they played?"

"Why did it have to be so loud?

"Why couldn't they play something you could dance to, instead of that techno crap?"

"I told them not to play the C*hicken Dance*.

"I hate the *Macarena."*

"The *Electric Slide* is out; how could they not know that?"

I don't even want to get started on the costumes. That's right. It is no longer a bridal gown. These days, the bride and the groom, and their ridiculous entourage, seem to all be getting bedecked in some costume that is supposed to represent a theme of some sorts.

"We were going for the *1920s look.*"

"We were going for that *Gone with the Wind* look."

"We wanted that *John Gotti gangster* look."

"We were going for the *Phantom of the Opera* look."

Why don't you go for the *Sesame Street* look? The groom could be *Oscar the grouch* and the bride could be *Miss Piggy.* Here's my take on the whole damned wedding thing. If you want to make one of the most special days of your life a circus, be my guest. Just don't get upset if either you, or the groom, comes away unhappy after all of the planning and paying you had to do. It was your day to stupefy and you did just that. How about this instead? Bag any crazy outfits. Keep it simple. Invite the people that you want to invite, people that have *meaning and continuity* in your life. This doesn't include fifth cousins because you feel obligated to invite them. It's an easy system. If you feel any obligation to invite someone, and they have a connection *to so and so* and if you don't invite them, they will have hard feelings, they are out. You actually have to *want* to have them there for no other reason other than *just because you have to invite them.* They should make you feel special. They should care about you and have your best interest at heart. This will greatly reduce the number of guests you invite, or should I say, the *clown count,* and will give you, the bride or groom, the opportunity to visit guests you actually want to chat with, people who you wish you had more time to talk to more often. If you are having hundreds and hundreds of guests and are hoping to get a lot of money as gifts, then recognize that this isn't a wedding at all. It is a serious *For-Profit Event,* and it is *all about the money* and you are content to suffer through, performing your roles as the *happy couple.* If the parents are picking up the tab, they may initially solicit your input, but ultimately it is less about you and more about them. It is now their circus and you, ultimately, are performing as their featured guest.

In my parent's time, there was an in between version of this joining of two families. It was kiddingly called a *football wedding.* You told your friends you were getting married. They said something like *don't worry we'll take care of it.* And they did. They invited hundreds of your friends; they all chipped in and bought beer and other assorted drinks.

They made a stack of sandwiches and had the reception in some hall someplace and as the guests arrived, they would throw them a sandwich (like a football) and hopefully they caught it. If not, they would grab another one from the stack and try again. Everyone had a great time, including the bride and groom. It was nothing fancy, and the loving couple, in most cases, lived happily ever after, even without a prenuptial agreement. Well, in any event, there were far fewer divorces back then, that's for sure.

Here's another suggestion. Spend more time planning your life together and discuss what is most important for you to do as a newly formed family unit. Spend less time thinking about the seating arrangements and the choice of flowers and that very, very special day. After all, it is only one day, and you have your whole life ahead of you. In the balance, which is more important?

Note to self: Fire all the wedding planners.

38. Boxer Shorts

There comes a time in every man's life when he is faced with one of the biggest decisions of all, Boxers or Briefs. This is an evolutionary decision. As infants our parents make a choice for us when they put us in diapers. The diaper is merely the precursor of the brief. As we get a little older and enter into the next stage of our life and move out of diapers, we naturally progress to *briefs*. In an effort to celebrate this extremely important transition, we might be afforded the additional luxury of the *Underroo*. For those of us who are unfamiliar with this bold but utilitarian fashion statement, they weren't just ordinary briefs. They were the serious work of some brilliant marketing genius. And if you were lucky enough to be between the toddler stage and *the tween* about 40 years ago when they were invented, you actually got to wear them.

What made them extra special? They included a matching top, and they were made for both boys and girls, alike. They typically featured a character from the popular entertainment media, especially from the superhero comics. In my day, we only had the *Davey Crocket* brief. I was twice blessed and was even more fortunate because my parents actually got me a *Davey Crocket* hat too, complete with the raccoon tail. This was the 1950s, and Fess Parker really made this famous American a house hold name. I can now finally admit to you, however, that I was always disappointed because I had to wear pants *over* these super cool undies. Nobody would get to see these uniquely bedazzled, special, tidy whities.

Then the teen years roll along. The *underoos* are definitely out at this point, unless you want to become hospitalized from an *atomic wedgey* administered by some guy named Duke in the locker room after school. This is an automatic, and would be one of those rarely *acceptable* forms of bullying in today's world. If you wearing the *Underroo,* at this point, shouldn't you simply expect the wedgey? Something happens to young men during that awful time called puberty and it has less to do with the darkening of the voice and the sprouting of whiskers than it does with the enlargement of something which is sometimes referred to as the third leg. Here's the question: can the *brief* contain this ever-growing package? Should you elect, at this point, to graduate to *boxers*? Some of the older boys do, and they look a little silly, because invariably the shorts that they get look huge on them. Additionally, they offer nothing in the way of support. Remember Kramer on *Seinfeld,* when he was concerned that his sperm count was being affected by his wearing briefs? (The evidence is pretty clear at this point: wearing briefs and otherwise constraining the testicles does in fact reduce the sperm count.) As that particular episode progressed, it was clear that Kramer was in his typical panic mode. He couldn't make the adjustment. With no support, he was "flipping and flopping." He couldn't live that way. He initially came up with the solution to wear nothing at all and joyfully proclaimed the immortal line:

"I am OUT Jerry and I'm LOVING it!"

Let's get back to the real world. Grown men get to choose. I wore briefs for probably longer than I care to admit it, and I thought that boxers were the province of older men. I am finally an older man. I wear boxers now, and when I put them on, I think of myself as a young Rocky Graziano, as the beautiful middle weight that he was at one time, eagerly stepping into the ring. You can't quite catch that image if you are wearing briefs.

Note to self: No tidy whities for me.

39. Starting a Cult

I should feel a certain amount of reluctance to say this, but I don't, so I am just going to say it: people are sheep. It is not an accident that the word pastor translates as "shepherd." And certainly, I mean no disrespect, because the Good Lord Himself referred to his followers as *My Flock.* It is true, however, that some very jaded people (in my opinion) do, in fact, refer to Christianity as a cult. I will argue that it is *not* based on various aspects of its different dogma and cultural interpretations of the creed in general. I also, would be totally remiss; however, if I did not disclose to you that I am a dyed in the wool Roman Catholic. It would be the acme of disrespect for a religion that I have ascribed to for most of my life. I additionally have respect for many other religions that include Judaism, Buddhism, Taoism, and others and I will include my Muslim brethren here, too. All religions suffer from misinterpretations of their actual beliefs. These days there is some serious condemnation of many Muslims that have been radicalized, and I will concede that their behaviors are simply not cool. Radical anything is almost always a bad thing and I find it equally disdainful to be subjected to some of the malarkey that one hears from some of those fringe groups of fundamentalist Christians out there, as well. But let me move more toward the premise here and discuss cults as opposed to *religions.*

There are numerous differences and one could take several college courses that will outline the myriad of these differences in a cult versus a religion. Let me simplify the entire model for you. A cult is a system of beliefs that would be considered by the average schmo to be just plain "goofy." Stick with me, because that is a really broad-brush stroke. So to clarify, let's consider the followers of one of the more celebrated cults in recent history: The *Heaven's Gate Cult.* Now for those of you who are too young to remember, it was started by an incredibly scary looking guy named Marshall Applewhite (1931–1997). It was an American UFO religious millenarian group founded in 1974 and based in San Diego, California. It made round the world headlines on March 26, 1997 when police discovered the bodies of 39 members of the group who had committed mass suicide in order to reach what they believed was an extraterrestrial spacecraft following the Halle-Bopp Comet. If you didn't know the details of this cult, at this point you might be saying to yourself as you scratch your head, "Hmmm, sounds reasonable to me."

And then again, maybe it doesn't sound so reasonable, so let's kick it up a notch for you. This cult had some unusual requirements if you elected to become a follower. If you were a man, you were expected to demonstrate your faith in the Leader by self-castrating yourself. (Yikes! That's gotta hurt.)

Now I'm thinking. Hey wait a minute, where can I sign up for this?

Is it me? Or *are you out of your cotton-picking mind?* Are you telling me that among the score or so of believers that wanted to leave the earth with this Bozzo that no one said, *I think you're asking a little too much here and this sounds a little weird.* Some of the other beliefs included the notion that Jesus had been reincarnated and came back as a Texan. I need to ask what part of Texas was he from, because if you say Dallas, I might buy it. If it was Austin or Houston, that would be too much to accept. Come on, how crazy are we going to get? This is the kind of stuff that makes for Cult-City. OK, you are probably thinking, this was a very extreme and isolated case. Would I shock you if I told you that there over 3000 officially recognized cults in the USA alone? Some make the *Heavens-Gate* people look positively mainstream.

I had a friend who didn't cook very much; while I was visiting, I asked if there was anything to eat in her house. She suggested that I should take a look and see what I could find. I opened one cabinet and found several boxes of lasagna. I looked in several more and found more boxes of lasagna. I quickly discerned that since there were no fewer than 16 boxes of lasagna in her house that she belonged to a cult in which they worshiped Lasagna. Why not? She didn't seem to be hurting anyone. It was as good a belief system any other. It got me thinking. I could have my own cult. Heck, we know people are essentially sheep and they will follow anything and anybody if you just put it out there enough. Some people will think you are nuts when you tell them you worship *wood.* Others will say, "You know what; I have always felt a special presence when I am around *wood.*"

Bingo, you've got your first follower. Start taking donations and you're in business. Throw in a few crazy rules and regulations and you have cemented the cause. Don't go with the castration thing right away, that's kind of a deal killer for most guys.

Note to self: I've got it. We can worship Hot Dogs. Who doesn't like Hot Dogs?

40. People of influence

One of the things people get upset about each year is the selection of the *Person of the Year* in *Time* magazine. You will hear conversations that sound like this:
   "I can't believe they picked him."
   "I think it should have been…"
   "You know those selections are always so political."
   "Well, I think that was a great selection, for a change."
   "Wow, how could they pick that idiot?"
   Regardless of who gets picked by the great secret panel of judges, it is always a controversy. Perhaps that's a good thing because hopefully it encourages some substantive dialogue. What most people fail to consider is that it is less about popularity and more about influence. Ironically, too, it is like the phrase we hear at weddings, "for better or for worse." That's why we frequently see a lot of really bad *hombres* getting the cover. We found Hitler there with his smiling face (1938) and (lovable Uncle Joe) Stalin made it twice (1939 and 1942.). Even the Ayatollah Khomeini (1979) found himself sitting for the portrait on the cover. There are very few who would not argue that these people did some amazingly despicable things. Nonetheless, they influenced an awful lot of behavior throughout the world and made a dramatic impact. Even if the impact was virtually all in the negative, which, based on the criteria is neither here nor there.
   Sometimes, there is some behind the scenes nonsense that affects who the ultimate selection will be. One such time is when they wanted directors Michael Moore and Mel Gibson to share the spot together. When it comes to the film genre, there could not be two more polar opposites. The year was 2004 and each of these controversial directors were singled out for their work, particularly for the films they had each released that year, *Fahrenheit 911* (Moore) and *the Passion of the Christ* (Gibson). It sounded like an interesting pronouncement and it was sure to stimulate a myriad of conversations around the water cooler the day after it came out, and it would probably sell a few extra million issues, too. All in all, it seemed like a great pick all around. The editors made the necessary arrangements and both of the Hollywood icons agreed to

do it. They were all set to fly Gibson up from Australia, and at the last minute, he calls them and says:

"I'm not doing it. I've thought it over and it is not the right thing to do."

So, they put George Bush (the second) on the cover.

It is an interesting scenario each year and it always sparks a bit of controversy. But here's my question to you. Who had a greater influence on your life, Mel Gibson, George Bush (Senior or Junior, whichever), Stalin, Charles Lindbergh, or *your mother*? Review the entire list for the past 100 years or so and then throw *your father* at the end for the same comparison. You might add your favorite teacher's name as well, or one of those people that you fondly describe as your mentor. As far as I'm concerned, those are the persons of influence that matter the most. In all but the rarest cases, those people will not only not get a magazine cover; they probably won't even get a richly deserved *thank you*. How sad is that? It makes us ask where our priorities really are, when we make these serious and conspicuous omissions.

Here's something else to think about when it comes to influencing others. Maybe the person to be singled out is *you*. I think that each of us in our own way was put on this planet to do something to make it a better place. That being said, we need to figure out who it is we want to influence and what is it we want to change. Hopefully, when they read our eulogies, there are lots of people around who get to say things like, "And, he did this for me…,"

"And she did that for me…"

"And if it wasn't for them, I wouldn't be the person I am today."

That's being a person of influence whose influence was more worthwhile than all of those other movers and shakers we see on the *Time* Magazine cover each year.

Note to Self. "I am a person of Influence."

41. Dog walking

Let's talk about the art and the science of dog walking. Unless you live in the country and have the luxury of living on a farm where you can simply let your dog roam free, you pretty much have to surrender to the discipline of walking the dog. There is another, more dubious possibility. This occurs when you see people living in cramped, NYC styled apartments. Pet owners there frequently have one of those little dogs, you know the ones that pretty much look like spiders that need a haircut. In these most fetid of conditions you sometimes see a pad by the door where the tiny mutant creature is allowed to wet and make its daily deposit there. This is a reasonably despicable solution to the inevitability of one of nature's most obvious dictates and it is neither enjoyable for the beast or any of the human inhabitants of this urban domicile. This is where somebody needed to really step up and simply *walk the damned dog.* Many fathers will tell their kids that they are not having a dog because they realize it will fall onto them to walk dear old Fido. The kids will rant and rave and sometimes the parents will relent, insisting, "OK, but you are the ones who are going to have to walk that damned mutt. When it rains, and when it snows, you are going to have to take him out to do his business."

It's a good plan. It is a critical announcement, too. It is especially important because the father has clearly stepped up to the plate and has declared to everyone that he is the authority figure and that he is the ultimate force to be reckoned with in the family; he has spoken. The only problem is that rarely does his decree make it through to the second week, before the kids forget their obligations and Papa Bear has to assume the role of the official dog walker. That's the way it works in most households in America. For me, it is different. I have mentioned my rescue dog, Louie. I specifically got him so that I could walk him. I figured there would be times when I would blow off the gym and being compelled to walk Louie 3-4 times a day around my South Buffalo neighborhood would be a good thing for both of us. It would force me to walk. It was an exercise regimen for both of us. OK, in my zeal to report nothing but the truth here, I have to tell you that since he is an early morning riser, 6: 30 a.m. on the nose, there were times, especially when there was a foot of snow on the ground, when neither of us wanted to head out into the wind. Nevertheless, we both did, and I would like to think we were each the better for it. You cannot believe how remarkably happy he was after he made his first deposit of the day. Of course, he knew he was going to get a reward when he went back to the nice warm cozy house, so it wasn't all bad for him. It wasn't all bad for me, either. I came back to a warm cozy house too. By then my coffee was ready and I was right on schedule to set about my day and would hop into my shower. It was a great symbiotic arrangement.

Something I hadn't considered is how well I got to know the neighbors. I would meet other poor unfortunates who had to walk their beasts, and after a while, they would say good morning to me. After a while longer, they would actually stop and we would let the dogs sniff each other's butts and we would exchange more substantive pleasantries. Invariably, we would all agree that we were glad we were not dogs and we could remain standing and simply say hello and that was sufficient. I have to admit, I never really came across anyone on my daily walks who offered me a butt that was worthy of smelling. That's OK; I am good with that. And as an added benefit to my daily routine, I got to meet those early morning people who didn't own dogs. They were OK too. I never would have gotten to experience them either. It was all good.

But here is the biggest thing that occurred while I continued with my dog walking. I got to have a better relationship with my dog. I would talk to him and he would learn my moods and my moves and I would learn his. Now everyone remarks what a great dog Louie is when we are in mixed company. They can't help but say, "How well behaved he is. He's a remarkable dog."

I am not going to disagree. I think Louie is remarkable. But what is more to the point is, we are more remarkable; Louie and I kind of function as a unit. We now have a sense of short hand together. He understands me. Certainly, he is a smart dog, don't get me wrong. The thing is, I think we have both gotten smarter as a result of our daily walks and everyone around us gets to see the benefit. Having a great dog is one of life's greatest pleasures. I think all dogs are great. A well-trained dog is even better. If you want a well-trained dog, there is no substitute to spending a lot of time with the dog, and there a few ways better than taking him for a regular walk.

Note to self: Take a walk. Oh, and make sure you bring the dog with you.

42. Life Expectancy

There is a wonderful clip from the TV series called *the Newsroom* in which one of the characters, Will McAvoy, goes off on a rant about how *America is not the greatest country anymore*. If you haven't seen it, it is seriously worthy of your googling and catching the *YouTube* version of it. It is sometimes referred to as *the most honest 3minutes on television*. It is a true *bubble buster,* especially for all of you who are to be included in the *sheep list* and who are relentless in their incessant chanting to the contrary. One of the statistics he quotes has to do with the life expectancy. At the time of the episode in 2012, we were 47th on the list. As I write this, we have climbed up the list and now stand proudly at 31st. Shall I offer a proud "whoopee do," here? I think not. So, having stated this, it certainly begs the question: who is ahead of us and why?

It might not come as a surprise for most of you that Japan tops the list with a combined age for sexes at just over 86 years. Maybe it is that Zen thing that puts them at number 1. Additionally, it could be reasoned that, at least from a dietary basis, they would be in a better position than we are if only we took into consideration their significantly greater consumption of fish and vegetables. If we looked at other factors in their lifestyles, we might have to scratch our heads a bit because they appeared more stressed in their occupational norms, and they have been subjected to much larger doses of radiation. I am not just singling them out because of Hiroshima and Nagasaki. Surely neither of those events was a good thing, but let's add the massive contamination in 2011 with the earthquake in Fukishima. Many are saying that the contamination will last for hundreds of years. Here's what Kendra Ulrich, Senior Nuclear Campaigner at Greenpeace Japan had to say.

"The government's massive decontamination program will have almost no impact on reducing the ecological threat from the enormous amount of radiation from the Fukushima nuclear disaster. Already, over 9 million cubic meters of nuclear waste are scattered over at least 113,000 locations across Fukushima prefecture."

And let's not forget that a lot of that radiation spilled into the ocean and all those fish that our Japanese friends love to incorporate into their healthy diets will apparently come, for a while at least, with a little extra zest and a super, special zing. I am just going to throw this out there: I will bet you that we might see their life expectancy numbers start to drop a little, based on this. That radiation thing just can't be all that good for you.

But there is something I noticed on the list that really stuck out for me. Remember in high school social studies when we learned about something called the *Romance languages*. These were the five languages that weren't so much all that romantic as much as they traced their roots to Latin, the language of Rome. They included French, Spanish, Portuguese, Romanian, and Italian of course. Here's comes the big "*ahah*" on the list. Four out of the five countries that are responsible for these languages are way above the United States on the list for life expectancy. Which one didn't make the cut? You get a gold star if you said Romania. That got me thinking.

What does France, Spain, Italy and Portugal do that is so different from us that they are that much healthier than we are? I wasn't sure, so my conclusion is totally based on speculation. I immediately thought: well Romania falls short because they clearly have had a vampire issue for hundreds of years and nothing seemed to indicate that they had gotten a handle on it as of yet. Do you really want to take a trip through the Carpathian Mountains after sunset? I know I don't.

But let's get back to the other four. If you have ever visited these countries you realize they share a lot of things in common. The first thing is that they have a diet that is rich in two major elixirs, red wine and olive oil. Now French cuisine is noted for many of the heavier cream sauces and a lot of those have *beaucoup fat* in them, but based on the theory of the *French Paradox*, that red wine and olive oil combo seems to cancel the suspected deleterious effect. Here's something else these countries have in common. Much like the Japanese, they too, consume more fish and vegetables. That's true for the Italians as well, and contrary to popular belief, they don't eat all that much pasta (even though the Italians in America do.) It is combined with lots of vegetables, and of course, fish. All of these countries have major coast lines that allow them to have vast supplies of seafood. We have a big coast line too but we are a meat-based country and it is not an accident that Noel Coward referred to us as the *United Steaks of America.*

There is something else that these countries all have in common. They all share a more carefree lifestyle. They are less driven by keeping up with the Joneses and more concerned with getting the families together for Sunday dinner. The last thing worthy of note is they all do something that we don't. They walk everywhere. We, on the other hand, think nothing about hopping in our car to go to the corner for a quart of milk. I will have to admit my observations on all of this are just that, observations. There is nothing supporting my conclusions that would approximate science, but maybe we can take a lesson from them here and live a lot longer, or, at least, live a lot happier. And what the heck, I really like the whole thing about going home for lunch and having a midday meal with my family anyway.

Note to self: Perhaps we should take a look at our lifestyle.

43. The Name Game

OK, here's another Louie story. Some of you by now have started to think I am a little obsessive about this dog, but he is a great dog, and of course, he should warrant a great story right from the beginning. I probably need to begin by telling you about his predecessor, Mr. Reilly. Now Mr. Reilly was a Sheltie. For those of you, who are not familiar with the breed, suffice it to say he looked like *Lassie* if you threw him in the dryer. He was easily mistaken for a miniature Collie, but in fact he was a Shetland sheepdog. They are without a doubt one of the smartest breeds of dogs anywhere. People would comment on how smart he was and I would agree and go on to tell them he was adept at Microsoft Word, and Excel, but that he wasn't entirely proficient with PowerPoint. They would look askance at me and I would further explain that it wasn't that big a problem, since he tended to do more back-office work and very few presentations, so PowerPoint wasn't really all that essential for him. Unfortunately, Mr. Reilly got old and after bringing so much joy to all of our lives for nearly 14 years, he went on to his reward.

After a year or so, I was seriously in dog withdrawal. I started looking for another great dog. I think all dogs are great, but I had some special requirements for my fast-paced world. I wanted, if possible, to get a *rescue dog*. Mr. Reilly was actually the only dog I ever got from a breeder. I have always had wonderful dogs that were recycled and, with so many unwanted animals out there, it just seems like the right thing to do. I started to look in the local pounds. It was seriously disheartening. Virtually every dog that I saw was a Pit bull, or a Pit bull mix. Now don't get me wrong, these can be, and frequently are, wonderful dogs. Regrettably, so many have been abused and even more have suffered from the seriously bad press that it was inconceivable for me to bring even the most award-winning Pit bull into my office. It simply would not work. I wanted a dog I could take to the office with me every day. I have always brought my dogs to the office. For those of you who did not read the original *Potato Chips for the Soul,* I run a Real Estate office when I am not writing books or doing speaking or acting gigs, and I wasn't about to leave a dog home for 8-10 hours a day. That's just not right on any count. So, I needed a great little dog that would get along with my staff and would be a great good will ambassador for everyone who would come in to do business with us. Louie, the lovable half dachshund/poodle mix, hit it out of the park from day one. Here's how I found him.

I had no luck at the *pounds*, so I started looking in the personal ads in the newspaper. I even looked on Craig's List. That's where I spotted this little fugitive. I saw an ad describing him and his name was *Louie*. How are you going to turn down a dog named Louie? I drove up to Niagara Falls, NY to scope him out and learned that he had been *adopted out* to a family that had two other foster dogs. I looked at all 12 and half pounds of this shy and very scruffy little dog and asked why he was dyed blue. He looked like a smurf. The nice lady explained that her children really loved him and thought it would be fun to decorate him for Halloween, so they dyed him blue. I paid the adoption fee and asked her if she had his papers, indicating what shots he had, etcetera. She told me I would have to go back to the pound to get them. OK no big deal, so I drive to beautiful downtown Niagara Falls and arrive at the pound and they tell me they have no record of a dog named Louie. Son of a bitch, (literally) I think to myself; scammed again. After further investigations, the nice lady at the computer says, "Wait a minute, what did you say his name was, Louie? No, there is definitely no Louie in our records. What was the address you said you went to when you picked him up?"

I told her the address and she was quite relieved. Then she responded.

"Oh, you mean *Fuzzy*. That dogs name was *Fuzzy*. They must have changed it."

I have to tell you I was not amused and somewhat taken back.

"Do you mean to tell me that I am traveling with a dog under an assumed name? Are you telling me this innocent looking creature is actually using an alias?"

She was even more perplexed now than when I first arrived. She looked at me as though she was not quite sure how serious I was and she cautiously added, "You do know you can change his name too, if you like."

I fired back with, "How ridiculous, then he really won't know who he is. *Louie* is his name and I am sticking with it. That's what's wrong with this country. Nobody knows who they are anymore!"

I am willing to wager that she was happy to see me go. You will be pleased to know that since he is no longer low man on the totem pole with two other giant dogs eating all his food, that Louie is up to a whopping 19 lbs. and is living large all the way. He has the run of the office. It's true, and he goes everywhere with me. If I don't bring him into the office people get quite concerned. Since he has a bit of a swagger when he walks around sporting his red bandana (and since he looks a little like Lamb Chop from the Sheri Lewis days), I gave him a gangster name. Officially; he is *Lamb Chop Louie* (sort of like Bugsy Malone). Most people just call him *Louie.* And for the record, I washed him 4 times to get the blue dye out and now he is styling.

Note to Self. You gotta know who you are.

44. Paper or Plastic?

There is no way to avoid this final question if you do your shopping at your typical supermarket in America. The question is pretty simple, but depending how you answer the question, it is fraught with some serious sociological and ecological overtones. You could simply flip a coin and play the odds, but *lookihere, pilgrim*, you didn't think you were going to get off that easily, now did you? OK, go with the plastic. I might have added, *go with the plastic, you selfish, ecologically ignorant, bastard,* but perhaps that would have been too kind for the likes of you. What the hell could you possibly be thinking? Those damned plastic bags you are using are not at all bio-degradable and are going to be in some landfill for at least the next 20,000 years or so, and you don't care. Someone should give you a big punch in the nose. Plastic? What were you thinking? How about joining the human race? Gee, you think to yourself: why is everyone getting mad at me? It isn't my fault. Why did they offer me the choice in the first place, if it was going to cause this big hullabaloo?

Yikes! OK, you have been warned, so let's go with *plan b*. Pick the paper bag.

I can't believe it. What are you stupid or something? Go ahead; kill a few more million trees while you are at it. Who do you think you are? What makes you so special? Was the earth put here for your sole amusement? Sure, eventually, after 100 years or so, those brown paper bags will be fully decomposed, but in the meantime, let's go ahead and deforest the entire *rainforest* while we are at. You do know these are the lungs of this planet we call mother earth, don't you? You and your kind are suffocating us. HELP! HELP! I CAN'T BREATHE.

Is there a third choice? Well, yes there is buckaroo. You can bring one of those reusable bags that people have been sporting all over Europe for the last 70 years. On the East Coast here, we have a store called Aldi and they have an even better idea. You can go in and grab one of the boxes that the food was shipped in when it came into the store and you can stack your groceries in one of them. The best part is the box is free. Then, when you get home you can cut the box up and put it in the recycling can. If you really want to be a *super greeny* you could also bring that same box back with you again, and again, and transport your goodies without all the guilt and grief we have been trying to lay on you right here. Either way, it is all good.

Life is kind of tough some times. Having to make decisions like these shouldn't weigh all that much on your seriously beaten down brow.

Paper or plastic, indeed, do you know who you are talking to, here? Maybe I will just put one of those plastic bags over your head for five minutes and stuff you in one of those nice, brown paper bags and see how you like that.

Note to self: it's the seemingly little decisions that can put you over the top sometimes.

45. Traffic

In today's dog eat dog, technologically advanced society, there is almost no way to avoid it. Having said that, if one is to survive, there has to be a reasonable effort to either deal with it or perhaps, my little Obewan, master it. I do a lot of driving and I will do anything to avoid traffic, if possible, and that is the first step toward mastery. If one is forced to commute and highways are the only choice you can make in your dismal effort to get you from point A to point B, an essential exercise is *avoiding the peak periods.* For most working squids, this means rush hours. If you are forced to drive during rush hours in any of the major metropolitan areas like NYC, LA, Chicago or Boston, suffice it to say that if you do it for any length of time, you will seriously diminish your life expectancy by a minimum of 2-5 years. Whether you believe that or not is not important. You will also be subject to personality disorders that will require some sort of self-medication which will probably lead to alcoholism or some similar substance abuse problem which will ultimately yield a divorce or two.

Ah, it's a wonderful life, isn't it? To further exacerbate the misery of commuting, you also need to recognize that you will be spending anywhere from 10 months to 3 years actually being behind the wheel. This is a really bad deal no matter how you cut it. Perhaps, you can learn to deal with it. Maybe you can explain it away to your friends and neighbors by saying things like, "It's not bad at all. It's only 90 minutes each way (that's an extra 60 hours a month). I listen to my tunes and make the best of it. Really, I don't mind it."

I don't mind a barium enema either, but I would really rather not have to get one every day. Then you have the reality of contending with being alert constantly, and hoping that some nit wit doesn't slam into you. Hey, it's dangerous out there. Not everyone is as good a defensive driver as you are, you know.

Here's something else to add to your personal to *deal with list*: rude drivers. I am not sure where to start with this one. How about the slow driver in the far-left lane, which is supposed to be reserved for drivers who want to use it for passing even slower drivers. You are in a hurry and all of a sudden you slide over into the passing lane and you get behind some lummox who is pretending it is a beautiful Sunday afternoon without a care in the world. Would it be rude to just shoot him? Then you get to deal with the lane hopper. These guys cause more accidents and almost never seem to get personally involved with them. They just continue to hop until they are out of traffic. Don't get me started on these sons of bitches. But my all-time number one, favorite, most aggravating thing when driving in traffic, are the drivers who do not how to merge.

It is really a simple thing and so many people, with the best of intentions and a vast amount of misspent manners, do it wrong. This is where you use the *zipper. The zipper* is the most efficient way to enter and merge into traffic going in the same direction as you are. It has been studied and endorsed by engineers and this is how it works. When one is attempting to merge into traffic, they drive to the very end of the line and one car lets them in, then the next car lets the next car in, and so forth. It looks like a single tooth of the zipper and the zipper is able to slide right up your fly. For some strange reason, if you have a line of twenty cars, some people think it is impolite to force the last guy in the line to let you in and they think you should have merged way sooner than that. They think it is wrong if they see you racing ahead of everyone else to get to the head of the line. Frequently, there are other drivers who have this misspent sense of automotive chivalry and they too will attempt to merge sooner rather than later. Now we have car number 20 jumping in, car number 12 deciding it is his time, and car number 3 saying:

"Yikes, I had better get over before it is too late."

Imagine yourself trying to zip up your pants that way. The best that you could hope for is a broken zipper and you will have to go get a different pair of pants to wear that evening. What I find truly amazing is that if you are in the lane that is actually in the regular traffic flow and you have passengers in the car and they see approaching drivers attempting to do the zipper, and you are the last guy who is supposed to allow the oncoming car to merge, they will get adamant and shout in your ear:

"Don't let this bastard in...God, I hate guys like that. Can you believe this jerk?"

If you are the wise driver who knows about the zipper, you might be so foolish as to want to explain the efficiency of addressing the correct way to allow for merging traffic and at this point, I will simply tell you, don't. If you do, you will be met with an unbridled sense of hostility that will truly take you to the next level of road rage. The zipper must be accepted as an article of faith. It cannot be explained to the uninitiated. I wish it could. If you try, they will simply think you are pathetic (for letting those sneaky drivers in) and you will have to take solace in the fact that they are among the many morons who will continue to contribute to the aggravation of your daily commute.

Note to self: Traffic, learn to deal with it.

46. Lifetime Warrantee

"…. And the best part about this thingumabob, Mr. Consumer, is that it comes with a lifetime warrantee."

"Oh, thank goodness for that, Mr. Salesperson; whose lifetime?"

Warrantees or Warranties, depending how you spell it, can fall into one of the biggest scams that we have ever seen come down the pike. The dialogue above addresses one of the more subtle points of this warrantee business. What the heck is a lifetime warrantee? Let's suppose I am buying a waffle iron and the salesperson tells me it comes with a lifetime warrantee. Are we talking about my life or the waffle iron's? I will presume it is the former, primarily because, does anyone really know the life expectancy of a waffle iron? What if the waffle iron is forced to endure a really difficult life in a house where people eat waffles at every meal and smoke cigarettes and drinks shots with dinner? I am willing to wager that this particular waffle iron is not going to last as long as one that lives in the country and only gets used in the summer time, and or, on weekends. So that we are clear: They couldn't possibly be referring to my age when they use that term. If I am over 65 years old and you are 22, are they saying we get the same warrantee? Yours would have to last an additional 40 some odd years. That's one industrial strength waffle iron. Maybe what they are saying is that we guarantee that this product will work no matter what. If not, return it or whatever, no questions asked. That would be a great warrantee.

There have been a number of companies that have predicated their success on this kind of 100% customer satisfaction thing. One of my first jobs after I got out of college was at Brooks Bros. in NYC at their flagship store at 346 Madison Avenue. It was an amazing experience working there at this iconic bastion of conservative upscale fashion and, I learned many things there which I will share with you in some of the upcoming episodes in the book.

One of the more admirable things about this, the oldest men's clothing store in America was their incredible return policy. They would take a shirt back even if you were wearing it after you fell out of a speeding car. I always thought that was unfair. I could understand if a product was seriously defective. Absolutely, the company should stand by the quality of the product. If, on the other hand, there was some kind of user abuse, one shouldn't be able to take advantage of the company. What if you were one of those stunt men who they set on fire in all those movies with the cars that explode all the time? No matter, that was their policy and I saw it tested one day.

This guy comes in and wants to return a pair of shoes, of course, with no receipt or anything, and he didn't volunteer a reason. It was very *pro forma* on the stores part. It never dawned on the costumer that he *wouldn't* get his money back. The salesmen looked at the shoes that appeared to be nearly new and was very gracious, but he was clearly stymied because he did not know how much to credit the customer's account, because no one could remember the last time this particular shoe was sold. They finally went to Moe Greenburg, the oldest salesmen they had. He had sold shoes in that department for more than 50 years. He stroked the tiny beard on his chin like no ordinary shoe sage and told everyone that he remembered when they carried it; he went to the inventory archives, but they only went back 40 years. He grinned with an air of recognition and dated it at least 45 years old. He smiled and apologized for the delay and they credited the account. No questions were asked. He apologized again, for any inconvenience. He wrote on the credit slip: poor wear. Here's the rest of the story: the guy who brought the nearly new looking shoes was in a wheel chair. I remember thinking: how much wear could those shoes have actually gotten? Later on, Moe told some of his coworkers that he recalled the very day he sold a pair of shoes like that; it was the day after the Japanese bombed Pearl Harbor. He couldn't remember why that memory stuck in his head. It just did. He told us, as one might suspect that, it was a very quiet morning that Monday. He only made 2-3 sales the entire day. People were staying home mostly because they were upset by the news. Now that's a company that stands behind the product. *L.L. Bean* has a similar policy, as does *Lands End.*

When they tell you it is lifetime warrantee, make sure you know whose lifetime they are talking about, and if it simply means forever. If it is, you are in luck and you can be reasonably certain you are getting a good deal. You might have to pay a bit more, but it will invariably be worth it. Frankly, it is also a much better way to do business. Most companies put you through the Spanish Inquisition before they will fess up and admit that the product or service was no good. It kills them to give you your money back and when they are compelled to make any such transactional adjustment, their return policy will frequently require an encyclopedia of paperwork and a papal character witness. What's that all about?

Note to self: There are very few guarantees in life that are worth it.

47. Coffee Cups

If one were asked to explain the meaning of the word *infinite,* a reasonable response would be the actual number of kinds of coffee cups there are in the in the world today. I might have been close if I limited the scope to just *in my office.* It is pretty amazing, really, when you realize that a little less than 100 years ago, nobody was even drinking the stuff. People toiled for 12 to 16 hours a day and nobody got anything that even remotely looked like a coffee break. Today, it is more than likely that you are taking 2 or 3 of these 15-20-minute opportunities to bilk your employer out of work time. To compound the issue further, this ritual is then carried out on a daily basis and you are working less than an 8-hour day. And since you are one of those trained professionals who have probably elevated this mini siesta into a highly developed art form, it is reasonable to wager that you have your own signature cup, as well. My, my, my, how times do change. But let's get back to those blasted cups. They come in a multitude of sizes, from the small espresso sized to one that looks like it could accommodate power boats and people who water ski. Now, I have to tell you the guy who is consuming 2-3 of those big-ass bad boys has got to have some serious bladder issues. Just the sheer volume of liquid that he is forcing through those tired old kidneys of his has got to be nothing short of astounding.

Then, of course, they come in multitudes of materials that range from, plastic to fine bone china and from ceramic to porcelain. Of course, for those who choose to not make the personal investment, there is always the cardboard or Styrofoam controversy. Everyone knows that the latter is much cheaper and offices will go down kicking and screaming before they will give them up. Most CFO's will tell you to screw the environment when it comes to going big on cardboard. It has to be a least a penny a cup more. I guess that is not happening. Companies will even consider giving up on the whole idea of supplying disposable coffee cups if they are forced to consider the environment. Now there's an idea. In the meantime, we are seeing more and more companies that have chosen to resolve the matter once and for all. They are simply putting their own logos on company supplied ceramic cups. This further contributes to the avalanche of coffee cups that occurs when you open any cabinet where they are contained. I think an extremely hazardous condition has been created in many offices by this new policy.

One may never know when one's number is up, but every time they open a coffee cup cabinet, the possibility definitely exists where 10, 20, or 30 cups could easily come cascading out on top of the unsuspecting worker. I fully expect to find somebody one day lying on the floor amidst a mountain of coffee cup rubble with only his or her feet visible. Perhaps when I look at their bloodied and unrecognizable bodies, I will see shards of smiley faces and pieces of words like BOSS or QUEEN or BITCH. I am not sure why one would want to have these words on their cup of choice, but we have all seen them. Can you only imagine how difficult it would be to go the family of the recently departed and tell them how you found their dearly beloved and then have to tell them:

"...and they never even got to drink that last cup of coffee."

Some people are extra fussy and they bring their coffee from home in specially designed ergonomic travel mugs, only to arrive at the office and race back to the car to get their personalized mug. God forbid someone is using *their* mug. We wouldn't want anyone to confuse who the actual BITCH is by having someone else drinking from the wrong mug under false pretenses. Then there is the situation where many of your lovable fellow employees insist on using their own cups and never seem to want to wash them. It is their inalienable right to simply leave them in the sink, isn't it?

"Don't worry, Stan; I will be happy to wash your coffee cup for you. It is the least that I can do since I am only a lowly peon and have nothing better to do than wash your dishes for you."

Note to self: Wash your own coffee cup, schmuckhead

48. Shingles

OK, this is going to be in the way of another public service announcement. I was about 45 and I was driving to work and I started getting this incredible pain all throughout my chest. Of course, like most guys, I thought, *man, what the hell is going on here, did I sleep in the subway last night or what?* I continued driving for about another 5 minutes and the pain wasn't getting any better and I thought, *oh don't tell me, I am having a friggin' heart attack, well that's just great.* I decided that discretion was called for, so I drove immediately over to the Mac Emergency center on Southwestern Blvd. in Orchard Park, NY. I was shocked that they saw me right away and the doctor examining me, told me after 20 minutes or so, in a heavy Indian accent, "Well, I've got good news and bad news."

Oh, that's great, here we go, let's have it.

"The good news is you are not having a heart attack. The bad news is you've got the shingles."

I wasn't even sure what shingles was and he explained to me that it was a virus that lingers in one's system sometimes for 20-40 years but only if you have had the chicken pox. It tends to manifest itself as a bit of a rash on one's side, like shingles on a house; hence the name. I assured him I didn't have a rash. He asked me to pick up my shirt again and he showed me the tiniest bump of a blister and said, "That's the shingles."

You can only imagine how flabbergasted I was because it was so minute and yet it was still incredibly painful. He went on to explain that sometimes people get a rash all over their bodies and sometimes it takes up space only on the nerve endings inside. That's what I had and it was the seriously more painful of the two types. He gave me a script and sent me home in a new found agony that was nearly surreal. But do you know what the worst part of shingles was for me? It was when I actually told people I had it. They became obsessed with consoling me with stories of people that they knew who had it, or they would regale me with their own tales.

"My sister had shingles, and she went blind."

"My next-door neighbor had them, and he died."

It was almost like these would-be comforters were lining up so they could take their best shots at me. Finally, I was met with the worst one of them all. I had a business acquaintance named Scott and he told me that he had had shingles and all he could do for the pain was lay in an oatmeal bath all day. Now Scott was, how shall I say, large and in charge, and all I could do in my own agony was imagine this beached whale of a guy laying in a bathtub moaning and I was convinced it was time to simple say, "Check, please."

He followed this horrific description of his painful lament with the mandatory, "And, you know what the worst part was?"

Please God, there is worse? Then he gave me his great reveal.

"They were so much worse the *second time* I got them."

That's it! I am out of here! You could get them more than once? I experienced the true sense of the word terror for the first time. You cannot imagine my sheer joy when I heard that you can get a vaccine, a shot to prevent shingles. I ran out and got it faster than you can say, "Give me that God damned shingles shot now or I am going to have to kill you and your entire family."

I didn't actually say that, but as you can imagine, I didn't waste any time. So here is my gift to you. If you are over 35, go out and get the shingles shot now! Very few doctors will even discuss it with you until you are 60 (since the chances of your getting it goes up to 1 in 2 at that age). If you never had the chicken pox, you can skip it. Most kids are lucky today, since they got vaccinated for that particular childhood disease. If not, be warned. You may have to pay for it and it might even be expensive if your insurance doesn't cover it. Either way, it is your choice; the money, or out of your mind, exceedingly, agony type pain. Or if you are really unlucky, you might just go blind or die. How much fun is that?

Note to self: I already got mine. This one's for you. Go get a shingles shot.

49. The Perfect Pizza

Some of you may have heard the expression that, "Sex is like pizza. Even when it is bad, it is not that bad." I am willing to wager that some incredibly goofy guy said that because I suspect women do not share this sentiment. I will concur with them and state for the record that I think this is a lot of malarkey, too. Based on this and other silly theories, it seems like we have all been reduced to suffer in the land of total mediocrity regardless of our wants and desires. I have no desire to get too profound on this. I just want to tell you; I want a good pizza, god damn it. Now, pizza comes in multiples of shapes and varieties and, frankly, we have gotten totally out of control when it comes to not just making a great pizza, but one that passes for pizza at all. Let's start with the basics. It should have a crust, some herbs like oregano, some olive oil, tomato sauce, fresh mozzarella cheese, and maybe a topping of some sort, like sausage, sliced meatballs or pepperoni. It should not have a stinking pineapple on it. If you are from Hawaii and you think so, why don't you just cover the whole dammed thing in a grass skirt and stick it in your… ear. Just because you can put anything you want on a pizza doesn't mean you should, and after a while, that *creature* that is now cooking in the genuine wood fired oven bares almost no resemblance to a real pizza.

Don't even think about discussing the infamous frozen pizza. Go eat a broom and be done with it. Throw some tomato sauce on it just to make it look good. It's not going to taste any better no matter what you do. OK, I can hear someone out there from Iowa saying, "Well, wait a minute; I buy the *so and so pizza* and it tastes really good."

My response to those poor deluded folks is, "You are just wrong."

In French, they have a specific word for those circular excuses for a pizza and I believe they call it "*merde.*" Even if you don't speak French, I think you can translate it. A pizza has to made fresh, and you have to use fresh ingredients, end of story.

All of that taken into consideration, I will concede there is some flexibility in your selection or the type of pizza. You can go with round or rectangle (also known as the Sicilian pizza). If you are going round, the next decision is thin or thick crust. My preference is *thin* because, as a purest from NYC, it isn't a pizza unless you can fold it and eat it with one hand. If you are going to be a *thick crust* person you could be faced with another choice: deep dish or regular. Deep dish is also known as *Chicago style*. If you live in Chicago, you cannot understand how anyone would eat anything else. It is not really a snack food by any stretch of the imagination. It is a meal, and a serious one at that. For me, I want a thin crust only. I love a lot of extra mozzarella cheese on it, and sliced meatballs just to give it an extra dimension.

But the thing that goes by with the least amount of fanfare and should justify the most respect is the sauce itself. Most of the sauces that are used today are nothing but some sort of prepared crap that shouldn't be fed to a dog. A great pizza deserves a great sauce. You will know a great sauce when you taste it. Make no mistake about that.

As an added aside, there are many stories and myths that surround the making of the first pizza. This is my favorite, though decidedly apocryphal. The first pizza was made for consumption by the soldiers in the Roman army. They would take a bit of stone ground flour and mix it with some water and roll it out onto their shields and let it cook in the sun. When it was *properly baked*, they would throw some olive oil and some oregano or whatever they could get their hands on it to dress up their little pie (*pizza* is pie in Italian), and that is what they survived on when they were in the field. I am not sure how true that story is, but I will bet you it tasted perfect after a hard day at the office killing all those barbarians. Either way, one thing I can tell you: I love a great slice of pizza. In Buffalo NY, where I live right now, many will argue that theirs is the best. They're really quite militant in their convictions on this particular subject. I beg to differ with them. First of all, a plain pizza there automatically comes with pepperoni on it. I really could skip the peperoni. I'll eat it if I have to, but that's like saying: *I'll have sex if I have to*; what's that all about? Also, no matter what they tell you, they all feature the standard thick crust. The choice really is thick or thicker. If you try to order a plain pizza, that is, without pepperoni, you have to ask for a Neapolitan. Yeah, that's what I want, and I will put any old pizzeria in Brooklyn against the best pie in Buffalo and tell you the one in Brooklyn is the one to beat. Of course, there is always Johnny's Pizzeria in Greenwich Village too, if you really want to be living.

Note to self: "A pizza, a pizza, my kingdom for a pizza." A hungry Shakespeare, while writing Richard III

50. Young at Heart.

OK, now that you are getting older, say into your mid fifty's, you might have found yourself on some of those awful dating sites. This is further presuming that you have one or two divorces under your belt. Perhaps you may regrettably be trying to start your life over again after becoming recently widowed. It is not a fun proposition no matter how you cut it. Then you have to sort through, depending on your preference, a myriad of fat, balding, older, men, (all of whom are lying about their age) or a series of plumpish women, some of whom appear to be really angry and very specific on their wants and do not wants list. Many of these women seem to want someone to take them out to dinner all the time and are not willing to *give back* anything in return. That implication probably sounds crass but let me expand on this for a moment. I recall counseling my former mother-in-law, when she was in her mid-seventies and recently widowed. I cautioned her if anyone offered to take her out to dinner, she should make sure that she didn't order the lobster. She wasn't sure what I was driving at and she was quick to tell me that she quite enjoyed lobster very much. I told her, OK, do what you want, but if somebody buys you a lobster dinner, he might just be expecting something in return (wink, wink). Since she had been out of the dating game for nearly 40 years at that time, she blushed when she realized what I was getting at and muttered, "Oh, my..."

"Oh my…, indeed."

The next challenge that one has to overcome on these sites is learning to decipher the code. Whenever you see the phrase: *young at heart,* it means anything but that. That usually means, if it is a woman, that the individual likes yard sales, making quilts, enjoys an occasional night at bingo and can probably eat you under the table when the dessert tray comes around. It does not mean that she enjoys any of the activities that people who are 20-25 years younger actually enjoy such as dining and dancing, going to rock concerts, and having frequent romps in the hay.

If it is a gentleman who uses this description for himself, it means he only dozes in front of the TV 4 nights a week, and goes camping only in the summer time. In the fall he goes moose hunting. This *young at heart* thing really gives an indication of one's age since it stems from the song "Young at Heart," which was sung by Frank Sinatra back in

1953. Checking my age meter, I was 2 years old back then. Considering the song's age, it might invoke a particular resonance with you. That is presuming that you would be at least a generation older than I am. That places you well into your 80s. I am not sure how much disco dancing you are doing as an octogenarian. Moreover, I am willing to speculate that if I go to the *Crisco Disco* this Friday night, just the sight of one of these former cougars (who is now old enough to be a snow leopard) out there on the dance floor is going to have me going in for shock treatments the next day to bring me back to reality.

If our *young at heart* friend indicates that she is into concerts, you can be reasonably certain that when concert night comes around, she will probably get duded up in some very retro outfit with platform shoes and a possible headband and the dress or jeans that she is sporting will go a long way toward accentuating the ubiquitous muffin top. It is not going to be a good look and if it is one of those head banging concerts you may want to start banging your head before you stop by the house to pick her up. The male counterpart version is similarly not so attractive either. Suffice it to say, that if you have entered into the world of senior dating, it is indeed a jungle out there.

Note to self: Here's a novel idea. How about aging gracefully?

51. Writer's block

There comes a time in the life of every writer when he or she sits down at the keyboard (few people pick up a pen these days if they are about to be writing anything serious) and BAM! It is as though the train has decided to *not* leave the station. There is no accounting for it. It is simply inevitable. It seems to happen less frequently with those writers who are accustomed to working on deadlines or who write all the time. It is kind of like mothers who simply cannot get sick. They are forced to rally, in spite of the way they feel, since the entire family unit seems to shut down without their constant and relentless contribution to the social order. Writers who fall into this group are in a very different category than say the non-published dilettante who has been working on the great American Novel for his or her enter life. This second group will experience that all too familiar block all the time. They may go months or years without writing a word and chalk it up to a block, but the reality is that they really aren't writers. They are people who want to be writers. There are many exceptions to this, of course. Harper Lee (*to Kill a Mocking Bird*) is definitely a good example since she didn't write all the time and had a lifetime dry spell, until she was forced to write that appalling prequel to her classic which would have been better *not* to have been written.

In my opinion, (most) real writers write. Margaret Mitchell may have only written one book in her life time and it may have been a best seller that defined a generation, *Gone with the Wind*, but she worked at the *Atlanta Journal* and wrote every day.

One of the things I really enjoyed about the TV series *Sex in the City* was when they would show one of the key characters, Caroline "Carrie" Bradshaw, working through the denouement of each episode at her computer. She showed the discipline that a writer must surrender to if they are in fact obsessed with belonging to the craft that makes one a writer. Today, there are many vehicles available that allow a writer to work at their craft. Something, Shakespeare, Hawthorne, Melville and the other giants didn't have at their disposal is this thing that we call *blogging*. Blogging, whether you look at it as a ridiculous example of technological self-aggrandizement or an incredible grass-root attempt to change the thinking of current society, is at its core, first and foremost, another way the writer tries to reach an audience. Few would disagree with me when I state that most of it crap. Many writers who use blogging as a part of their work go on to reach much broader audiences. Consider Julie Powell, the author of the blog that begat the fictionalized book and further begat the movie *Julie & Julia*. In 2002, when Ms. Powell began her quest to cook every recipe in Child's *Mastering the Art of French Cooking* (in a year), I am not sure she really knew where it would ultimately take her.

How about Tim Ferriss who started a blog called *the 4-Hour Work Week*? Many business people and CEO's considered it well-written and very thought provoking. From this modest foray into the world of writing, he subsequently launched his book in 2007, T*he 4-Hour Workweek* published by Random House, and marketed the book mostly to other bloggers. (That's a pretty big audience, by the way.) Today, he is a major big shot on the speaking circuit, but I am sure he still gets a bit of writing in from time to time.

I make it a habit to write something every day. It isn't important that I write something that is going to change the minds and hearts of men. People who set out to do that usually wind up writing nothing, since that is just too overwhelming a task. If you are going to take up the craft, I would extend one bit of advice to you. This is true regardless of whether you are Carrie Bradshaw or Tim Ferris or yours truly. Write about something that you think you might know something about; something that is on your mind. The sexy Ms. Bradshaw wrote about the ever-changing world of dating for single women of today. Interestingly enough, her style included lots of questions and she didn't always come up with solutions or answers to those questions. She frequently left that up to her readers to discern. Me, I'm just writing about things that I observe and that perplex me. I might choose to write about some business issues and how the playing field seems to be changing all too often in most of the markets around the world. Other times, I may write about things much closer to home. As in: when was the last time you told your wife or significant other that you loved them. Sometimes, when I am stalled, I simply turn away from my subject and write a few emails or a note to someone I care enough about to send a hand written note and my writing mechanism gets jump started. Either way, I'm writing about it right now and screw that damn writer's block thing. Who needs it?

Note to self: Now, where was I?

52. You're on my list

Some of you may remember my discussion of my dear friend's granddaughter Vienna in the original *Potato Chips for the Soul.* She is an extremely precocious young lady and several years ago, when it was becoming clear that she was a fan of mine, we had an interesting exchange. She was about 7 at the time and she was starting to act up a little and her grandmother, who she adores, set her straight in a very authoritative but loving way, and I added, "And you better shape up, Vienna, because otherwise I will have to put you on my list."

Well, you would have thought I threatened to have her drawn and quartered. This enormous tear started to emerge from her left eye, and she burst into borderline hysterics and begged her grandmother, "Ya Ya, please don't let Brendan put me on his list!"

I was torn between having to chuckle because of the ludicrous-ness of my idle threat and crushed because I had upset this little urchin unnecessarily. I immediately jumped to her rescue and assured her I wouldn't have to put her on "the list" if she listened more appropriately to her YaYa. Thank goodness, we became friends again.

This encounter, however, taught me something. I realized that people do have lists and whether or not you are on the list might just make a difference not only to you, but to those who hope to appear there or not. In some circles, these might be referred to as one's s*** list. There could be serious ramifications if you make that list. Today, it seems that all of the decisions in Washington are based on either getting onto someone's list or staying off of someone else's. Currying one's favor is the law of the land now, rather than doing your job and showing integrity. Is it any wonder why most would agree that we are going to hell in a handbag? I am not going to deny that in years gone by there wasn't a very far reaching and definite *good old boys network* and it had major implications both in business as well as politics. It just seems that today this mechanism seems to have taken on an entirely new dimension of inappropriateness and *the means* is keeping everyone from getting even close to a *justifiable end.* These days, doing a good job seems to have become so much less important than this relentless jockeying for position. And generally speaking, whether it is in the canyons of Wall Street or on the hallowed Senate floor, it is just not a good thing.

In the political arena, it is a popular argument, to blame the *two-party system* for all of this back scratching. There might be something to that, but that notion seemed to be shattered by a good friend of mine who happens to be Israeli. He relished our system and condemned his own, which had at the time of this writing, no fewer than 34 official political parties. The best that they could ever hope for in the *Promised Land* was what is called a coalition government. Talk about the art of compromise. Let's not forget that it was a coalition government that elected Hitler, who led one of the several minority parties in Germany. If that is the case, what's a fellow to do? I am not sure. I guess it was just a very elementary lesson that Vienna taught me that day. There are lists everywhere. Just be careful which one you are on and which one you are not. It might make a profound difference to you someday.

Note to self: Now, where is that list?

53. I danced with Gregory Hines.

For those of you who don't know who Gregory Hines is, or perhaps I should say was, he was probably the best tap dancer of his generation. He literally grew up in the business and was part of a family act with his father and brother back in the 1950s, called *Hines, Hines and Dad.* His *hay day* as a soloist was from the 1970s, through the 1990s and he was one fantastic, tap dancing son of a gun. Back in the early 1970s I got the bug to be an actor in NYC, and in my travels, I lucked out and took a part time day job at Brook's Brothers on 44th and Madison. It was a great gig, they paid a lot of money, and the best part was it was like a road company of out of work Broadway actors who were trying to make ends meet without waiting on tables and or driving a cab.

One of the people who befriended me was a gentleman named Wayne Sheridan. He had been one of Agnes Demille's dance captains. Ms. Demille was one of the most famous choreographers back in the 1950s and through the 1980s. He had worked with her back in the 1950s in *Brigadoon* and *Pajama Game*, which both ran on Broadway for seemingly forever. He realized that there were enough struggling actors working the main floor at Brooks Brothers and he eventually wrote a musical about the place called *From Brooks with Love* which ran *off Broadway* to a good bit of fanfare. Before that, however, he started giving dancing classes for a number of us who worked there. I studied ballet and tap, and it was clear from the get go that Wayne was an amazingly gifted dancer. Now for the record, it was never my intent to become the next Gene Kelly or Fred Astaire. One of the things that most actors do, however, is take singing and dancing classes. They do this so that perhaps they can sell themselves as actors who sing and move well. This would be as opposed to singers who act and move well or dancers who sing and act. These latter groups frequently wind up in the chorus, making the star look good. I took dance classes for nearly 6 years (ballet, jazz and tap) as a rudimentary part of my training and it was all good and well worth it.

After studying with him for a bit, I decided I wanted to take classes with other teachers and expand my growing abilities. I thought maybe I would take a tap class with Henry LaTang. Now this was pretty brazen on my part because Henry was considered to be the best tap dance teacher in New York at the time. He was in his mid-seventies, a little paunchy, and appeared to be your average grandfather type. His class was very different than any other class I ever attended up to that time, and by then there had been several. Typically, there are some loosening up exercises at the start of each class. Then you work on a combination (a series of steps that help to build a full routine.)You would practice the combination over and over and work out the kinks, and then at the end of the class, everyone would get a chance to glide across the floor and show how well they could execute the steps.

That's not how this class was going to be. Henry got up at the front of the studio. He did a quick tap step that looked like one of those moves that you would expect the lead character in the Wiley Coyote cartoon to do. You know, where the feet are all blurry and smoke comes billowing up from underneath. He did it once. Then he walked out of the room, never to be seen again. That was it. That was the class. He showed you the step. Now you do it. I would be lying if I didn't tell you I thought to myself: *Yeah right, are you out of your cotton-picking mind, or what?* No matter. That was the deal and that's how Henry taught. I was pretty much done at that point, but I pressed on and tried to make the feeblest attempt at doing the combination. I was pretty bad and was totally out of my element. As I was trying to do my pathetic shuffle, ball, change, I looked up and out of the corner of my eye I saw Gregory Hines. I was so ossified at having just watched Henry do his thing that I hadn't noticed this living legend standing next to me. He was attempting to do it too. He seemed to get virtually 90% of it the first time. He kept drilling it over and over again and he pretty much had it after about 5 minutes. He kept to himself. He didn't look at me condescendingly. There was no indication of him thinking: *Man, that's one pathetic white boy next to me.* In fact, at one point he smiled at me almost as if to tell me, *go ahead kid, keep trying, you'll get it soon enough.* It was a cool moment. Just to be in the same room with this amazing talent was extraordinary to me. But to be next to him in the same class was nothing short of fantastic.

Wayne taught me an extremely important lesson and I will pass it on to you. He asked me at one point if I was a dancer. I meekly replied, "Well, I am taking some classes and trying to learn..."

He interrupted me and asked me again, "Are you a dancer?"

I stumbled over my second response and started to add, "Well, one day I am hoping that I can say that I am but, in the meantime, I am..."

He asked a third time, but this time, he cut me off completely and finished the question, by saying, "I didn't ask how good a dancer you were. That's not the point. I asked you, are you a dancer. You either are or you aren't."

"I'm a dancer."

Note to self: Gregory Hines may have been a better dancer but he stood next to me in class. Beat that.

54. Hi, honey…

I always smile when my lady love greets me with this all too familiar salutation. It makes me happy to hear her say this because I know that she is genuinely happy to see me. It doubles my affections for her and makes me think to myself, *wow, that's just the sweetest greeting, isn't it?* I don't know how many people have heard this greeting over the countless millennia but I'm sure it is a pretty large number. Perhaps the first person to use this moniker thought of the very essence of honey and was making a simple comparison of the sweetness itself. Let's be frank here, honey is sweet. It has been used as a flavor enhancer for literally thousands of years and was the sweetener of choice long before the emergence of sugar cane. But of all of the ingredients and discoveries in our long course of what we call human history, honey has been something that has never really been given its due. For the record, it is close to being a nearly magical substance.

Any kid in school will tell you it comes from bees, right? Let's expand on this a little. In order to produce 1 pound of honey, 2 million flowers must be visited. That's a helluva lot of flowers and some serious heavy lifting on those little bees' parts. One of the things that some of us will take note of is that there are different kinds of honey, and based on the kinds of plants or flowers the honey bees visit, there can be an incredible difference in the flavor. I like buckwheat and wildflower the most. Depending on the part of the world you are in, there is a multitude of differences because the wildflowers that one sees in the southwest of our country are very different than what one would encounter in New England or Ireland for that matter. I really love food, and I have been heard on more than an occasion or two trying to describe certain foods. Eating oysters reminds me of what it would be like if you could eat the ocean. Drinking tequila (Patron) for me is like drinking the earth. Eating wildflower honey gives me a sense of breathing in the entire countryside from whence the honey originated.

Here's another factoid about how difficult this substance is to collect. The bees in a hive must fly 55,000 miles to produce a pound of honey. Clearly, this is some serious hard work here. We read in too many parts of the Christian and Hebrew bibles how honey plays a part in the development of our lives and throughout western culture. The Hebrews were led out of bondage and servitude and promised a land that was to be theirs forever, *flowing with milk and Honey.* John the Baptist subsisted on honey in the dessert. And the Quran and some of the Muslim writings take it even further. In the *Sahih Bukhari,* we read that the Prophet said, "Honey is a remedy for every illness and the *Quran* is a remedy for all illness of the mind; therefore, I recommend to you (both) remedies, the *Quran* and honey." Either way, honey is a truly miraculous liquid. If it is sealed, it will last for literally thousands of years. It doesn't spoil; its use as a medicinal for covering injuries, wounds, and bruises is nothing short of amazing.

Here's one last thing to consider. An average worker bee makes only about 1/12 teaspoon of honey in its very short lifetime (4 to 5 months). That's a lot of work for so little and we can now see that this is absolutely amazing stuff. The next time your beloved greets you with "Hi, honey," recognize that she isn't just saying you are sweet and uttering a simple throwaway line. She/he is telling you that you are wondrous and special and something that is really hard to come by and they are blessed to have you in their lives.

Note to self: "I am lucky to have you, honey."

55. Moving Day

Few things cause more stress in a person's life than moving from one place to another. Even under the best of circumstances, it is a day that is fraught with one aggravation after another. Here are a few of the simpler tasks that have to occur to create a smooth transition. First of all, the utilities in your name have to get canceled in the place you are exiting and reconnected in your name at the destination. These can include: gas, electric, water, garbage pickup, telephone, and internet. This can also include cancelling and switching over other services that include: Fios, cable, or the satellite dish for your television. That's a lot of phone calls, a lot of listening to music on hold, and at least 9 conversations you have to have with people who sound like you have made it your mission to bother them. This is where you really have to suck it up though, because if you get porky with anyone of them, they can simply put you back on hold for anywhere from 10 minutes to a month, or they can reconnect you to another division for faster response time. If you fall into this latter abyss, you just need to presume whatever service you were looking to adjust will not happen when you need it and perhaps that means you will be sitting in the dark for a few days or shivering in the cold until you settle down a little and make nice to these frustrated bureaucrats.

So far so good; now we are on to the next piece of wizardry. This is where you have to coordinate the movers. More times than not, if you are purchasing a house and are required to move from one place to the other, there might be a title company and or attorneys that arrange for what is called the closing or the settlement process. Regardless of who is assuming this role, please expect nothing other than super last-minute notice as to when the actual transition is to occur. Most places in the United States have "on or about" dates for the actual closing and much like a pregnancy date, they know how long a pregnancy is supposed to be so they come up with *a kind of sorta* target date. What you telling me then is that *the movers are on hold, right?* Yes, that is exactly what I am telling you; and sometimes the movers book other jobs because they want to keep their crews working. Then you make the call and just magically hope that they will appear at your doorstep. Sometimes they do and sometimes they don't. It is in the *when they don't* category that most people resort to hysterics, f-bombs and massive quantities of alcohol laden drinks to get through the next 24 hours. Right around this point, it becomes abundantly clear that most of what is about to be transported needed to be wrapped or safely put into boxes. That incredible Ming vase which has been handed down from generation to generation cannot be simply tossed onto the sofa, as it is being loaded on to the truck. A single object like this might take 20 minutes to get wrapped properly.

Now here's the good news. You can have the movers pack everything for you and most professional movers will do a great job and offer the promise of almost no breakage. Or you can do it yourself and further aggravate yourself. Certainly, the do it your self-option is much cheaper. Novices rarely realize that it is extremely expensive to have the moving companies do it for them. I say if you're aggravated already, do it yourself and see if you can put yourself into a full scaled seizure. Go for the foaming at the mouth thing and everything and be done with it. Go big or don't go at all. One thing we can guarantee; moving is one big pain in the butt. That's why anyone with any sense puts it off whenever they can. Oh, and one other thing; don't forget to change your address at the post office. I suppose you don't have to and perhaps you can just hope that the guy that is moving into your place will be kind enough to continue to pay your bills. Wouldn't that be nice? I wouldn't bank on that if I were you.

Note to self: The only good thing about moving is you find out who your friends are.

56. The "well" is deep.

The word "well" in the English language is a funny thing. It can be used as a verb as in: tears *welled* from her eyes. It can be used as an adverb as in: works *well* under pressure. It can be used as an adjective: All's *Well* That Ends *Well*. We have our good friend, Billy Shakespeare, to thank for that one. It's funny how no one ever calls him Billy anymore. Obviously, it can be used as a noun, as in: a deep hole made in the ground through which water can be removed. You know, a *WELL*? You big lunk-head, it's that thing with a bucket, and wishing, and all that sort of folderol. But for all of the usages this four-letter word begets, it is as an *interjection* that I take the greatest exception. You know, when it used to indicate: resumption of discourse or to introduce a remark. To clarify, this is as in the case of every politician who ever opened his/her mouth to speak and used it to start their sentence. Every time I hear a politician do this I am tempted to say, "Let the games begin."

This is where you get to have some fun and do a little experiment. Watch the evening news or take a glimpse at any interview that appears on the various social media and wait for a politician to get asked a question. If the person questioned begins the answer with the word "well...," you can be assured of one of three possibilities:

- They will want to avoid answering the question and they will use it as a pause.
- They will use it as a bridge to cross over into a world of total nonsense and obfuscation and leave the listener with no other choice but to say, "Huh?"
- They will use it to tell one incredible bold face lie.

Don't believe me? Try it. It will make you laugh out loud, really.

It is the best "tell" to determine if someone is looking to throw you the curve ball or simply pull the wool over your eyes. Some of our more renowned politicians were huge "well-ers." Ronald Reagan couldn't say anything without taking a pause to collect his thoughts and he would always commence with his jovial and fatherly:

"Weell, it's like this," or, "Well... balancing the budget is kind of like renovating a kitchen. It always takes a little longer and costs a lot more than you thought it would."

I paraphrased these, but I'm sure you can hear him saying things like this. I think in Ronnie's case, he wasn't saying "well" for the more nefarious usages. It was merely a folksy pause, and nothing more. On the other hand, if you look at how Hillary Clinton uses it, or worse, how her successor as Secretary of State, John Kerry used it, you will clearly see how the word "well" is only used as a *truth checker*. That is to say, that once they utter the word, all vestiges of truth are checked at the door. I had the occasion specifically to listen to John Kerry in an interview recently (and this is several months after he was no longer serving as Secretary of State) and he was asked a fairly simple and direct question and he droned back with "Well..." and literally after two minutes, the only thing the interviewer could have been thinking to himself was, "Boy would I love to tell this guy, are you f###ing kidding me, or what. What a crock of s### that was."

Would that be wrong? I don't think so, and until someone starts challenging career politicians when they attempt to sail the curve ball past us, we can expect it to be business as usual in Washington. In the meantime, start truth checking your friends, too, when you see them trying to throw you into their own "wells." For better or for worse, it is time we put a stop to all of this subterfuge and start being a lot more frank with one another.

Note to self: *Well*, **I was going to say this, but I opted for that instead."**

57. The Three Most Dreaded Words in the English Language

Now how is that for a teaser of a title? For George Costanza on *Seinfeld*, they were the words "I love you." He had never said them before, and finding himself in his mid-thirties, he finally mustered the courage to say it, only to discover that the girl he said them to simply responded with, "Hey, do you wanna get a pizza?" Not to be discouraged, he subsequently discovers that she is deaf in one ear. So obviously, she couldn't possibly have heard him, so he tries again a few days later. The next time there is no doubt she hears him and she sheepishly looks at him and says, "Yeah, I know, I heard you the first time." This was not the response he had hoped for and I would have to admit, as his side kick Jerry told him, saying *I love you* and not getting an *I love you* back is quite a big matzo ball to lay out there. It could cause a lot of stress in a person's life.

For me and for some others out there who might be less romantically obsessed, the three words I absolutely dread are: *Some Assembly Required*. I think my last marriage officially went down the toilet because my wife, at the time, just couldn't grasp what those words meant to me. I literally get palpations and hives when I see these words. Here's the deal. I have very poor small motor skills and a relentless aversion to detail work, and simple things like even turning a screw with an Allen wrench will put me over the top. My idea of hell is to be forced to sit and assemble a jigsaw puzzle: you know, the kind that has 1000 pieces and are of scenes from *around the world.* Some people find it relaxing, I get it. I even admire those that can spend hours in their own personal woodworking shops in their basements. What a great sense of accomplishment it must be for them when they assemble a life-sized version of the USS Enterprise out of plastic deposit bottles and from the thousand or so nuts and washers they have found scattered about their garage floors for the last few years. I, on the other hand, begin to hyperventilate as soon as I see those three little words on the outside of the box. Actually, I am anxiety ridden long before I even open the box. I mentioned that the "ex" put me over the top one time too many. Let me tell you the story.

First of all, it is important that you know that I made no bones about my aversion to putting things together. I was clear. I was adamant as I expressed my limitations, even in the cases where it said, *so simple even a 5-year-old could do it.* I think I am confident in saying that I have some other talents; it is just that the *assembling* thing isn't one of them. Now after a few years of being forced to admit defeat with bloodied fingers and f-bombs galore, the bride decides we need to get one of those gazebos that one sees at *Home Depot* or *Lowes* or in any garden center. I looked at her and stated the obvious in fairly emphatic but in the most affectionate of terms, "This looks great, just don't even think of having me put this son of a bitchin thing together."

The salesman who has overhear me gently chides me with how easy it is and how he put one together in little under an hour. I smiled and reiterated my position. All of my cards were on the table.

We get the damned thing home, and the *former Mrs. C.* condescendingly mentions that she is more than willing to help me, and after all, "How hard can it be?"

We open the box and I am immediately struck with what it must be like to be a politician discussing the deficit in Washington these days. I don't see millions, I don't see billions, and I am literally looking at *trillions* of screws, washers, lug nuts and a litany of tiny metal pieces that I cannot even name. In an effort to save face and perhaps prolong this failing marriage another month, I grind my teeth and acquiesce, and resentfully tell her, so that there could be no hope of a misunderstanding:

"I will give it one hour."

After the hour was up and we were no further along than when we first opened the box, I took my bleeding fingers and my beaten down ego and called a local handy guy and had him come over to put the f***ing thing together. I heard almost as many f-bombs from this guy as I would have uttered myself and he had every imaginable kind of power tool available in the Western Hemisphere. Just as I was paying him, I watched him wipe the buckets of sweat from his brow and he looked up and added, "You do know that you have to take this down at the end of the season, don't you?"

Before I could even begin to get the words out of my mouth to ask him when I should have him come back, he completed his thought.

"And don't even think about calling me."

Note to self: I do not assemble things. I get someone else to do it regardless of the price.

58. So Let's Paint the Living Room

So, what are we thinking, maybe a little *Landlord White* just to play it safe? Well, maybe we could jazz it up, just a little bit, and go with one of those myriads of off-white colors. I mean really, that *super stark white* is just too antiseptic looking and such a bore, isn't it? Granted, it is safe, but surely we can always glitz it up with some super nifty paintings, couldn't we? How about some photos that look like cool black and whites, as featured in *Life* Magazine? Now you are talking. Let's get artsy! Who are we kidding; can anyone tell me that one of those Elvis paintings on the signature, black velvet backgrounds won't look great no matter what color you decide on when you boldly go where no man has painted before? Well, hold your horses' buckaroo; you are not getting off that easily.

Have you been to a paint store recently? It is a pretty scary place, especially when you approach the wall with all those paint chip colors. There are 30-40 shades of white alone. When did white evolve beyond itself? Apparently, it has, and now those of us who really wanted that basic Landlord look have gotten sucked in and we are considering, *Linen*, or *Antique White*, or *Cloud White*, or *Marshmallow White*, or *Surgical Room White*, as distinctly different and more favorable variations. My darling friend, Marilynn, recently selected, after much painstaking and neurotic angst, a color that actually turned out to be truly a game changer. The only problem was the name: *Lavender Suede*. Having a dining room painted the same color as the name of a cheap, burlesque stripper, is, to me, quite disconcerting. It is almost impossible to say the name without drawing it in and thrusting your tongue out and elongating it so that it doesn't sound like a nasty bit of seduction. Try saying it: *L-A-V-E-N-D-E-R Suede*. See, it took you at least 3 seconds to say it, didn't it? You feel disgusting now too, don't you? It's a bad name, but a great color and it really brings out the shade of amethyst in a nearby stained-glass window that she has in that same room.

Of course, she wasn't through yet. The living room had to get freshened up, too. She dipped her toe in the myriads of off whites, and what the hell do I know, this one looked as good as that one. I mean, I am not exactly an art critic. Come on, who are we kidding here? One color is as good as another, especially in that ever-growing *beige* category. Finally, we had a winner. Are you ready?

Somehow, I don't think you are? How about: *Yuma Sand?* Now if you are like me, you probably have never been to Yuma, Arizona. I have no way of knowing what color the sand is there and, I suspect, neither do you. Is it all that different from all of the other sands around the world? I have heard of certain beaches where the sand has a pinkish hue and of course, many of the islands in the South Seas have volcanic sand that look positively black. Is the sand of the Sahara a different color than the deserts in the American Southwest? Apparently, the answer is yes, or perhaps it is all a big case of simple marketing. Either way, I have to tell you that *Yuma Sand* looks seriously fabulous in her living room and I am glad she went through the painstaking process of finding just the right color. It's a *Wow and a half.* If nothing else, it gives us some humorous talking points when people ask, "So what the hell color is this anyway, it sort of like a creamy, yellowy white or something?"

"What are you blind, or just plain stupid? Any dope knows that's *Yuma Sand.*"

Note to Self: "The world is a cavalcade of color."
Walt Disney

59. The sequel

For all those media junkies out there who can't get enough of a good thing, it seems whether it is a favorite book, or movie, or TV series (and now even video games) there is an obsession with just giving us a little more. Hence, we have the *sequel.* To ensure that there is no confusion here, let's make sure we are talking about the same thing. We are not talking about those white birds we see along the shore line at Cape Cod or Jones Beach. Those are *Sea gulls.* And we are not referring to that nice Jewish couple who lived across the street from us. They are the *Segals.* We are talking about the continuation of a story, as in *The Godfather* and the sequel to that, as in the *Godfather 2.* This example might further confuse us because there was a subsequent sequel to the *Godfather 2.* Amazingly they decided to call it: *Godfather 3.* Oddly enough, this second sequel wasn't well received by the critics, but it had one of the best lines of any of them. Remember when Michael Corleone says, "Just when I think I'm out, they pull me back in."

Yeah, that's from the third one. I actually liked that one, since it finally completes the epic morality play and all debts get paid. Here, we see the completion of the tragedy. We see the end of this tale of one family's journey to assimilate into the American culture.

Now for the record, sequels are not modern inventions at all. Nearly 2500 hundred years ago, Homer wrote the *Iliad* and quickly followed it up with the arguably more famous *Odyssey.* The Bible has an *Old Testament* and it is followed up by an even more convincing statement of faith in its sequel, the *New Testament.* Alexander Dumas wrote *The Three Musketeers* and then did a spin off with the *Man in the Iron Mask.* Mark Twain gave us *Tom Sawyer.* The resulting accolades and hardy reception he received from that classic compelled him to give us the complete backstory on the even more famous *Huckleberry Finn. The Robe,* based on the bestselling novel by Lloyd C. Douglas, introduced us to *Cinemascope* and literally saved 20 Century Fox from going under; it was so well received that it had to be followed up by *Demetrius and the Gladiators.* I just can't get enough of those Lions eating those Christians. How about *The Wizard of Oz?* Now, most of us are familiar with the heartwarming classic film with Judy Garland from 1939. What most of don't realize is that the author, Frank L. Baum, wrote an entire series of books and several sequels that were favorite bedtime stores 20 years before the *silent* version of the film ever even came out. Hey, when we like something, we like it and we just can't get enough. Unfortunately, sometimes we go a little haywire.

How about those *Transformer* movies? The first one was schlock and God only knows how they keep cranking out even more schlock. What about the *Fast and Furious* films? I have lost count and I think they are up to number 8 by now, and I have to ask you, what are the odds that there are cars that crash or get blown up in the next film? We have truly become stupefied with this series. You know what I find exciting. When they come up with a great series, or film, or book and they kill off the most important characters, so clearly, they cannot have a sequel anymore. Here's a great example: *Breaking Bad.* With one of the greatest climaxes in the history of Hollywood, there was no way they could do a next chapter. But we loved it so much that they were forced to figure a way to do it. If there is a buck to be made, they will come up with a solution and "ta dah," they did. They developed the *prequel*; the story before the story. In this case it is called *Better Call Saul.* With three seasons down, it is just beginning to find its audience. I am all in on this one, too, and I love how they tell the story of how Jimmy McGill, the struggling attorney, evolves to become Saul, the super slimy lawyer for crack dealers.

Then we have the masterpiece of sequels in the *Star Wars* saga. It had the audacity to start out somewhere in the near middle. It starts out on episode 3 or 4, (I'm not sure) and then it wanders all across a myriad of galaxies over 40 years in actual production time and comes out the other end to tell the complete story. Sequels on top of sequels and prequels on top of prequels; that's a lot of space garbage no matter how you lift it. We love it, don't we?

Note to self: When it comes to sequels, may the force be with you.

60. The Dysfunctional Family Feud

One of my favorite skits on the old *Saturday Night Live* show was their rendition of *Family Feud,* appropriately called the *Dysfunctional Family Feud.* The question came around to team one and it was as follows: Name a convenient tool or appliance that you would expect to find in your kitchen. The contestant quickly shouts out, "an AX!" You had to laugh and you also had to think to yourself, *Yeah, that's pretty much what I was going to say,* if you grew up in America. Not sure how we got here, but I think it is safe to say that virtually everyone out there grew up in a dysfunctional family, one way or the other. The only question left unanswered is the degree of the dysfunction. No one grew up in an idyllic family like *Ozzie and Harriet,* or *Leave it Beaver,* or *the Donna Reed Show.* It might make for some great television, but it doesn't have anything to do with reality, which is probably closer to the family as shown on *The Munster's.*

In many parts of the inner cities these days, less than one family in four has a father figure at home. More than half of the marriages end in divorce and most families are blended, with half siblings either through blood or marriage. A really scary trend these days is family units with children from multiple partners totally devoid of even an attempt at a marriage. When the adults are questioned on this, the typical response is something like, "Well, we haven't gotten around to it yet," or my favorite is, "Well, we aren't ready to make that kind of a commitment yet." Excuse me? Let me explain something to you; those little people running around in need of shoes are what I would call a really serious commitment. Compounding these issues is the fact that more people are on food stamps and public assistance than ever before in our entire nation's history. Does anyone think that's a good thing? I didn't think so.

Some of us baby boomers grew up in households run by fathers who were members of the *Greatest Generation.* There are no arguments here; they were truly the greatest. They fought in a terrible war and came back and didn't say boo and just picked up where they left off. There was no PTSD. They toughed it out and more times than not, they simply didn't talk about it. If on occasion they had to resort to using a little alcohol (medicinally), so be it.

If we are being honest, however, a lot of those guys that served in WWII were pretty messed up. If they came back from Korea, they were probably worse. And the guys that served in Viet Nam were the most scarred of them all, and they not only didn't get a hero's welcome when they returned, they got spat upon. Let's bring the women into the mix. How many of our parents stayed together for the sake of preserving the family unit, or for religious reasons? In these scenarios, the mothers bared most of the burden and frequently suffered in silence. That sure makes for a happy family, doesn't it?

How many shotgun weddings were there? I can remember hearing a comedian doing a routine about growing up Catholic in the 50s. He went on to explain that you pretty much had to get married to a gorilla if you got pregnant back then. That was true, too. This is not the stuff that makes for a full and productive family life that stresses good values. It creates an environment that is much closer to fighting for your life, with *survival of the fittest* being the watchword of the day. Add to this that with 3, 6, or 12 children, sometimes the father had to work 2 or 3 jobs and was never home and the mother might have to have a job outside the home as well. That presents an entirely new set of constructs to contribute to dysfunction. In the end, we are all less than kosher in the mental hygiene department. Even the rich and famous families like the Kennedys don't get to escape the wrath of a less than hospitable upbringing. So, what's a fella to do then? This is what I say. DEAL WITH IT. Just stop trying to use your personal dysfunctional shortcomings as an excuse. Believe me, nobody has time for that and they just might tell you to, "Go play it on the ukulele."

Note to self: Nobody really cares about your personal dysfunctions.

61. The "S" Factor

In my second book, *The 7th Sense, the Key to Effectiveness in Life and Business*, I described a phenomenon of which we should all become aware. Let me explain how I deduced its existence. Suffice it to say as a writer and an actor, I love words. I love the sounds of words, the etymology of words, and the nuances of their connotations as opposed to their denotations. Because of that, I strongly related to a bit that the actor Orson Bean did on the old *Tonight Show* with Johnny Carsen. It was evidently humorous enough so that another comedian named Tim Allen ripped it off word for word and did it 15 years later for another generation of laughter enthusiasts. Being a word smith, he went on to proclaim that he loved words too, but we all had to agree that some languages simply sounded better than others. Take the word *Butterfly* for example. It's certainly a very nice word, in English. It is made of two lovely, but smaller words, Butter, which is nice, and sounds yummy, and fly, and who doesn't think that flying isn't a cool thing too? *Butterfly* is a great sounding word. In French, however, it is spectacular. The same word is *Papillion.* Can't you just hear the magic in their version of the same word and see how the word *butterfly* pales in comparison.

Let's move on to Spanish. The same word now becomes *Mariposa.* I love this one. Can't you just hear Antonio Banderas seductively whispering in your ear the word *Mariposa*? Who cares what it means? It sounds awesome. This pretty much continues until you get to the word in German. Here it becomes, *Schmetterling!* It sounds like a prehistoric bird or some sort of a dive bomber swooping out of the skies. WATCH OUT! THE SHMETTERLINK IS ABOUT TO GRAB US. Run for your lives." I thought this was pretty funny.

I happened to be incorporating this story to make a point one day at a meeting I was conducting and right in the front row, unbeknownst to me, was a very nice lady who just happens to come from Germany. Just as I got to the punchline, she smiles enthusiastically and interrupts my pontificating and proudly proclaims, in the sweetest and gentlest of voices:

"Yes, and in German it is the most beautiful word of them all, *Schmetterling!* I love that word. *Schmetterling*, it is beautiful, *nein*?"

OK, so now I had a problem and had to come up with a different ending. The good news is that it forced me to realize something. What sounded funny to me didn't sound funny to the native speaker at all. So based on this observation, it forced me to promulgate a theory. Whenever one tries to do something or say something that is unfamiliar, or foreign, most people will ridicule the idea or try to put it down in some way.

It further occurred to me that this *Schmetterling Factor,* as I now refer to it, manifested itself so much worse with the people who were closest to us. What happens when you tell your wife or a family member that you are thinking of starting a new business or going to hairdresser school or whatever? If it is something that was unexpected or not consistent with their understanding of who you are or what you do normally, they will immediately try to put you down, or make fun of the idea. Strangers may join in, but they tend to be less vociferous in their criticism since they don't know you as well. Remember the movie *Rudy.* This poor kid had his heart set on playing football for Notre Dame. Not only does his family make fun of him, but they try to convince him to knock it off and hope to get him to come to his senses. It sounded foreign to them. It sounded ridiculous. Almost to the last frame of the movie, his father tries to console him and talk him back into reality by explaining, "Rudy, we're Ridickers. We work in a steel mill. We can't play football for Notre Dame."

He was trying to impose *his* limitations on his son. This is exactly what happens with our friends and closest allies. They will impose their limitations on us.

Beware of the *Schmetterling Factor.* If you have an idea or if you want to say something that is inconsistent with what people are used to hearing from you, expect that you are going to get knocked down and mocked, and probably more so by the people who are closest to you. If it makes sense to you, who cares what others think or say? Act boldly, and choirs of angels will come to your aide and assistance.

Note to self: Act boldly, and be ready to spit on the *Schmetterling*.

62. A good night's sleep

Some of us baby boomers out there might remember the familiar sign-off at the end of each episode of *The Waltons*. We would see the house at night with a few of the windows lighted and each of the characters would utter a few words like "good night, Jim Bob," or good night, Jane" or "good night, John Boy or whomever," and each of the bedrooms would go dark and this peaceful Virginian family would go off to curl up peacefully in the arms of Morpheus. It was a much less complicated time to live in, and it is an easy wager to make that since the times were less hectic back then, we can assume that the Walton's probably got a better night sleep than most of us today. Granted, they had their big problems to deal with, too. They had to deal with puberty, unemployment, sickness, death, dating, all of those constant worries that we have. On those matters, they weren't able to beat the rap even way back then. What's different now, however, is the addition of such perversities in our society as the continual assault of social media, the ever increasing incidence of cyber bullying, sexual predators in our neighborhoods, the rampant use of illegal drugs, the devastation of traditional values in the home, the lack of trust in our government, and all of the rest of the things that we accept as a normal part of the regular social order in Western Civilization today. It might be the right time to simply say, "*Bring on the good old days.*"

How the hell could anybody sleep knowing that they have to wake up to all this new crap?

If that wasn't bad enough, even if you didn't worry about these things, you still might have trouble sleeping. You could still find yourself frequently turning and tossing. Why would that be? Is it possible that maybe you are sleeping on too soft a mattress? I never cease to be amazed at the number of different mattress commercials we will see during the regular span of even one *Law and Order* episode. It used to be that maybe there were two different kinds of mattresses, hard and soft. Today we have gone light years beyond that and can have extra firm, medium firm, and super firm, and, perhaps, there is a mattress that is just called *rock* or *rock hard*. This last category might simply be a piece of granite with a pillow attached.

There are the *tempurpedics*, the mattresses that divide into two different levels of firmness or that offer the husband one setting and the wife another all in the same bed. There are mattresses with coil springs, and those without, some that have special top layers of foam and others that do not. I have a tough time thinking about all the differences just in the mattress selection and I find myself staying up worrying that perhaps I made the wrong choice and my back is going to suffer when I get up in the morning. Maybe it won't give out tomorrow, or the next day, but I know for sure, based on what I just heard in the last commercial, that it is only a matter of time before I emerge from my nighttime slumber and look at myself and discover that I have become the *Hunchback of Notre Dame.*

"WHY, WHY," I ask myself over and over again.

I will be spending perhaps a third of my life on my back and spend 5 years searching and researching for the perfect mattress, only to have failed miserably. Now, I am *Quasimodo's* clone. I have no one to blame but myself and each night I will retire to my lair, jump into bed and find myself on a mattress that could have been harder than even the granite I should have gone with when I had the chance.

Making matters even worse, now I have to contend with the fact and barely have the strength to deal with the issue that somehow Hillary Clinton lost the election. *What Happened?* Hey, what a great name for a book. I suppose the answer is, she lost. Perhaps if I read her book, I can get a better handle on her defeat and move beyond such a simplistic answer. Since I am never going to sleep again, what's a fella to do? I will read that book and reread it again. By then if I'm not asleep, I guess there is no hope.

Then to further complicate things even more, I have to determine if I should get a full-sized mattress, or a Queen sized, or a King, or a Hollywood, or a California King sized version? Do they actually have Kings in California? Who knew? Do they sleep with crowns on their heads or are they optional?

Note to self: Go to bed early and get some sleep.

63. A Sharp Stick in the Eye

We have all heard the expression: "Well, it's better than getting a sharp stick in the eye." Haven't we? Sure, we have. The problem with that is most people have never had that experience. There might even be the possibility that the stick in the eye might feel good? I mean, how would you know unless you really tried to stick one in there? Well, ladies and gentlemen, boys and girls, and children of all ages, I'm here to tell you, I have had a sharp stick in my eye. As you might have suspected, it wasn't as amazingly pleasant as this lead-in might have suggested to you. Allow me to proceed and ramble on for you.

When I first bought the farm in East Aurora, NY, I decided that I would be more comfortable if people didn't hunt on my property. This is not because I am anti-hunting; it was because I just didn't want people shooting up my woods all over the place. I also didn't want to be out walking with my dog and have to duck from an errant bullet that might find its way toward my head. To ensure that my wishes were heard and my rights were protected, I proceeded to post the property with *No Trespassing* signs. These bright yellow signs added the further admonishment of *No Hunting, NO Fishing, No Parcheesi Playing, No Dancing Girls*, etc. It is important to note that to be enforceable, they had to be placed no more than 100 feet apart. Now, if I simply walked in a straight line up and back on my 30 plus acre parcel, that would be well over a mile. If you are doing your calculations, that's a lot of signs. It was considerably more than that because I had to walk up hills and over creeks and follow a more circuitous route since the lot was extremely irregular. It offered an extra challenge but either way it was as they say, so far, so good. I took the following items along with me, together with at least 100 signs: a hatchet to cut down small branches, so the signs could wrap smoothly around the girth of the trees, some small nails, and I even carried a large staple gun with me, just to make sure I got the job done right.

All went well until it was starting to get dark. I had one or two more signs left. I took out the hatchet and proceeded to chop off a small thumb sized branch that was more like a knot really. I lopped it off. Immediately, it shot into my eye like a bullet. Surprisingly, it didn't hurt, but as you can imagine, I was stunned. I subsequently learned that the eyeball has virtually no pain nerves in it. At this point, I couldn't see all that well out of that eye and I thought, *Hmm, this is not good.*

I considered my situation with uncanny clarity and analyzed what needed to happen next. It was quite amazing really. I thought I could simply pull out the branch and hopefully not take the eye with it. That was door number 1. My second option was that I could put down my tools and immediately head toward the house, which was about half a mile away and get myself to a hospital ASAP. I had the forethought to realize that this second option might not be as simple as it sounded. I would be required to walk back over exceptionally uneven terrain with rapidly diminishing light. Additionally, I would be traveling literally over hill and over dale and even over water and there was a good possibility that I might lose my footing along the way. There was the further possibility that I might be slipping into shock at some point as well. If I *did* fall, there was another possibility. The branch could get driven further into my eye and could go into my brain and I could die. I weighed the pros and cons for about 20 seconds. It was an easy choice. I pulled out the stump.

Two miracles occurred that afternoon. The first one was that I did not pull out the eyeball in it's entirely. The second miracle was that when I made it to the hospital, the doctor told me I missed blinding myself by slightly less than 1/32nd of an inch. Hey, what can I tell you, I'm a lucky guy? The funny thing about this entire episode was that by posting my property, the deer in the area must have all convened a deer summit conference because they quickly discovered that I had created a sanctuary for all of them. If you were named Bambi, this was the safest place to be in hunting season. Well, perhaps if you were a stripper named Bambi that wouldn't be true, but if you were a deer, this was the place to be. I literally attracted deer by the herds. They all wanted to hang out at my place.

I had to laugh when one of my neighbors, who was walking along the perimeters of my property, was nice enough to ask if I would allow him to hunt on my property. He asked, so I granted him permission. There was one house rule. He was only allowed to use a dagger. He thought I was jesting and presumed I was just being a wise guy. Truth be told, even with a dagger, anybody could have bagged a deer up in those hills. That's how many deer there were.

Note to self: It is better than getting a sharp...Wait, don't even say that!

64. The Perversion of Protest versus Respect for the Zipper

There is a very strange and innately sinister movement occurring in our country today. In the fall of 2017, there was an obsession with a number of NFL players who seem to resist standing for the National Anthem prior to the start of the game. What started out as a symbolic protest against racial inequality seems to have taken on a whole new life, and some say, it has completely divided our country. Some see those objectors as doing nothing more than joining in a peaceful form of protest. They conclude that if this right is infringed upon, it is definitely a serious threat to an inalienable right to free speech. Those who take exception see it as an utter affront to a symbol and an icon that most Americans consider to be sacred. It is something that should never be denigrated. For them, it is showing a blatant and despicable disrespect for *the Flag*. Who is right? Who is wrong? Permit me to give you a different perspective that might help bring both sides together.

I have trouble thinking that either side would overtly object to any American's infringement on the right to free speech. What the *flag respecters* are attempting to say (and their voice appears to be totally shut down by the media) is that disrespecting the flag is a perversion of protest. There is no way that disrespecting what many people hold near and dear to their hearts will ever win you over to an opposing view (which should be the actual subject of the protest, i.e. police brutality, racial inequality, etc.)

To compound the confusion, those that are "dising" the flag are appalled that the *respecters* cannot seem to grasp that they are not disrespecting the flag. How are they not thumbing their noses at veterans (together with all the first responders, the police and the fire fighters) and everyone else that fought, bled and died for that symbol. They proclaim quite emphatically that it is a stupid assumption and one that has nothing to do with the other. I have even heard people in the former camp say that this is tantamount to Rosa Parks complaining about bad transportation when she refused to give up her seat on the bus. This is a case of taking denial to a realm that is nuclear in the world of nonsense. None of that makes sense.

There are two facts and only two facts here. We have peaceful demonstrators who have chosen to exercise their rights to free speech, legally, albeit they have chosen what some would deem an incredibly inappropriate vehicle. Then on the other hand, we have people who find their disrespecting of an iconic symbol objectionable and insulting. Telling the second group that they shouldn't feel that their symbol is being insulted and that there is no disrespect intended is simply a major case of denial. It is as ridiculous as calling a black man the "n" word and explaining to him that you did not intend it to be offensive. You just wanted to get his attention. You were merely using it because it has historical significance. Come on folks, who are we kidding here?

Let's consider this dog-assed argument another way. For those of us who drive in major cities like Boston and NYC, we recognize a common scenario on the highway where on occasion we have to merge from one lane into the other. Engineers have studied the most efficient way to maintain traffic flow: it is called using the zipper. The person driving the car, who is attempting to merge, drives all the way to the end of his lane and then the driver in the next lane allows him to enter. All of the drivers then continue to alternate *one car at a time* in an orderly fashion. What seriously screws up the flow of traffic is when the line is backed up by drivers who think they need to merge immediately, even if the line extends over half a mile. Perhaps the justification for this is that it seems more polite than racing all the way to the front and skipping over the more orderly drivers who anticipated the merge and decided to get over earlier. It is further confounded when drivers in the second land refuse to let the other driver merge, as if to say, "I will show you; who do you think you are, trying to sneak in ahead of me at the last minute."

We see this all the time in smaller cities where traffic is never equal to the big cities and drivers consider themselves to be less aggressive. This is the way people feel. The problem is that they're reading the situation all wrong. The zipper is the most efficient way to move traffic. It has been mathematically proven. Do you want to get there faster or do you want to make political commentary and create road rage with your misguided driving habits?

The flag thing is no different. I respect your right to protest. Respect that you are denigrating something many hold sacred. If you simply want to assert that I am right and you are wrong, we are going to have nothing but pissed off drivers who can't get to where they want to in an orderly fashion. My hope is that, ultimately, in years to come, this episode of the kneeling football players will become a forgotten footnote in history, much like the *dimpled chads* fiasco in the Bush/Gore election at the start of this glorious century. In the meantime, could we figure a better way to address your grievances? There has to be a better way to create a constructive dialogue? And finally, could we all please stand together for the singing of the national anthem? There is no law requiring us to do this. I don't have to say: "(God) bless you," when you sneeze, either. It is just a great custom that most of us feel is appropriate.

Note to Self: **Let's all figure out why we are standing in the first place.**

65. Respect for Whale Watching

Several years ago, when I had the good luck to be living on Cape Cod, I sent my family out for an afternoon of whale watching. I knew that they would love it because being upfront and close to these magnificent animals is, as the millennials would say, "just amazing." Having grown up on the eastern seaboard, I have had many occasions to see whales bouncing around. It is always a fascinating event. It was not that I was jaded or bored by the experience; it was like living in WNY and taking Niagara Falls for granted. By the way, living in Buffalo, NY now, it is standard bill of fare to take any and all visitors from out of town to *See the Falls* pretty much as soon as they arrive. But let me tell you about a time when I had the ultimate whale watching adventure.

It was the summer of 2008 or 9 and the people I worked with asked me if I would like to go tuna fishing. Four of us set sail that morning on a beautiful sunny day and hopped aboard a 22 ft. Boston Whaler with twin 100 horse power Mercury Engines. I was all in; who wouldn't want to go tuna fishing off the coast of Hyannis. The small craft could fly along at around 36 knots, and once we got out of the harbor, we opened her up and cruised at a top speed for about an hour and 15 minutes. At this point, we were well into the shipping lanes where the tuna and the whales abounded. Along the way we slowed down long enough to catch some huge blue fish (about 36 inches or so). We threw them back since we were after tuna that day. Frankly, I was glad we would ultimately strike out in the tuna department, since I was absolutely spent, having used up all my muscle power reeling in the blues. What I hadn't expected was the added bonus of cruising along with the whales. At one point our little craft was in the middle of a herd of whales that numbered at least 30. They were all around us. We were close enough so that if I wanted to, I could have leaped from the small vessel and mounted one of them like Captain Ahab did In *Moby Dick*. We could smell the blow holes, we were so close. Incidentally, I would not necessarily describe myself as a *blowhole aficionado*, so I will just say for the record, it is not a particularity pleasant smell. At one point, I must have looked concerned, since one of my ship mates assured me, based on our immediate proximately to this multitude of behemoths, that we were safe. We weren't in any real danger of the whales capsizing us. There

155

was no need to worry. Actually, I hadn't considered that as a possibility until he brought it up, but it was all good, and I was as close to going on a *Nantucket sleigh ride* as I am ever going to get. It was an out of body experience. It made me think of the incredible fearlessness of our ancestors who faced death frequently in a feeble effort to make a living, hunting down these awesome creatures. It gives one a new respect for what a hard day's work consists of some times. As I told you earlier, we struck out in the tuna department, but we scored big in the making it real, whale watching department.

My wife at the time asked me if I was going to be disappointed the morning I sent her out with her brother to go whale watching. I knew whatever experience they were going to have aboard that big commercial ship that morning would pale by comparison to what I had experienced. I also knew they would have the time of their lives within 45 minutes of leaving the port at *Woods Hole.* When they returned that evening, they were truly moved. My (wife) was in tears describing the majesty she had witnessed. Barney, my brother-in-law, doubled down and he went on and on to tell me what a great time he had. I knew they would. How could they not?

Whale watching: it's a cool thing to do anytime.

Note to self: Go whale watching any time you can and be humbled by the majesty of nature.

66. Handy guys

It is no secret now that I am the least handy guy you will ever meet. The three most dreaded words in my vocabulary are always, as I have explained, *Some Assembly Required.* I live in awe of those guys who can whittle a suspension bridge out of a bar of soap. I worship at the altar of those real men who have shrines in their garages, with every imaginable tool for every conceivable job, all neatly arranged with each screwdriver mounted according to size on those ubiquitous pegboards. These are the men who embrace woodworking like a mother embraces a newborn babe. For them, WD-40 is like a hair tonic. Kerosene is an aftershave. And, ironically, they tend to clean up incredibly well in spite of their undying willingness to get their hands dirty. It is just in their DNA. They know how to fix stuff.

I bought a simple rolling kitchen cart several years ago and, of course, it had those three dreaded words right on the outside box. No matter; I was not dissuaded. I was figuring of course, *how hard could it be?* An hour or two into the process I acquiesced and silently admitted my personal failing and made the call to Mike, my handy guy. Now Mike is a great guy and, I should add, he is merely one of an army of *Handy guys* that I routinely employ. The saddest part of my reality is that I need to call in *the team* much more than I used to, since the few handy skills I might have had years ago have sadly waned to the point of being non-existent now. Basically, my handy skill set has been reduced to *painting*, and I am not all that good at that, either. I tend to just slop it on, so my Michelangelo skills are reserved for slathering rather than brushing with little hope of any precision. I am great on a porch or a basement.

But let's get back to that rolling cart that I tasked Mike to assemble. I had screws and shelves all over the floor, without the foggiest notion of which was an A or B screw and where any of them went. Yes, don't even dare ask me if I was following the instructions! Of course, I was. The instructions were not just difficult to follow, they required a magnifying glass to read, and as you can imagine, they were written in the standard Mandarin. As I gazed across the floor, I could see I had a surplus of screws to washers and somehow, and I know this doesn't seem possible: I also had what appeared to be too many shelves, as well.

Now that's where I started to get really crazy. I made the most valiant effort that I could, but I was so done.

My daughter stopped by to visit the doddering old man, and I have to tell you, she is incredibly smart. She's a lawyer for God's sake. I was convinced that surely with her logical mind, between the two of us, we should be able to put this stinking thing together. She even had the added advantage of being a woman and everyone knows that women are smarter than men. Regrettably, we quickly learned that she had inherited the spastic, non-handy, gene, from her father, and we were both at wits end exchanging the appropriate number of F-bombs in the process.

Mike arrived almost with a red cape blowing in the wind and a giant S on his chest. He came in and had the stupid thing assembled with one tool in little under 5 minutes. He didn't say much. He resisted the impulse to say what everyone in the room knew he was thinking. *What a pair of losers.* I was grateful for his lack of condescension and for his innate assembly skills and had him do several other odd jobs while he was there. If memory served me correctly, I think I asked him to build a garage or something. I didn't want him to think that he had only been summoned for this stupid shelf thing.

I am saddened to confess that I am less of a man for not possessing the handy gene. I take little solace in the fact that I can do other things and they can't. We simply can't do it all. Somehow, my ability to prepare a roasted chicken breast with a beurre blanc, white wine and tarragon sauce pales by comparison to being able to install a float in a toilet. Writing a book will always seem insignificant to rewiring a lamp. Speaking in front of a group of several hundred will always take a back seat to working a belt sander. How could a woman not be really turned on by a guy in a leather tool belt with 4 inches of erotic butt crack on display?

Note to self: Everybody sing: "It's so nice to have a man around the house." Sadly, for me, it is never hammer time.

67. Turning the clocks back

How many of you just said in your own head: "Spring ahead, Fall back?" Now if you said it in some else's head, that would really be confusing. Either way, I always say it when it is that time of the year. Now I have to admit the day we turn the clocks back is one of my favorite days of the year. On the east coast, we do it on a Saturday evening in early November and I always think: *I am just so appreciative that I get an extra hour of sleep.* It doesn't bother me that soon afterwards I will be driving home at 5: 30 p.m. and it will be darker than the inside of a cow's stomach. It doesn't unnerve me in the least that when I leave the house at 6: 30 in the morning, it will be pitch black out there and I will think to myself, *now I know what it must feel like to be a coal miner.* All I know is that on that one day when the clock goes back, I get to punch that big fluffy pillow for one more solid hour. What a gift. It is almost like that one extra hour is going to make up for all those 14-16-hour days I get to put in for the entirety of the rest of the year. Now, I know in my heart of hearts, that it doesn't make up for it. So please, please, I am begging you, don't ruin the illusion for me. I just love that extra hour. The one thing we cannot get more of is that thing called *time* and somehow each of us receives this magical blessing at this wonderfully special time of the year and everyone gets a single hour of it. Of course, we lose it in the spring, but there you go spoiling it for us all.

This year, I received an extra bonus. It was about 7 p.m. I remember thinking that this was the night the clocks go back, as I was walking down the street toward Conlon's, the corner bar in my neighborhood in South Buffalo. I was practically salivating over the bonus of that extra hour, but perhaps that was just because I was anticipating one of the best corned beef sandwiches imaginable. My girlfriend Marilynn and I had decided to just have a "do nothing" Saturday night where we were going to order out and proceed to continue a binge watch of the *Walking Dead* on Netflix. It was a very pleasant 45 degrees and although it was now dark, 5 or 6 of the local pre-adolescent boys were playing street hockey with the goal right under the street lamp, so for them it was like *playing under the lights*. They were having a blast and they very respectively seemed to *press the pause button* on their game to let me pass by. I was impressed at how polite they were for allowing some old guy to interrupt their game.

But then I thought: *how cool it is for these kids.* It was like when I was growing up in Brooklyn 50 years ago. They weren't playing video games or sitting around inside glued to a computer screen. They were right outside their respective houses playing where the neighborhood grownups could keep their eyes on them. Of course, back in the old days, we were required to get the hell home when the first light came on, but now, you were getting an extra hour tonight.

I arrived at Conlon's, and it was a typical Saturday night with all of the locals very properly watching the college football game and I placed my order for two sandwiches. They were to be accompanied by two cups of the absolutely best clam chowder on the planet. It is hard to imagine that you could get great clam chowder anywhere outside of Cape Cod, but this place has it.

I asked for a Guinness and a shot of Jameson while I waited. Rachel, the always gracious bartender, warned me that they had a large party in the back room and I might have a bit of a wait; I suggested that it wasn't the end of the world and I told her with a grin that I might have to have second round if the need arose. She winked and responded in like kind, "And perhaps maybe even a third." The good news is that by the time I finished the second, my sandwiches were ready and I didn't have to become a sot. I made a quick exit just as the political conversations started to become slurred and the content began to devolve into a different and more unintelligible dialect. It might have had something to do with the round or two of Fireball shots that were lining up at the bar at that point for all of the revelers. It was the ultimate in local color. As I strolled up the street toward the house on Kenefick, the kids were still skating their brains out and they seemed to be having an even better time of it. Perhaps they only seemed to be having a better time just by me. It's possible the two Guinness's I downed changed the way I saw things. Perhaps, it might have had something to do with the two shots of Jamison. Either way, that night, those were the best dang sandwiches I think I ever ate. Perhaps it was the company waiting for me in the cozy living room. Maybe it was the alcohol. I'd like to think it actually might have had something to do with the rolling back of those darned clocks. Who knows, but for me, it was a perfect night.

Note to self: I love rolling the clock back.

68. Voting Day

Unfortunately, many citizens would probably tell us that the system is rigged and there is little to no reason to vote and that's why they don't. That has to be one of the saddest commentaries on life in the United States and the worst part is, there is, at a minimum, a kernel of truth to the belief that contributes to this "what's the point" attitude. At the national level, especially in light of the recent DNC scandals in the Clinton election, it is difficult not to question the purpose of casting a ballot. If the candidate has already been anointed, why go through the global charade of trying to raise money and throw your support for another candidate, now that you know the "fix is in." All of these things considered, I still take it as a somewhat sacred charge to go and vote on every Election Day. I usually respond harshly to anyone that pig headedly glowers at me and tells me this is what's wrong with the country, or that is what is wrong, and we should do this or that, and then follows it up with, "and that's why I don't vote."

To them I say. "SHUT UP! You are part of the problem. If you don't vote, you have nothing to say on the matter and you should simply be silent."

God knows, it is not a perfect system. It's a national disgrace that we have such a low voter turnout. At this year's election in Erie County, NY, it was just around 11%. The low number was attributed to it being neither a mid-term nor a presidential election year. Even in those years, however, the figure never gets to the 50% level. At the local level, one's vote is so much more critical, and I have known candidates running in some small towns who have literally lost by 5-6 votes.

Our country is a big organization and the purpose of all organizations is to serve the people who created it. The problem is that as organizations grow in size (or age), the reason for their existence shifts more toward sustaining the organization rather than serving the membership. As such, there is simply a natural tendency to become corrupted. Still, I am not dissuaded and I vote. I enjoy the whole process.

Here's another reason I have this curious penchant for voting. I love walking down to the polling station at the Dudley Library on South Park Avenue in South Buffalo. It is little less than a 3-minute stroll from my house on Bloomfield Avenue. It gives me a chance to consider who or what I want to vote for and gives me a bit of sorely needed quiet time. I go in and I am usually one of the first voters, somewhere between 25 and 50 on the count. I review the ballot and am disappointed as I am reminded that the Mayoral Candidate is running unopposed. Now don't get me wrong; I think the incumbent at this time, Byron Brown, has done a pretty remarkable job and I would vote for him even though he is affiliated with the party that I'm not registered with, but he shouldn't be running unopposed.

Let me expand on this point. Here's is the problem with cities like Buffalo. They have had a Democratic Mayor for 65 years. Cleveland has the same story with a 68-year run of Democrats at this time. I need to make something clear here. This is not about Democrat versus Republican. Common sense would tell us that it simply cannot be a good thing to have the same party in power for that long. It is impossible for them to not corrupt themselves with that long a run. The President himself is specifically limited to only two terms to reduce the specter of tyranny. If ever there was something crying out to make the system better, it is the entire notion of term limits for every elected official (especially in Congress).

This year, I see that there are three bills that have to get voted on as well. There has been a conspicuous lack of any debate or press coverage on any of them and that seems wrong too. Too many voters are simply uninformed. The media wants to barrage us with sex scandals and *how we get to keep up with the Kardasians.* Perhaps I am being a little heavy handed by placing the blame here, but I fully fault them for dumbing down the citizenry and keeping most of us in the dark. Maybe the *Illuminati* is manipulating the entire game after all.

I cast my ballot and I return the same way I came, and I walk past Tim Russert Park. That's this little vest pocket park right next to the library, and it is the most delightful little urban oasis anywhere you can imagine. He would be proud that it bears his name. (I may have mentioned it once or twice before this, but I live in the famed Buffalo native son's parish). It's funny how you can walk past a place all the time and not notice little things. I see this small plaque on a large boulder. It quotes the legendary newsman and reads, "The greatest exercise you can do for your heart is to bend over and pick someone up."

Tim was a remarkable man and was the absolute best at what he did. As a newsman, he was truly a giant. I sure miss him and his incisive reporting. In the city of good neighbors, he was a great neighbor. I think he would have had a field day covering the situation in Washington today. We would all have been a lot better informed if he was around. But he is not, and it makes it harder to go in and pull that lever each time on Voting Day.

Perhaps his reminder also serves to tell us we need to help pick each other up and attempt to establish a better dialogue. We need to talk about the issues. If we do, then perhaps next year when it comes to ballot time, each of us can be more confident that we did the right thing.

Note to Self: Don't forget to vote. It is your duty.

69. Talk radio

I have a confession to make. Other than NPR, I don't listen to music on the radio. I don't listen to music when I'm driving in the car. When I am driving, I listen to *Talk Radio.* How this practice evolved is of no matter, but especially when I am driving, I want to be more engaged than simply sitting passively listening to head banging music. Perhaps this is not the kind of advice one would expect to hear in a safe driving course, but I do the best I can to stay alert and try not to get so emotionally worked up so that I become distracted. If I am listening to a call-in station, I very responsibly use my blue tooth, hands-free device and try to get connected to the host and offer my two cents.

Now for those readers who haven't deduced my political bent at this point, suffice it to say that I am a slightly to the right of middle moderate. I have a strong eversion to hate mongering and all extremes. I loathe any speaker who relies on demonizing anyone who holds an opposing position. Unfortunately, there is absolutely too much of this these days.

I enjoy listening to Sean Hannity. He is extremely intelligent and is less strident in his opinions than most and he is not afraid to relent, if the facts bear him modifying his point of view.

Rachel Maddow conversely is so far to the left that she swings beyond the airwaves into a world bordering on fantasy. It's shame, because this is an incredibly intelligent person whose message has been lost as she becomes increasingly more strident. Passion without common sense becomes ludicrous. Having said all that, I long for the days when newsmen (and woman) actually made an attempt to report the news (objectively). Today, it is all opinion and editorializing. It makes it really hard to get the facts, so I opt for intelligence over volume in most cases.

What's interesting about all this is how *Talk Radio* has grown with respect to audience size. In the early days, the only talk radio guys were the shock jocks like Imus and Howard Stern who I absolutely detested. Yet they found an audience and many imitators followed in their shoes. Why is that? Perhaps it comes down to the old axiom about "finding a need and filling it." What was the need? Listeners (and subsequent viewers) wanted to hear the things that they were already thinking while knowing that no one had the *chutzpah* to actually say it.

Eventually, more moderate views became expressed and they found an audience. Somewhere along the way, however, something weird happened. As the movement to make everything either politically correct or incorrect, there became a severe polarization of opinions. And clearly the volume went up on both sides.

That's the part of *Talk Radio* I don't like. Back in the ancient times when Walter Cronkite would come into your living room, one could expect to hear horrible facts coming in from all over the world. When the public listened to him, they would hear him present the "facts" as they were, frequently disturbing, and many times he would attempt to point out who the villain was or was not in the narrative. There was never any ranting. There was no place for constant name calling and there was never a conscious effort to pigeon hole people based on a particular behavior.

The Fourth Estate has left the room and now we have been cast into a deep and perilous ocean that is simply called *the media*. So how do we find our way back to the safe shores of journalism? It is such a far cry from what we have now. Even the *New York Times* has been co-opted and what we have today is not even remotely close to "all the news that is fit to print." I am not sure how we get back to something that is closer to the truth. For now, I am stuck with *Talk Radio.*

Note to self: Talk Radio-is it really the best thing out there?

70. Rescue dogs

I love dogs. How could you not? To my way of thinking, they are, in many ways, so much more superior to humans that to even render the comparison is ridiculous. They simply want to love and serve. That's it. Now you can train them to do all sorts of amazing things along the way, but they still just want to do those two things. Nowadays, in this extremely materialistic world, we see people spending thousands upon thousands of dollars for so-called designer dogs. These are dogs that are already so overbred, and now they find themselves being introduced to another breed to create a new and funky kind of mutant version of the two originals. I would be lying to you if I didn't tell you that sometimes they come up with some pretty cool looking dogs. They do. The problem is that it is such an unnecessary and wasteful use of our resources and it borders on the perversion of the *vomitoria* in ancient Rome. What makes matters worse is there are so many dogs in shelters, wonderful dogs, smart dogs, well trained dogs that are literally *dying* for a good home. I have been blessed by well over a half a dozen over the years.

Let me tell you about Eva. Eva was a Belgian Shepherd that I got as a puppy around four months old. At the time, I was living in downtown Brooklyn and a friend of mine who knew I was thinking of having a dog convinced me to check out this dog. I never had a "Shepherd" before, but she swore by the breed and had a beautiful one of her own.

The story behind the story in this case was somebody thought it would be great to give this guy a puppy for his birthday not knowing he was allergic to dog hair, and so, there sat this amazingly sweet animal tied to a chain link fence in a remote part of Queens. I saw her and made my claim on her in a heartbeat. At the time, I was living in a studio apartment on State Street, complete with a Murphy bed. The dog hadn't been trained yet, but that was of little concern since I have trained dogs before and I had the most important thing in my possession needed to train a dog, being able to spend a tremendous amount of time with her.

The lummox I got her from told me she was outside because she was too dumb and peed in the house all the time. With me, she was house broken in one day. It is pretty simple if you know that a dog won't soil or pee where it sleeps or eats. In my studio apartment, she was never out of my eyesight and whenever she looked like she needed *to go*, I would take her out, she would do her business and I would give her a treat immediately afterwards. It is basic operant conditioning.

Making matters more interesting was that when I needed to sleep and I had the Murphy bed down, the dog would sleep under me almost like it was in a cave. I think she liked it and it tapped into her wolf like heritage. You know, the cave, and the master by her side thing. Since I had the added luxury of being able to take her with me to the office every day, the same drill applied and she would rest comfortably under my desk. Other than the hair, she was the perfect dog. (Shepherds need to be brushed constantly.) When she was in her *first position* (under my desk), hardly anyone was ever aware that there was a dog in the room. She was positively brilliant and when people would comment on how smart she was I would tell them, "Well, yes, she is very good with *Microsoft Word* and *Excel* but she struggles with *PowerPoint*, but then again, how often does she really need to use *PowerPoint?*"

After Eva died (and that is a terrible story, with more on that later), my sister-in-law at the time told me I needed to get another dog. She told me about this huge Yellow Lab at the Orchard Park Shelter, so I checked him out. This dog turned out to be one of the best good will ambassadors for dogs anywhere. Some super shmuck-head thought it would be cool to dump him off on the highway. Fortunately, it was only about a mile from the shelter. He must have looked unimaginably pathetic. I was told later that the poor creature stayed at the base of the exit waiting for his owner to return for a full day before someone called the Dog Warden. Anyway, by the time I came along, he was on his last week and I was told that they were getting ready to give him the gas pipe. I saved the day for him, and when I brought him home, I was living on this gorgeous 30-acre horse farm on top of the hill in East Aurora, NY. As soon as the dog spied the half acre pond, it bolted from the back door of the car and made a mad dash and did a swan dive that would have made an Olympic diver jealous. All labs love water. He looked like the great white whale out there frolicking in the middle of the pond, so I appropriately named him Moby (Dog). We had him for about 10 years and he brought more enjoyment to my home than I can begin to tell you.

There have been others and I will discuss them all in greater detail. Today I have Louie. He is half dachshund and half poodle, and this guy really should have the words "soon to be a major motion picture" after his name. He deserves his full story for sure and he will get it.

I have been told that *rescues* make the best dogs because they know you saved them and they are eternally grateful. It might be true. I cannot say this with scientific certainty. One thing I do know; I cannot tell you how much joy each of them has brought to me and my family. I didn't pay thousands of dollars for any of them. The all ran the price from free to the nominal adoption fee. But make no mistake about it; each of them was worth a million bucks to me.

Note to self: Love my rescue dogs.

71. The Public Library

Historically, most of the greatest writers in the world have come from big cities. Why is that, you ask? Well, maybe you didn't, but now that I have called it to your attention, aren't you at least considering why that might be true? Prior to the internet, the greatest libraries in the world were all in big cities. Writers tend to do research when they write, and that is where you would find the most important resources for the work that was required, such as looking through books and important and famous documents. I love libraries: big ones, small local ones, private collections, presidential libraries, and most importantly, public libraries. There is a unique sensation and feel that one gets by the turning of actual pages. I love the smell of the books there. There is a distinct scent that can only be found in a library and it is unlike any other space in any other building. It is a combination of fragrances derived from the dust and the dust jacket covers, and the smell of the different papers that are used, and the various glues in the bindings. Part of the aroma also comes from those all too familiar oak tables and chairs occasionally wiped down by a spritz of *Pledge.* In the more hallowed Law Libraries, surely, we will pick up the additional aroma of the leather-bound captain's chairs.

Nowadays we can throw in the extra flavor of the photocopy machine, together with the fragrance of computers. And then lovingly, there is the smell of wet, woolen, hand knitted sweaters, worn by older readers who come to the library on a daily basis, if only to get out of the house and catch up on their reading for FREE. As I get older, I think that I too may find myself reading along with some of the other *gray hairs.*

The Public Library opens up a magical world for readers everywhere; what a wonderful place it truly is. You can go in and borrow a book for up to three weeks and return it for no charge and with no questions asked. You can take up occupancy and read the daily newspaper or any magazine you might want to read for free and retire into your own private world. You can sit with like-minded, thinking people who actually might have something interesting to say, but be warned: you have to *speak quietly.* THERE IS NO SHOUTING and cell phone conversations are not allowed. How civilized is that? Talk about a *safe free zone.*

Here's another thing that our best spent tax dollars do. Many times libraries are used as polling stations. They serve as meeting places for block clubs and civic groups. In general, they become go-to spots to provide an environment to share all sorts of necessary local information.

Here's the sad part about all of this. Today, because of smart phones and the internet, we are beginning to see libraries close all around the country. All of the wonderful benefits I described in the previous paragraphs will go by the wayside as the trend continues and a large slice of the quality of all of lives will be taken from us. Critics will tell me that this is all just a bit of nostalgic nonsense. They will compare my observations to those romantic days of horse and buggy transportation. They will tell me that it may have seemed like fun back in 1900 (you know that whole thing about the *Surrey with Fringe on the Top*) but that it was slow, smelly, hot in the summer, and frigid in the winter, and moreover, it was extremely dangerous and unreliable.

So, to be fair, I should say that I am not sure the analogy holds true when discussing the public library. Dangerous, I am not sure how? Unless it is that having a population that reads regularly might be better at free thinking. They will certainly be better informed and, indeed by definition, more well–read, and yes, that is something we should definitely be concerned about and absolutely consider to be dangerous. I dare say no one will argue with you as I make one last point: there is no question that our society has been ferociously dumbed down in the last two generations. Don't believe me; ask the next three people you meet at random, if they have been in a public library in the last 6 months. Yes, you should be concerned at the number. If anyone says yes, ask them if they were there to read or return a book?

Note to self: See you at the public library on Saturday.

72. The United States Post Office

What an amazing institution it is: the U.S. Post Office. It actually predates the signing of the Declaration of Independence and the Constitution. If it wasn't for the Boston riots in 1774, there would have been no creation of the Continental Congress and the beginnings of an independent government. And if there was no creation of the Continental Congress, then a year later in 1775, there would have been no need to appoint Benjamin Franklin as the first postmaster general, in charge of the newly created Post Office Department. So out of this very stormy beginning, we have this wonderful part of the Federal government taking care of delivering our letters and packages for what is getting close to 250 years. It is a relatively amazing success story especially considering when you typically look at how the federal government runs things. It is nearly impossible for them to get anything right. This time they did.

Now I know there will be the naysayers that scoff and mention any number of inefficiencies in the Post Office, and how right now, there are a number of competitors in the private sector that can beat the pants off them on any given day. For example, our friends with the big brown trucks at *UPS* seem to do a great job. I would never say they don't. *Federal Express*, or *FedEx* as they are more commonly known, is right up there with them, as well, with outstanding service and their own very highly competitive rates. I am good with all this. Surely, there are lots of others, too, that offer similarly effective delivery services. All of that is legitimate, but there are two things the Post Office simply kills them on every day.

First of all, let's look at the buildings. In virtually any municipalities, the Post Office building is probably one of the signature structures to be found. In some cities, they are neoclassical, architectural gems. One of the most spectacular of them of all was the one in Buffalo, NY which sadly closed recently and was taken over by Erie County Community College. It was and is a work of art. There are several in NYC, but the mother of them all is on Eight Avenue around the corner from Madison Square Garden. It is a true modern marvel and it is worth a trip to the Big Apple just to go this Post Office. Regrettably, in the smaller towns and suburbs, we see more modern structures but all of them have one thing in common; if the building itself isn't amazing, the location always is. They've got the convenience thing down pat. The private companies can certainly give the historical founder of the business a run for its money on service, but the buildings themselves seem to almost always be located in remote parts of town and have that definite warehouse look to them. It may not be a big deal for most but, I tend to be a traditionalist, and since we have brought up the service thing, let's talk about it, because that is the second big difference.

Here's something I am amazed at. How often do people lie about mailing something from the post office and tell people it got lost in the mail? My favorite lie that old line, *the check is in the mail.* Very few people can even say that line and keep a straight face, or have to back it up with some sort of an additional truth qualifier such as, "No, no, it is: really it is."

I don't know if I am a statistical anomaly or not, but I have never sent anything and had it lost in the mail. I cannot recall anyone telling me that that they sent me something (if I believed they actually did) and discovered later on that it was lost. I am over 60, so that is an incredible record of success. Don't get me wrong, there are lots of pieces of mail that go awry: The Post Office makes no effort to deny it but statistically it is insignificant and that is amazing. Let's add another feat of amazement to the pile.

Now I know that many people that will complain about how expensive it has gotten to mail a standard letter. So, let's consider this based on cost increases on everything across the board. That way, it is nothing that should shock anyone. But let's think about something. Currently, the rate for delivering a standard letter is 47 cents. I think it was 2 cents when I was a kid, but let's go with the current rate because who cares what it was way back when. For 47 cents, I can put an extremely important communication on a couple of pieces of paper and stick it in an envelope, put a stamp on the outside, and pretty much in one day, somebody will *hand deliver* it across town for me. In 2-3 days, they will *hand deliver* it to the opposite coast 3000 miles away. Can you get anyone else to do that for 47 cents? That is truly the 8th Wonder of the World. None of the private companies can do anything remotely close to match that.

Note to self: It is tough to beat the United States Post Office.

73. Making a nation great and keeping it that way

It is an odd thing these days that a candidate for president can run for office and have the slogan *Let's Make America Great Again,* and literally millions of people seem to be up in arms over it. Much of the exception that people take has to do with the man and not the slogan, but many others have hostility at the implication that he shouldn't have said it at all. The criticisms run the gamut from:

- What makes you think it is not great already, to
- When was it really great, and finally
- It was never really great in the first place.

On this last point, *I* get to take some exception. If it was never great, then why is it that millions and millions of people have made the tireless crossing to get here in this century? They did so in the last century and the one before that and many of them died along the way. Suffice it to say, if we can narrow our focus, it is reasonably certain that most of the immigrants who came to our shores (my ancestors and perhaps yours) came here for two solid reasons, freedom and opportunity. Both of these can be fused into what has become known as *the American Dream.* I am going to stick my neck out here a little further and declare that these two elements still exist and this is one of the reasons we have a heated debate and an immigration issue that seems to increase when we have positive spikes in the economy (like we do right now.)

Let's shift gears a bit and get to the second part of our proposition: how does one keep it great? Here's the conundrum: *Greatness* is a constant. Once you achieve greatness, that's it. *Mohammed Ali* was great. After he stopped fighting, he was still great. Now one might argue that he was a great fighter, *in his day,* but that is a meaningless qualifier. He was great: End of story. If America was ever great, and I believe it pretty much was from the signing of the Declaration of Independence to today, it is great; case closed. The second part of the question is not how do we keep it great (since it already is), but how do we sustain the parts of our culture that we have taken for granted, when we consider our greatness. The answer to that is simple and can be said in one word, involvement.

Great families crank out great kids. Those kids go on to become established as great citizens later in life, and they have parents who are *involved* in the upbringing of the children. This is by no means to praise the virtues of the overly protective helicopter parent. Come on, we know what it looks like when the parents are involved. Conversely, we see a multitude of problems arising in many inner-city families. There is clearly less involvement when we consider that there is a lack of a father figure in nearly 74% of the households. We look at that and scratch our heads and ask why? Why do we have all these problems: crime, truancy, teenage pregnancy, higher rates of unemployment, a higher than usual high school dropout rate, etc.? Is there a big mystery here? Are we this stupid, that we have to ask the question?

We see memberships in Civic Associations like the Lions Club, Kiwanis church groups, and the Masons drying up like we are stuck in the middle of the Sahara and we ask why is it that people are so out of touch with what's going on in their towns? We see a voter turnout of 11% and wonder why the wrong people seem to be consistently getting elected and we see church attendance down virtually everywhere. Is it any wonder why things have changed, and America looks less like it used to look? The greater portion of the population is plugged into reality TV, and their children are busy playing video games and using *fidget spinners* to occupy their time, instead of doing homework, or household chores, or simply getting a job.

Fewer and fewer people are involved in the important aspects of what goes to make a life for a family and a community, and we wonder why our country seems to be going in the wrong direction and not quite as great as it used to be. If we want to have the country that we want to have, then it will be limited to each one of our personal commitments to getting involved in what we want in a better life. If we all choose to sit on the sidelines, and let someone else vote, someone else do the research, someone else volunteer, and someone else make the decision, you can rest assured that when we talk about greatness, it will be in the past tense and have little to do with the way life is today.

Note to self: Do something, get involved.

74. Let me buy you a drink

There is a strange ritual that exists in bars all over the world and, depending on your location; the ritual can vary a bit. It is the ritual of buying a drink for someone else. Let's start out with your standard shot and a beer bar joint. You boldly declare, "Buy my friend here a drink."

At this point, the bartender either says nothing, and just brings another beer or whatever the person was originally drinking or he gently tells the lucky guest that you are proffering a free libation, compliments of you. If there are no drinks in front of him, there is the option of accepting or declining. Accepting it is what is expected. I recently declined one simply because I had been there for a while and I knew that it was time to go and one more would have potentially put me over my limit. These days no one wants a DWI and, unfortunately, it is really too easy to get one right now. In this scenario we were safe; there was no harm and no foul. When I run into this fellow again, presuming his memory is still intact, it is conceivable he will offer to buy me a drink, mentioning that he owed me one from last time. Therein lays the paradox. He offered to buy me a drink that night because I bought him a drink earlier in the evening. If I didn't buy him a drink, he would be under no implied obligation to reciprocate. There is no net loss or gain on this transaction. The question is why I bothered in the first place, since the presumption that he would buy me a return drink always existed.

Version two of this ritual can be dangerous and can kick the stakes up a lot higher. I offer to buy you a drink and, much like Moe Green in *the Godfather,* you are deeply offended and declare, usually in a loud voice for everyone in a 30-block radius to hear,

"YOU BUY ME, I DON'T THINK SO; NO, I BUY YOU."

There is a small possibility of the two coming to blows, but usually and hopefully, we go back and forth a few times and it becomes settled and one guy winds up paying. Sometimes a skilled bartender will intercede and try to embarrass both of the would-be combatants and ask everyone to make up their minds so he or she can move on to the rest of the people at the bar whose tongues are hanging out by this time. Another option is to simply leave the bill lying there between the two to eventually figure it out for themselves. It can get sticky. The worst part is both parties might end up feeling slighted and then one of them feels the extra obligation of buying one in return. Yikes! Maybe everyone should buy their own stinkin' drink and we can avoid all of this "Hail hardy, good fellow, well met" nonsense.

There is an extra funny episode on *Seinfeld* where Jerry tries to buy dinner for his parents. It doesn't go well. His father is beyond upset. He is insulted and won't hear of it. He insists on paying. Of course, he doesn't have enough money to pay and he has to get the owner of the restaurant involved so he can assure him that he can go back to his hotel and get more money and, as is expected, a general mayhem ensues. Of course, Jerry ends up paying. Now his father has to attempt to unknowingly slip the cash into Jerry's wallet later on in the show. At the end, Jerry is walking down the street and suddenly realizes how much he hates that old wallet he is carrying and throws it away (with the cash his father put in it.) There are at least 3 more wrinkles to the plot line, but as you can see, this buying you and you buying me thing is out of control.

Something I find equally amusing is that if the guy already has a drink, some bars will literally make up another drink (or grab another bottle of beer) and back up the drink. The night before my Army induction physical, the beers were 6 deep at the bar. As you might imagine, it wasn't pretty the next day. Some bars will simply put a shot glass upside down in front of the drink. Really cheap joints, or bars that cater to a younger crowd, put little plastic cups up that are supposed to hold a quantity equal to a shot glass, but they look more like thimbles. Sometimes the lucky drinker walks away and doesn't actually ask for the drink. In some instances, there might be several shot glasses stacked up in a holding pattern. This gives the bar a super profit margin. They will charge for the drink but they don't have to actually make it. Giving someone an extra shot glass might get someone a free drink, but it has none of the panache and lacks all of the grandstanding of declaring to the world:

"Buy my friend a drink here."

Where we really go down a scary path is when a man offers to buy a drink for a woman. Notice, I didn't say lady. That would have been too politically charged these days, and I, right now, only want to address this stupid drink issue.

Note to self: Buy your own stinkin' drink.

75. Respect for Acting

Like most people, when I was a younger, I had little or no respect for acting. What I mean by this is that I had no respect for acting as a craft, as a performing art. Typically, any art form demands years of training and a discipline to apply various techniques in an effort to give the artist a chance to display the uniqueness of his or her talent. Most people think it is, in a word: easy. All you kind of have to do is *say your lines and not bump into the furniture.* I remember attending a scene study class at the HB Studios in the West Village in Manhattan back in the mid-1970s. My good friend Andy, who was secretly aspiring to be an actor, invited me to see him do *some work* in a scene study workshop and I said sure. He did his scene and afterwards, when we were walking home, he asked me what I thought. I was always a bit of a ball buster so I asked him, "So you have to go to class for that stuff?"

I knew I was being a punk then, and later on I learned how much of a punk, when I decided to start studying the craft myself because I found the entire thing so intriguing. I never thanked Andy for that night, but it was a pivotal moment in my life. I learned that one of the founders of that studio, who I eventually got to study with, Uta Hagen, wrote a book that is a classic in the world of acting. It is called *Respect for Acting* and rarely will you find an actor who isn't serious about his or her work, who hasn't read it. Most actors blanch, or chuckle, when people ask them, "So how do you remember all of those lines," because, as important as it is to know your lines, that is only the beginning of the process. The great actor Peter O'Toole made an important distinction on this point and emphasized the difference between knowing one's lines and studying them. Anyone can learn to recite lines much like a parrot. Knowing one's lines allows the artist to embrace the meaning of what is said so the when he or she speaks, it is as though they are being uttered for the first time. It seems like the words just came into their minds and they are giving them voice for the first time.

Then there is the skill of understanding the characters intention and going through what they are feeling. What makes for a wonderful night in the theater is when we no longer see the performers and they become the person they are supposed to be on stage. This can be fascinating for the audience and many times dangerous for the actor. When we see actors cry on stage, many times it is because the actor has to tap into some deep sense memory and summon up very unpleasant feelings from their own past. The emotions you are seeing in these instances are real. It is not unusual for them to experience real pain, and because of this, many actors encounter some issues that interfere with their lives off stage. Some have succumbed to nervous breakdowns (i.e. Frederick March, in *Dr. Jekyll and Mr. Hyde*). Many people speculate that Heath Ledger met his early demise because of his dedication to the craft and his obsession in embracing the role of the Joker in the *Batman* movie. Less catastrophic but certainly at a minimum, actors can also experience a personal intrusion into their normal lives. The tabloids often reveal that it is not uncommon for actors to become difficult to live with before, during and after a performance. This is especially true when a role demands a high emotional investment. There is a helluva lot more to the craft than simply saying the lines and the most embarrassing part of this rampant disrespect is our culture's inability to separate the craft from one's *celebrity*.

There is a tremendous wealth of talent that takes to the stage all across our country, but by and large, unless you are a household name in a TV sitcom, or a Soap Opera, you will be much like Rodney Dangerfield and "Get NO Respect." This totally negates the value of the craft and short changes both the artist and our culture.

I had the good fortune to catch a production of Arthur Miller's *The Crucible* at the *Kavinokey Theater* in downtown Buffalo recently. Many people might know the play because they were forced to read it in high school. It made for a complicated and boring read way back then. The actors in this particular production, many of whom I have had the pleasure of working with, breathed so much life into those characters that the point of Miller's play became so obvious and it was difficult, if not impossible, not to be tremendously moved by the individual performances. What seemed to be a play about the witch trials in the late 1600s clearly was a social comment about the issues summoned up during the McCarthy years. The actors forced us to see how clearly the hysteria and fear of *being accused* back then could easily serve as a tableau for today. They also made us feel badly for their character's individual plights as they lived on stage *in the moment*, as they moved us to feel the anxiety and pain of being falsely accused and having to go to the gallows and leave their loved ones behind. Good theater with great acting is so much more than a simple treat to behold. It is a pearl of great price. It is a Renoir painting. It is precious to the core of our culture. Regrettably, it gets little to no respect in our society.

"Didn't I see you in a commercial somewhere?"

Note to self: Always show respect for great acting.

76. Olive Oil

Few things are more delectable or make food taste better than a touch of rich Olive Oil. Now this is where it gets complicated: what kind of Olive Oil should you use (and when should you use it.) Like most people, I have been taught by the media to use only rich *Extra Virgin* Olive Oil. The famous foodie Rachel Ray uses so much of it that she has been forced to abbreviate and now simply calls it E.V.O.O. She practically slathers herself in the stuff on every show and adds it to everything she is cooking. I jokingly tell people I use it on everything too and even put it on my *Cheerios* in the morning. (I don't actually.) But it is pretty amazing stuff, and, evidently, it is one of the best things you can eat to ensure a healthy lifestyle.

I have always been amused by the category *extra virgin* since, to my way of thinking you either are *a virgin* or you are not. I mean, come on, what's that all about anyway? Either way, *Extra Virgin* olive oil to those people who live on a diet of *fast food only*, is that magical substance mostly used as a salad dressing, but it has so many other uses.

If you want to make great salad dressing, one of the best is a simple splash of the special stuff added to a whisper of rich Balsamic vinegar. Hit it with a dash of salt and pepper and it makes for a salad dressing so perfect that you will be accused of being a gourmet. Another thing about this special elixir is that it is uncompromised by heat, and thus, it is perfect for sautéing. There is a time and place for cooking with butter, but many times olive oil is the way to go for both taste and personal longevity. Now here is where the fun begins.

There is a tremendous range of tastes and textures when it comes to selecting a good olive oil. Much like picking a good red wine, the differences are stark and vary by region, country of origin, freshness, and time of harvest. Add to this, the different actual olive varieties, each with a particular flavor, texture, and shelf life and you really have a study.

Being half Italian I always presumed that most of the olive oil in the world came from Italy. How shocked was I to discover on my first trip to Spain that *they,* in fact, were the leaders in olive oil production. It was fairly self-evident, since it seemed that everywhere you went on the Iberian Peninsula there was an olive grove. There was no escaping them, and they were spectacular in their ancient beauty. (Olives have been growing there for literally thousands of years.) For the record, Spain produces nearly 6 times the olive oil that Italy does, which rests comfortably in the number 2 slot in world production. Few things are more delectable than to have some bread dipped in some fresh extra virgin olive oil accompanied by a piece of manchego (cheese) and a glass of Temprenillo. I am in heaven.

As would be expected, olive oil is produced in most of the countries surrounding the Mediterranean; and, I had the great fortune to recently sample a wonderful bottle of the golden liquid from Tunisia, which really gave me a sense of the range of flavor that existed. These days, it is not unusual to see olive oil shops cropping up in malls and small towns and, frequently, they offer *tastings* similar to craft beer emporiums and wineries. It's fun thing to do on a rainy afternoon. Now let's enter the twilight zone.

What is the world coming to when we see massive *counterfeiting* of olive oil? It has been proven that there are some companies that have been caught mixing imported olive oil with alternate oils (such as soy). They then falsely market the blend as authentic olive oil and add to the label things like, "Made in Italy," for example. Unscrupulous dealers seem to be lining up to dupe many an unwary consumer. This rampant marketing of fraudulent olive oil has forced the European Commission to take action by offering a 5 million Euro reward to catch profiteers and to stimulate better methods of authentication. I cannot tell you how disappointed I was to discover this and to learn that so many brands we see sold in this country were suspect. "Mother of Mercy," is there nothing sacred?

Today we see another assault on this sacred oil. There are commercials now extolling the virtues of corn oil; yes, corn oil. You see advertisers quoting serious facts proving that it is superior in every way to olive oil. This makes as much sense as when the Pork Producers got together to convince people that it was the *Other White Meat* and it was extremely low in fat. IT COMES FROM A PIG, for God's sake. No one calls anyone a skinny little pig, do they? It is always, "You big *fat* pig!"

On this point, there is nothing more to be said other than, "…so much for truth in advertising."

Here's something else to consider. If it is that good for you, can you consume too much olive oil? The people who live in Crete incorporate nearly a cup of olive oil every day as a natural part of their diet, and they live longer than just about everyone. I guess the answer is, no. One caveat on this is worth mentioning. I remember reading in Fromer's guide to Spain, that one should be careful if you weren't used to a lot of olive oil in your diet. They use it prolifically there. Fromer's warning said that it could *catch up* to you. When I made my first trip to the Iberian Peninsula, I definitely wasn't used to it, and it did, catch up to me, if you know what I mean.

Note to self: Extra Virgin Olive Oil; get the real stuff.

77. Moby Dog

As I mentioned in a previous story, I was going to give you a more complete version of the Moby Dog story. It really starts with the very sad tale of the demise of his predecessor, my beautiful Belgian Shepherd, Eva. My former wife thought it was a bad joke that I named her Eva (even though I had the dog before I met her.) I told her it was short for Eva Braun, you know as in another German *bitch,* so I thought it was appropriate, but she still thought it was in bad taste. Regardless, Eva was a wonderful dog and another rescue. When we left NYC and moved up to the farm in East Aurora, this incredible docile dog would have a habit of sleeping lazily in the driveway. Make no mistake here, she may have seemed like an innocent sleeping beauty, but she was up in a nanosecond and ready to protect at all costs. She was brilliant in her ability to sense any *real* threats, and consequently, she was in neutral gear 99% of the time. There was no wasted energy.

One fine day, the neighbor across the street, who was having a considerable amount of work done on his house, walked up my driveway and knocked on the side door. I noticed a large truck that had backed into my driveway a few minutes before that, in an effort to make a three-point turn. But I didn't think anything of it. I greeted Mark, my neighbor, who was a great guy with a nice family with 3 adorable little children. He was stuttering and stammering and visibly upset. Through all of his yammering, he confessed that his workman had run over my dog that was asleep in my driveway.

I ran out to the dog and she seemed fine initially, and then I could see the blood oozing from her mouth. I rushed her to the emergency room at the vets, but it was too late. I was crushed. I had her from a puppy and she was the best and smartest dog I ever had.

I wasn't angry with poor Mark. I felt doubly sorry for him. It wasn't his fault. It was truly an accident. If the shoe had been on the other foot, I would have had to have been institutionalized; I would have been totally devastated.

My sister- in-law, Margie, knew how upset I was and she told me about this great yellow lab that was approaching his last days at the pound. At the time, my daughter Alice was a toddler and I had some concern about bringing another large dog into the house as a replacement. You don't always know what you are going to get with an adoption. I went down to the shelter and this giant of a yellow lab was pacing back in forth and barking and literally jumping out of its skin. I looked at what I would ultimately come to realize was a true gentle giant and thought *this dog is crazed.* I declined nicely, explaining that I could not take the chance with a small child at home. The next day, I get a call from the lady at the shelter and she begs me to come back and give the dog a second chance. She suggested I take him out of the cage, and walk him around for a bit. She told me, "He will settle right down. He was just nervous because he had been in the cage for so long and I think he realizes this is his next to his last day."

I stood outside the cage, and nervously grabbed a *two by four* that had been laying around, just in case. I would not have hurt the creature, but I wanted to make sure I could defend myself, if the need arose. The door swung open and the dog leaped at me like the *Hound of the Baskervilles.* Then, he ran past me two or three times in the yard to blow off some steam. Finally, he rolled over exposing his throat in the ultimate submissive position, and it was almost as if he was trying to say in a perfect British accent, "I am so sorry dear boy; I hope I didn't startle you. It was just that I found that terrible cage ever so confining. It would be just delightful if I could come home with you and be your number one dog. Really, it would be just lovely, old chap."

I took him home and I seriously thought he was going to start singing songs on the way. This was one happy dog. As soon as I parked the car, he leaped from the back seat and made a bee line to the half-acre pond and launched himself like a Saturn rocket. He swam a few laps back and forth. At one point, I think he was actually doing the backstroke He looked like Herman Melville's "great white whale" and truly seemed to be in bliss consciousness. I decided to call him *the Moby Dog.* Moby was the best, most lovable dog, you ever met. When Alice got a little older, he would take her for rides around the pond. The kids who lived nearby would all come over and sit at the edge of the pond. They loved to watch him dive off the end of the dock. He brought so much delight to all of us, and we never would have got to experience having him if it wasn't for the tragic loss of my Eva.

I could bore you with so many other wonderful stories about this perfect example of God's better handiwork, but I won't. He loved to go on little road trips with me; to the farmers market or into town. This will sound funny to some of you but he always seemed so proud to be with me. It was like he was saying, "Yeah, this is my owner. He's pretty cool, isn't he?"

It so thoroughly disgusts me to hear that some imbecile just threw him out of his truck and left him on a highway to fend for himself. I am ever so grateful for having him.

Note to self: It is just another great example of the specialness of rescue dogs.

78. The Blue Water Tower

I hate traffic. I will do almost anything I can do to avoid it. Having traveled about the country extensively, I have come to recognize specific traffic patterns; peak times to particularly avoid certain highways and what I need to do to get around situations that are sure to make most people seriously mental. Some places are worse than others. Having grown up in NYC, one would think that it is the worst place to be, but as bad as it is there, with time spent in traffic averaging 73 hours; it is only in the fourth-place position. No, the accolade of *numero uno* in the traffic department goes to the *city of the angels*, Los Angeles, Ca. (with an average of 81 hours a year.) So, we can keep this in perspective: if you need to drive in these places, expect to spend well over 3 days of the year sitting in the car listening to talk radio and sucking down exhaust fumes. Hey, do we know how to have good time yet or what? I cannot tell you how shocked I was to learn how bad it was in the serenity filled city of Seattle. It has an average of 66 hours. Making matters worse, it is probably raining there for about 60 of them and most people there are *Sleepless* anyway.

Fortunately, for me, I now reside in the Queen City (Buffalo, NY) and there is little or no traffic there. They boast an average commuting time of just 19 minutes. Because of this, there is a popular expression, which states: "You are always 20 minutes to anywhere you want to go." Oddly enough, it is mostly true, too.

Here's another feature of living in this driver's paradise. Because of Buffalo's proximately to Lake Erie and the nearby foothills of the Appalachian Mountains, a series of microclimates are created naturally. This gives rise to a sub-corollary of the previous expression.

"If you don't like the weather, wait 20 minutes or, drive 20 miles."

This is also remarkably true for the most part. Something I also find somewhat comical is when I hear some of the people in the neighboring suburbs like East Aurora (which has a population of less than 10,000) or Clarence (about 20,000), complaining about "all the traffic." It is nothing when one compares it even to normal times on the L.A. freeway, but I guess it is all relevant.

This brings up the situation that exists with the infamous *Blue Water Tower* that everyone talks about all the time. This *landmark* which is located just east of the city and can be found right alongside the road that merges the I-290 with the I-90. It provides a perfect bottle neck. At a minimum, it will delay the regular flow of traffic twice a day. So quite obviously, I do everything I can do avoid traveling near the *Blue Water Tower* during those times of the day. You know you are going to get stuck there, so why would you go that way? There are numerous alternate routes. Pick one. Every city has these well-known bottle necks. I chuckled when George Costanza was mentioning one of these infamous slow down points on a particularly funny episode on *Seinfeld*.

"Nobody gets to beat the Van Wyck (expressway.)"

Being a native from the Big Apple, I knew that was absolutely true. I have been stuck on that damned Van Wyck too many times to mention. I am not sure if this statement had the same impact with all of the viewers in Peoria, IL, or to the drivers in Buffalo, but every town and city has their own version of the *Blue Water Tower*. Avoid it, dummy.

The *Blue Water Tower* can provide a good analogy for life. If you have trouble with alcohol, wouldn't it make sense to avoid some of the bars you used to frequent. Maybe you are a degenerate gambler and you have been fortunate enough to come to terms with your addiction. Perhaps you even have embraced a good 12 step program to help you deal with your problem. Wouldn't it make sense for you to stay out of that casino? You know which casino I am talking about, the one that has that great restaurant in it, which makes those super terrific fabulous sandwiches that you just love. You need to tell yourself: *I am not going there. It cannot happen.*

Where (or what) is your *Blue Water Tower*? If you are not sure, it is possible, even if only slightly, that you do not have one. I somehow suspect that you aren't as observant as you think you are, or you just have a higher threshold for pain than the rest of us. Perhaps you think there is no alternative, and you just have to get stuck there. Maybe the *Blue Water Tower* is your ultimate reality? I happen to think that there is always an alternative and I don't know about you, but I am going to find it. I am not going to get stuck because of the illusion of bad karma.

Note to self: I always have an alternate route around the *Blue Water Tower*.

79. Can we talk?

Some of us may have some fond memories of the comedienne, Joan Rivers. Others might still be mad or disappointed in her for blatantly betraying her friend and colleague Johnny Carson. Most people might have forgotten that little incident, but Johnny never did. He never forgave her for secretly going behind his back and signing a contract through which she would host another nighttime show directly competing with his own. I would concede that it was a douchebag move on her part, but others might say: *that's show biz.*

Either way, everyone would agree that she was a pretty funny lady. She was famous for a number of other things that included an inordinate amount of plastic surgery and irreverent comments. Toward the end of her life, the former would literally kill her, and while she was waiting to go under the knife for that last time, everyone would have had to have described her as looking like a mannequin. In the meantime, few seemed to escape her caustic barbs. It was amazing how she was able to get away with it. She had a familiar conversational bridge that always started out with her looking into the camera and asking the audience very seriously, "Can we talk?"

This was frequently followed up with a second version of the same question when she would again ask, "Can WE talk?"

It became her signature line, much like Rodney Dangerfield's "I get no respect."

Her asking this one rhetorical question would almost always prompt a laugh all on its own. Then she would immediately go into one of her routines and tear down this person or that person in her very own uniquely sarcastic way. It was never very nice but it was always very funny. Often times when I am trying to make a point, I have quoted her and said:

"OK, as Joan Rivers would say, can we talk?"

I like to punch it up a little bit and say the word *talk* in an exaggerated New York City accent so that I get the right emphasis. It also gets me a hardy chuckle or a gentle laugh, and this further tees-up whatever message or point I am trying to get across. At this point, I have seemingly blanketed my listener into a formidable circle of trust, and I can say pretty much anything I want and it will be accepted. It is a powerful technique. When I ask this question, I am no longer a salesperson, or a teacher, or a presenter, or a speaker. I am a close confident and a friend who wants to share something on the q.t.

"As Joan Rivers would say, can WE Taawlk?"

Try it out for yourself. It is magical, the way it breaks down even the most cement like resistance. Joan Rivers gave some us more than just a few good laughs.

Note to self: "Can we talk?"

80. Binge Watching

Did you know that the format of the *Novel* actually introduced a brand-new form of literature? Many may not realize this, but it wasn't even that long ago. In fact, the word itself translates from the French; it means "new." For those trivia fans out there, the first novel was *Robinson Crusoe*, by Daniel Defoe in 1719. Prior to that, if one were to put pen to paper, it might be in the form of a poem, or a play, perhaps a biography, or maybe even as an historical document. The point is, the simple act of storytelling has had an evolution, just like everything else.

Now let's fast forward into the earliest part of the 20th century. At this point, we see that many of the early novels have now become what we refer to today as classics. We see these stories being portrayed on the silver screen initially as silent movies and then as *talkies*.

Now let's continue. About 40 years after the first movies appear, we have the advent of radio, and then following quickly afterward we witness the ever-present TV. It was probably around this point that reading really took a hit and people began to become less literate. Again, there is a funny and somewhat tragic episode on *Seinfeld*. This time, George joins a book club. Of course, George forgot something important. He would actually have to read books if he was to be an active participant in this club. The first assignment was to read *Breakfast at Tiffany's.* As it turns out these days, many people would agree with George, and ask the question, why read the book, when you can just see the movie. So always looking to cut a corner or two, he goes to the local video store to rent the movie and of course it is out of stock. Now he is forced to sleuth out who was the last person to take the movie out, so he can access it. He then pays them a visit. This way he can watch the movie, making himself perfectly at home at their place. As is expected, Mayhem ensues, in a perfect "Seinfeld-like" fashion.

Today, we see video stores are gone and viewing habits have changed again with the emergence of *Netflix*, and *Hulu,* and *Amazon,* and several other on-line providers. We have instant access to movies 24 hours a day.

Many providers have even gotten into the act and started producing movies themselves. They are creating a myriad of mini and full-length series that totally bypass the regular movie house, so you can get your viewing fix without ever having to leave your home. This has created an interesting term for a new habit: *binge watching*. Now, anyone can kill an entire afternoon or evening, watching multiple episodes in the series.

The owners of these mega companies are pretty smart. They produce each series and release them as weekly episodes. They create a fan base that goes wild talking about what happened, and what they think will happen the following week, and then, when the year is up the series can be revisited in its entirety. Masterpiece stories like *The Tudors* and *The West Wing* and the *Walking Dead* live on in rerun heaven and one can *binge watch* any one of them and get caught up, so as not to be out of the cultural loop.

I can remember being shamed into watching *Breaking Bad.* Every actor I knew could not believe I hadn't seen it. How could I have not seen Brian Cranston in this tour de force role? I watched the first episode and afterwards I was more hooked on the series than some of the characters in it who were on methamphetamine. I *binged* the entire 5 season series in less than 3 weeks. There were times when I would be up until 2 a.m. I simply could not get enough of it.

Netflix has changed the way we look at movies and TV in general. We have had binge eaters before, and binge drinkers, and binge shoppers. Human beings because of their very nature seem to be prone to bingeing if they like something. Why would we think that their viewing habits and the way we get information would be any different? You are probably binging on *Potato Chips* right now. At least, I hope you are, the book that is.

Note to self: Bet you didn't know this was going to be a BYOB: Bring Your Own Binge.

81. Thanksgiving

If ever there was a holiday that has its own unique American stamp on it, Thanksgiving would have to be it. Let's start with the turkey. It is the classic American bird. Benjamin Franklyn admired it so much that he wanted to make it the National bird over the eagle. Oddly enough, I was at a dinner party recently and a gentleman there tried to convince me that the number one producer of turkeys in the world is the Ukraine. I couldn't believe it. I said to myself, *what the hell is that all about?* Thank God for *google.* I checked the next day because I couldn't live with this. The mere fact that some former Iron Curtin country was trying to muscle in on our beloved turkey would be too much for me. Well, low and behold that bloody, former commie, pinko bastard was wrong. We lead the world, and appropriately so, with more than one and half times the total for all other countries combined on an annual basis. I was shocked, however, to learn that Israel eats more turkey on a per capita basis. Who knew? But let's get back to Thanksgiving.

For most of us it is all about the meal. Some people will go on and on about who makes the best stuffing. I think I have that down with a sausage and sage, cornbread base, with candied pecans in it. It's pretty darned good. Some people go on and on about the mashed potatoes. I mean, who is kidding whom here? We're talking mashed potatoes. What's the big deal with mashed potatoes? Then there are the pie pontificators. I make the best pumpkin. I make the best sweet potato. I make the best banana cream pie. OK, stop right here. A banana cream pie has no place at a Thanksgiving table. This is how chaos is created. No one brought bananas to the pilgrims at the first Thanksgiving feast. I like banana cream as much as the next guy, but here it is just all wrong. It would be almost as absurd as Donald Trump getting elected president. Oh, wait a minute. Never mind.

After all the food is prepared, there is the annual gorging. The average person ingests somewhere between 2700 and 3600 calories at this festive family holiday meal. Considering the recommended intake is 1500 to 2000 on a daily basis, you can see how people are really blimping up at this meal. This is of course is followed by the mandatory carb crash where half the room is sleeping about 20 minutes later either in front of the TV watching the required 3 to 4 football games that are traditional on this day, or for the few truly pathetic, right at their places at the table. Sometimes their heads actually fall right into the mode part of the pie *a la mode*. It is not pretty.

And all during this annual *grand bouffe,* the whole point of "giving thanks" is forgotten. On this one day, we should all ask ourselves: what we are most thankful for; what is it that we are taking for granted that we should acknowledge to each other. If each of us was 100% truthful, we would be going on and on for hours, and we would never get to loosen our belts as the day normally requires. So perhaps we would all be better served if we went around the table and shared with each other 3 things we are specifically grateful for this year. Think about it. What are your 3 things? I have mine. The entire exercise will probably take about 5 minutes before you dive into that drumstick. This year, you should do it for yourself and family or whomever you are thankful enough to be sharing your meal. Heck, a lot of people aren't even fortunate enough to be having a meal, even if it is only at the local soup kitchen or city mission. Make it a point to be grateful this year.

Note to self. Share your thanks with those around you and give thanks for the blessings God has bestowed on you this year.

82. Can I ask you a question?

I can't believe it. It happened again. It never ceases to amaze me. I can be wearing anything, a suit, a tuxedo, and even painter's cloths, whatever; if I am in a store, any store, someone will come up to me and if they are nice, they will ask the above question. If they are a little less polite, they will just proceed to ask the actual question. I was in *Lowe's* the other day. I took 15 minutes off while I was at lunch just to pick up a few household items, and mind you, I am wearing a charcoal grey business suit. Do I look like I work at *Lowe's?* Don't get me wrong, there is nothing wrong with the people that work at *Lowe's.* I think it is a pretty good store and the service is certainly up to par and the staff is reasonably attentive.

But here is the deal. You can spot these guys a mile away. They are wearing bright red aprons that say *Lowe's* on them. By design, they are pretty hard to miss. They don't look like me, who at the time bore a closer resemblance to a fugitive from the set of *Mad Men.* This nicely dressed older lady walks right up to me while I am standing in isle 17 looking at the various kinds of door bells I might purchase and she starts with the lead-in I have described in the heading and without even taking a breath she continues:

"Would you be good enough to tell me where the filters are for the dehumidifiers?"

I am so used to these incessant interrogations whenever I sally forth into the world that I have simply stopped telling people up front that I don't work there. At this point, I have mentally conceded that half the time they wouldn't believe me anyway. I looked at her and inwardly smiled to myself thinking *here we go again.* I compassionately responded. "Now are you sure you need one for a *dehumidifier?* Because most people this time of the year would probably want one for a *humidifier.*"

She smiled back at me and ever so reluctantly admitted that, in fact, yes, that is exactly what she needed. OK, so far so good, I thought and then I lingered a bit, thinking; now which aisle should I direct her to because I wouldn't want to give her any misinformation. After all, I wouldn't want to do anything to tarnish the good name of *Lowe's*

"So, yes, where would I find them?"

I was stymied for a moment and I tried to look this way and that, trying to read the informational signs at the end of each isle. *Electrical*, no definitely not, *plumbing supplies*, possibly; I interjected a quick:

"Now let me think for a moment," but I could see she was becoming impatient. I heard a tiny sigh and hoped it was a respiratory condition and not her thinking she should just demand to see the manager.

"Well, it could be isle 9, or maybe 12."

I was toast. I knew it, but she as yet was still uncertain at my ability to track the illusive object she had requested. It was time to come clean.

"I really want to help you. You have no idea how much I want to help you, but since I don't actually work here, let me ask one of these nice people in the red aprons."

A very knowledgeable and amiable clerk pivoted immediately and told me where she should look and I thanked them. The woman looked at me and afforded a flimsy apology and told me she just presumed I worked there. I smiled and looked at myself in my grey business suit and asked her what made her think that. Her answer made no sense to me at all.

"You just looked like you worked here."

This happens to me all the time. I was on my way to a formal dinner, and I stopped in a bank one day to get some cash since the ATM was OOO (*out of order*; I was trying to baffle you with an esoteric abbreviation.). I was wearing a tuxedo and was all set to step into the line when a customer stopped me and said, "Do you work here?"

Now I have to tell you, sometimes it is difficult for me not to respond like a smart aleck. I warmly smiled as I asked her. "What gave it away? Was it the tuxedo? What do you think of this bank's new dress code? Is it too much, because I think it is really nifty?"

I was in the super market once looking to pick up some hot dogs. I was dressed in really grungy jeans and a ripped golf shirt that I use for painting and a woman confronted me and *insisted* I tell her where the steaks were. I refuse to be accosted. I told her in no uncertain terms that I didn't work there, but quite true to form, she wasn't having any of it. She seriously berated me because I wouldn't tell her. I thought she was going to deck me. Go ahead and laugh. My life was on the line this time. You might think I'm making this stuff up, but I am not. There are eyewitnesses that can attest to this last incident. I just don't get it.

Note to self: Maybe I should simply wear a sign that says, "I DON'T WORK HERE. Don't ask me for help"

83. Often and Early

We have heard the phrase above on numerous occasions. Sometimes it is included on some particular *invitational stems* to make the point that much more humorous. In Chicago, we have heard it as the popular: "*Vote* often and early." Many would argue that there has never been any voter fraud in the United States, but most people from the *Windy City* would tell you that it is simply standard operating procedure there. Their rich tradition in this department goes way back to the Al Capone days and I won't comment as to the current status. Ask someone who loves their famous *deep-dish pizza* and see what they say.

In theory, you should only be allowed to vote once and it should be counted once. But if you are dedicated to obstructing the election process, you definitely want to get out and cast your first ballot early, so that you can move to other polling stations and do the same thing elsewhere throughout the day. How hard could it be? I mean, it is not like anyone is required to check your identification, are they? OK, that's enough about this. I can already hear people out there telling me that this is all in my imagination. Let's move on and look at other places where the principle might be applied.

How about food? Eating often will get you fat, right? Not necessarily. Nutritionists frequently tell us that the *3 meals a day* thing is a bunch of crap. We should eat maybe 5 or 6 smaller meals every day, and in essence, move from meals to something closer to what we call g*razing*. If we are to have separate and distinctly set meals, we should have the larger meals earlier in the day so that we can use our digestion systems that much more efficiently.

Have you ever gone out and had a traditional 5-course, soup to nuts, meal? Have you done it lately? It is insanity. I cannot imagine how people actually used to eat like this. Of course, this was in the day of Diamond Jim Brady and President William Howard Taft. For those non-historians out there, these were some seriously rotund individuals, the latter of whom had to have a special bathtub made for him in the White House. (At well over 300 lbs., he got stuck in the one that was left there by his predecessors.) Eating a giant meal like that, late at night, is both uncomfortable and downright unhealthy, so that *often and early* thing starts to take on a much greater impact, especially if they are smaller meals with high fiber and low fat. Where else does the rule apply?

How about when it comes to sexual partners? Now hold your horses, honey. Do you really want to go here? Well, let's think about it. I have heard all kinds of statistics on this. One survey cited that the average woman has 5 partners over the course of a lifetime and a man around 8. I am not sure where they came up with this scientific evaluation. It is, however, reasonable to assume that you would want to get those multiple partners out of your system *before* you get married. If you are a guy and you get married, having your average of 7 more women to do the deed with, after you tie the knot, might make for some serious complications and a lot of "splaining" to do in divorce court. This is not a good idea.

How about the idea of prayer? If you are a praying sort of person, the "often and early" thing applies wonderfully. What's a better way to start the day then trying to connect with your maker and then to continue to do so all throughout the day? My Muslim friends have me beat on this one hands down. They are up at the crack of dawn and take a serious prayer break another 4 times during the day, and before they go to bed at night. That is both "often and early" and more importantly, consistent, and the best part is, it works really well for them too.

Note to self: "Often and early" is not such a bad idea after all. Well, sometimes it is.

84. Wearing many hats

Many of us have heard a familiar expression that describes a busy person. We say that "they wear many hats." It is a nice way of saying that they are forced to multitask on a regular basis or that they are frequently in situations that require them to be all things to all people. I have even seen funny cartoons of people that have a stack of actual hats on top of their hats to describe their daily plight.

That is not what I'm talking about at all. I wish to consider the man that literally wears a lot of different kinds of hats both for comfort and as a fashion statement. It really makes me angry when I think about how John F. Kennedy single-handedly killed the hat business for men in this country. Most people aren't aware of this. He had a giant melon of a head and he never wore a hat because of it. (Of course, we see him wearing one in the Navy, but that's different because it was a required part of his uniform.) When he was inaugurated President, they had to make a special Top Hat for him since they didn't come in a size 8. He was perfectly comfortable sporting his beautiful mane of thick brown hair and that was more than enough to start a trend, and overnight, men from east coast to west stopped wearing hats. It was a tragedy.

Prior to that, a man finished off his entire look with the perfect crown. He wore a hat that he looked good in, and that made sense, depending on the weather or the occasion. Thank God, we are beginning to see the return of hats on men. The *shaved head* look has become popular these days, but in colder climates most smart guys have figured out that their "chrome dome" is freezing up there.

A great cover up is seen in the *Tilley Endurable* line. A guy I work with who has elected to embrace that *Howie Mandel* look and he wears a *Tilly* and he looks awesome in it. It is smart looking and extremely practical.

I, quite to the contrary, was never swayed by Mr. Kennedy's fashion *faux pas* and always wore a hat. I should confess, it does add to what many perceive as my overall eccentricity. I consistently wear one during the colder months and I still wear hats on rare occasions in the hotter months. Many times, the hat that I pick is more of a cap, but I never wear anything that remotely looks like a baseball cap. If it is a cap, it more likely resembles the rounder, eight-piece variety, usually made of tweed, and something you would expect to see worn by gentlemen in a pub in either England or Ireland. I wear a linen version when I play golf. My slightly rounded face looks good in a cap.

When the snows start to fly, I always get a little more serious and usually sport a trapper's hat. They are almost always made of some sort of faux fur, and I cannot tell you what a difference it makes in terms of my keeping my body temperature where it should be. I sometimes look as ridiculous as George Costanza in his giant furry hat but no matter, if I have the big furry hat on, I hardly need to wear a coat. Some say that 50%; some say 80%, of your body's heat escapes through the top of your head. I have heard every kind of figure imaginable. All I know is, when I have a warm hat on my head, I feel a million times better.

These days, in the dead of winter in Buffalo NY, I have been sporting a Russian Soldier's hat called an Ushanka, complete with the Hammer and Sickle badge in the front, and there is nothing warmer. I think I could go buck naked and just wear this crazy hat and I would be warm enough in it. I don't quite have the moxy, or should I say, that I am not far gone enough, to put that to the test, but either way, my daughter tells me I look like I'm invading a country.

"You look ridiculous," She says.

I merely smile and I profess my love for Putin to her and she simply rolls her eyes at me and dismisses me as her crazy old dad who is getting crazier with each day.

When I'm not embracing the Russian look, I now find that I am doing the Beret thing. I was too young and just missed being a part of the beatnik generation, so Berets were out. Berets are mostly worn today by romantic old men who might be playing chess or feeding the pigeons in Central Park. Now that I'm an old guy, I have to admit, I like the look. It gives me a slight bit of that *je n'ai sais qua* and *savoir faire*. Of course, because I cannot stop at the mundane, I feature Berets in a multitude of colors and I particularly like the *Polish Army* soldier's look which comes in maroon. When I wear that with a maroon scarf, I think it looks especially smashing and my poor daughter, Alice, just rolls her eyes at me again. She says I look like an idiot. Then she takes the hat and puts it on her head and tells me how cute she looks. I must concede she does. But it isn't going to stop me from wearing my hats.

Note to self: A man isn't really fully dressed if he is not wearing a hat.

85. Holiday Moon

I am at a Christmas party, or at what has become more politically correct today, and is referred to as a holiday party, and I go over to the bar and ask for a drink. There is a gentleman standing next to me drinking some sort of festive looking concoction with all sorts of froth and red berries and glitter and I ask him:

"What's that?"

He says, "I don't know, but it's really good. I think it's the special drink of the night."

I finally close in on the bartender and I ask him, "What is this guy over here drinking?"

He boldly proclaims to me, "That's a *Holiday Moon*. It's the special drink for the night."

"A *Holiday Moon*? I thought that was when I dropped my pants down and showed off my butt and said Ho, Ho, Ho, and Merry Christmas."

He was not amused. And the guy next to me explained, "No, it's a Holiday *Mule*. You know, like a *Moscow Mule*. They just throw some pomegranates in it to make it look festive; otherwise, it's the same deal."

Oh, no wonder my joke fell on deaf ears. That got me thinking about all these crazy drinks that people order and the more ridiculous sounding names that get attached to them. How about *Sex on the Beach*? That's a mixture of ingredients that includes vodka, peach schnapps, creme de cassis (or Chambord), orange juice (or pineapple juice), cranberry juice, an orange slice and a maraschino cherry for garnish. Here's the question. How does this complex mixture of alcohol and fruit juices resemble anything remotely like having *sex on the beach*? There is no smell of the ocean and dead fish and sea weed. There is no sand to get into the tiny cracks of your secret orifices. (This last part of having actual sex on the beach never held any intrigue for me personally.) What am I supposed to do here, stick a maraschino cherry up my butt and say?

"Oh yeah, that's how I came up with the name of this drink?"

How about a *Sea Breeze*? For those non-mixologists out there, it is very refreshing cocktail containing vodka with cranberry juice and grapefruit juice. Let me state for the record. I grew up around the waters of the Long Island Sound. Then we moved over to the *South Shore* and my parents' house was actually on a street called *South **Breeze** Drive*, which was bulk headed overlooking *Great South Bay*. So, trust me; I know about some pretty serious breezes.

I have a thorough knowledge of winds which blow more like gales. I have even experienced my own share of hurricanes. What I don't remember, is feeling that not so delightful splash of vodka on my face mixed with cranberry juice (or pineapple juice for that matter), unless it was from an irate girl friend who was tossing a drink in my face. (I was always a gentleman and actually never was christened this way.) I don't recall pressing my face into the wind on the ferry that would take us over to the section of *Fire Island* called *Davis Park* and getting it lathered in the sticky concoction I have described here; sea breeze, my ass. Where the hell do they come up with these names?

Note to self: I won't even ask, "Who the hell was Harvey Wallbanger?"

86. The Road to Perfection

Philosophers and mystics alike have argued for years about the true path to wisdom and just how one can find that illusive *road to perfection.* Eastern sages have promulgated various practices from yoga to T'ai Chi. Even with, or should I say, in spite of the Beatles help, we have seen the rise and seemingly fall of *Transcendental Meditation* as yet another way to find inner peace. In an attempt to seek enlightenment, we have seen monks lock themselves away from the world while others choose to walk amongst us. So called gurus relentlessly pop up at all four corners of the world and the majority see their messages evaporate almost as quickly as they are verbalized. In most cases, that is justifiable, since some of their orthodoxies are downright ridiculous and do little but line the pockets of most of these who frequently are little more than spiritual charlatans and religious snake oil salesmen. We continue to embrace the ever so popular *mantra of the month* and still we find that we are pretty much no better off than we were before and that road to nirvana never seems to get any closer for any of us. What's a fellow to do?

Well, let's think about what it is we are hoping to find on this dusty trail to perfection? I say that it is dusty because so few ever get to actually set a foot on to anything that closely resembles the mythological path at all. Let's break the phrase down and start with the last word: perfection. I'm going to hang a premise out there that will either be accepted by you or not. I think that God, or the Great Spirit or the Higher Power, or whatever you choose to call the creator, has made everything *perfectly.* Many question the purpose of the mosquito and I have serious difficulty explaining the need for this disease carrying major annoyance. This is especially true considering that 50% of all of whom have every lived on this planet have died because of the malaria that is carried by this tiny and extremely annoying buzzing little insect. What possible benefit has this winged pest ever brought us? Who needs a mosquito? Perhaps in His wisdom He has provided us with this miniscule flying monster if for no other reason than to give us a failsafe system for population control. If not, I'm at a loss to determine its value. Nevertheless, I still think it is a perfect creation.

If one looks at a child born with severe physical handicaps, I would go further and state that within the scope of all of the anomalies, that child is perfect, in spite of the challenges it will face. There is a pleasant folk song that shares the familiar lyrics that "everything is beautiful, in its own way…" I believe that sentiment is true. Let's turn and consider the other words, the Path (or the road).

This is a little more complicated. If there is a path, there might be other paths that take you to places other than *perfection*. I think that's true, too. I suspect that if one has actually found a path that leads to *personal* perfection, it must have been easy to stumble along the way. One might stub their toe. Another might fall down several times and not have the strength to get back up or even have second thoughts and decide to reroute. Perhaps the path is always difficult.

Most people understand this and clearly take an easier route. I love what Jesus told his disciples, "Follow me because my burden is light."

So many misinterpret that statement, thinking that He was telling them that the burden wasn't heavy and that it wouldn't be difficult to carry. Quite to the contrary, He was telling them that it was light. It was *light* as opposed to darkness. One can see things so much more clearly in the light, can't they?

The greatest feat to finding the path is recognizing that you have to *choose* the path. Once you choose, you have to stay on the path and that requires a second choice because it is easy to decide to get off the path. The "light of the world" that Jesus brought was a simple choice and he offered a single commandment: to love one another. If you just did that, everything would fall into place. I offer no argument on this proclamation.

The path to perfection, as I see it then, becomes that much more difficult to find because it asks you to accept the perfection of all creation and it further asks you to take a simple action. I would extend the premise one step more and say if you wanted to get perfect at a task or a job or a situation, there is an additional requirement. You always need to choose to work on at least one thing to change that current situation. You cannot get closer to your goal unless you work on changing and improving that which you seek to change. Einstein tells us that nothing occurs in the universe without change and movement.

The road to perfection can only be found by choosing to change and taking action to do so.

Note to self: What am I going to work on today?

87. Hardwood Decking

I was driving in the car and approaching that part of route 5 just outside of Buffalo known as the *Skyway* and I offered my daughter Alice a challenge. Several days a week I will drop her at her office in the Liberty Building downtown, on my way to my office, just north of the city in a place called *Tonawanda*. How's that for another cool Indian name? This part of Western New York is littered with scores of other names that bare homage to our Native American ancestors. We have places named, *Niagara* as in the Falls, (West) *Seneca, Salamanca, Cheektowaga, Canandaigua, Ontario, Cattaraugus, Chautauqua* just to name a half dozen or so.

But let's get back on that *Skyway*. For those of you who are unfamiliar with this route, it is an elevated highway that was built in the 1950s to allow some of the tall freight ships to pass under it so they could get to the various mills that are built all along the harbor. The irony, of course, is that within 6 months of completion, most of the freighters by-passed Buffalo when they opened a better and more efficient route through the Saint Lawrence Seaway. Now, there is a movement to take down the Skyway, so all I can say is, thank God for sound urban planning.

In any event, I was stalled for a day or so writing my book here, so I asked her to give me two words. "I want you to think of any two words that come to the top of your head."

I had to endure a series of lawyer like, staccato exchanges back and fourths, such as, "Why are you asking me this? What do you mean? Where are we going with this? "

She relented and finally came up with "hardwood decking." I am not going to suggest that the choice of these two words implies any personality disorder or unusual mental fixation. This is reasonable, since she went on to further explain that she saw the phrase on a billboard we were passing and she simply read it to me. She also came up with "Outer Harbor," which she saw on another sign, so we will be discussing that next. But let's get back to the decking.

I thought to myself: *Hmm, Hardwood decking?* This would make some sense, since Alice just bought her first house and she is always talking about what project she wants to take on next, endeavoring to make her little *Adobe Hacienda* even more perfect than it already is. For you literalists out there, she does not live in an actual *Adobe Hacienda*. That would make no sense, since she lives in South Buffalo, the city in the Northeast that is synonymous, even in the summer months with the term *frozen tundra*.

We have several conversations about how a nice deck outside her kitchen, would look great. We both agreed that it would be pretty nifty and add considerable value to her house, *Adobe* or otherwise. We have also discussed who would actually be the one to build it and the name Stevie comes up; he lives in the house next to her. He is a great guy and a fabulous neighbor and he also happens to have the most amazing Bostonian accent you have ever heard. He has already volunteered his nephew Bobby who lives across the street. (That's pronounced *Bawbby,* by the way.) Now, I am not sure if *Bawbby* even knows that his hat has been thrown into the arena for this spring time project. No matter; I'm sure he will do a great job on it when the time comes.

As I write this, I think to myself, how lucky I am to have my daughter living across the street from me in the neighborhood that Tim Russert claimed as his parish (Tim was to most people's thinking, one of the finest newscasters NBC has ever had and was absolutely the proudest native son of (South) Buffalo in the last 50 years.) And yes, I live right in the same part of town that he did and it is almost like hallowed ground because of it. He was a super cool guy and the neighborhood that bore him is equally as cool as he was. Sometimes they call this the "city of good neighbors." It has certainly been true for me and I repeatedly tell people that I have lived in a lot of places, but Buffalo is truly the bomb (and South Buffalo which is just 8 minutes to the heart of downtown if you take the *Skyway* is the *MOAB*.) I'll bet you it will be even better when Alice gets *Bawbby* over next spring and he completes that deck of hers. I wonder if she will be using actual hardwoods or if she is going to consider that plastic stuff that is supposed to last 30 lifetimes? Maybe we should ask *Bawbby?*

Note to self: Sometimes it is about a lot more than just hardwood decking.

88. The Outer Harbor

In 1985 I moved to this little town outside of Buffalo NY called East Aurora. By anyone's' reckoning, it was and still is one of the cutest little towns in America. It has a Main street with an adorable *5 and dime* store called *Vidler's* and people from all over country go there just to see it. This pastoral slice of heaven boasts fewer than 10,000 residents and it is so safe that the kids can leave their bikes on the sidewalks outside this famous *5 and dime* (or anywhere in this little slice of time trapped Americana). They just expect that the same bike they left there is going to be there when they come out; and, they don't have to lock them up, ever. I don't think any of the kids even know what a bicycle lock is. Most of the people don't even lock their houses at night. It has quaint little shops and an old-time movie house complete with neon lighting on the marque. Did I mention that it boasts three buildings that are on the *National Historic Register?* Did I tell you that it is where the 14th President of the United States used to live when he first practiced law? For those obsessed with trivia, his name was *Milliard T. Fillmore* and he is famous for being the "Do Nothing" President.

When I first arrived there, it reminded me of *Brigadoon*, that magical little town in Scotland that was simply swept into the sleepy fog of the heather-bound highlands every hundred years. Did I further mention, East Aurora, the place I would call home for the next 20 years or so, is surrounded by lots of horse farms? It is the kind of town that simply doesn't exist anymore. The good news is that unlike Brigadoon, you can actually find it on the map. It is about 20 minutes southwest from Buffalo and it is prettier now than it has ever been. If you ever get the chance to visit, make sure you stay at the Roycroft Inn, which was made famous by its founder Elbert Hubbard, who spearheaded the American Craft movement (and died on the Lusitania.)

When I moved there in 1985, Buffalo was still a city very much on the decline, in spite of its being the second largest city in New York State. Conversely, it had a lot of things going for it. It was the home of the State University of New York at Buffalo. (Since my arrival, the University had grown significantly, as one might imagine.) Back then it still boasted having the largest inventory of historical homes in the United States. It was then and still is the only town to boast 5 Frederick

Law Olmstead Parks in it. There was something else that was praise worthy about this little town in the rust belt. It had this incredible waterfront which was strategically placed on the banks of the smallest of the Great Lakes, Lake Erie. Unfortunately, the harbor no longer played much of a role in freight shipping like it did prior to the opening of the St. Lawrence Seaway and it was considered a liability more than anything else. Eventually, the light bulb went off over the heads of builders and investors alike who saw the tremendous opportunity that lay right in front of them and they started to redevelop the waterfront.

One man can make a serious difference in all of this and that one man was a young congressman named Brian Higgins. He grew up and lived right down the road from Tim Russert; South Buffalo's other favorite son. He kicked the entire waterfront project into a seriously higher gear and now the place that is called *Canalside* (in light of its proximity to the Erie Canal) is attracting people from all over the world. In summer and in winter, it has become a nexus for the entire city.

In the 1990s and even into the early 2000s, developing the waterfront seemed to either be ludicrous or impossible. The Outer Harbor is the last stage of this part of the master plan for the improvement of the Queens City and it is well underway. The USS Little Rock, which is a retired battleship, is permanently docked in the harbor in the heart of downtown, and her successor and name sake has just been launched alongside her.

Let's think about this for a second. This is the first time in U.S. maritime history that such an event has ever occurred and where does it happen? Buffalo. This is significant. This is meaningful. This is without precedent. None of this would have happened if not for the indomitable vision and drive of Brian Higgins. Sure, there were countless others and scores of individuals who had a hand and will continue to be involved with the overall project. But Brian is the guy that stuck his neck out the furthest and got it done. I'm fortunate enough in that I get to include Brian as not just my Congressman, since I live in South Buffalo now; I get to call him my friend. I get to call him my neighbor. When I cross over the Skyway and look down at the emerging waterfront below, I'm constantly reminded that one man can make a difference. As you go through life, be that one person who makes a difference. Be the guy or gal that gets it done. Find that one thing that makes for a better life for all of us and *be there* when you are called upon to act.

Note to Self: Find *your* Outer Harbor and make it happen.

89. The Buffalo Bills

Even for those of you who could care less about professional football, the *Buffalo Bills* are a true phenomenon. They are a team that is a series of extremes and contradictions in a city that is likewise a series of extremes and contradictions. Before we tread into the world of theses polar opposites, let's consider the name. Lots of professional teams have names that make sense or that are at least understandable. We have the *Detroit Lions*, and the *Cincinnati Bengals*. One team is named after a lion and the other after the ferocious Bengal Tiger. We have the *Jacksonville Jaguars* and the *Miami Dolphins* and the *Seattle Seahawks*. There are too many others to list, but here are a few others to help make the point. We have *Giants*, *Jets*, *Titans,* and *Ravens*. They're all pretty simple to understand. On the other hand, what the hell is a *Buffalo Bill?* I know there was a famous character in the old west named Buffalo Bill, but what are *Buffalo Bills?* It is a goofy name.

Similarly, the city of Buffalo itself is a bit of misnomer. Most people think it is named after the animal, but are surprised to learn that some people argue that it is actually named after the French description of the city, or more appropriately, as they called it, *Beau Flueve.* This translates as *beautiful river,* or more specifically, the Niagara River. Unless you live there, or are a geography major, you wouldn't know, that's the river that runs alongside the city. And just a few miles downstream, it winds up going over those infamous "Falls. "You know: the ones where all those honeymooners from yesteryear used to be obsessed with visiting. Now let's get back to that football team with the goofy name.

The *Buffalo Bills* are a team that is all about superlatives. They are the only team to ever go to 4 consecutive Super Bowls. And as most people know, they are the only team to also ever *lose* 4 consecutive Super Bowls. They hold the record for being in the longest playoff drought of any team (18 years.) In 2017, they appeared in (and won) the snowiest game ever played. (Oddly enough, the fans that sat through the blizzard-like and blinding conditions that day absolutely loved being there.) How crazy is that? They also hold the distinction of playing in the greatest *comeback* game in NFL history. It is probably because of all of these idiosyncrasies that they have the most loyal fan base anywhere. It is really quite amazing. But here's the thing. I don't think this would be true in many other cities, but it just seems to make sense in a city like Buffalo.

When the steel mills started closing, Buffalo for the latter half of the 20th century was a textbook example of a city in decline and was forced to deal with enormous population erosion. Up until 2010, one would routinely hear people discuss the "Brain Drain." This referred to the steady stream of young professionals who would graduate from the 30 plus colleges in the Buffalo area and run, and I mean literally run, to seek employment in other cities. If you graduated from SUNY at Buffalo with a degree in business, your professors would actually give you a list of destination cities. Conversely, in 1900 it was the true "City of Light." It was the first city in the world to have electricity. It boasted more millionaires than any city in the United States. With its access at the end point of the Erie Canal and its incredible railway system, it was the gateway to the west. Two presidents hailed from there. One was assassinated there (McKinley.) Another one was inaugurated there (Teddy Roosevelt.) It is the only city that has 5 *Frederick Law Olmstead Parks* in it, and it has the largest inventory of historical homes in the nation.

And just when everyone wanted to count out the city that became famous for *wings* and reasonably corrupt politics and incompetent urban planning, we are witnessing the greatest comeback in the history of cities. It is reminiscent of those crazy *Bills* that came back in the greatest comeback game in NFL history. No one could believe it while it was happening and people still shake their heads in disbelief and amazement when they look at the highlight films. Back in 1993 they came back from a 38-point deficit at the half to win the game (by 3 points in overtime) against the *Houston Oilers.*

Now the *Queen City,* as Buffalo is called, is bouncing back and shocking everyone as well. The waterfront is thriving. The *Medical Corridor* is exploding so much so that it is attracting the watchful eye of doctors and researches all around the world. It is the home of *Roswell Park,* the number 1 cancer hospital in the nation. The downtown, with all those historical homes, has become one of the hottest Real Estate markets anywhere. Only in "chip on the shoulder," blue collar, down and out Buffalo, would you find a team as beloved as those roller coaster ride *Buffalo Bills.* Somehow, they just wouldn't make a lot of sense anywhere else. Perhaps it is because *they are* in a comeback town?

Anyone who watches them play, just kind of knows that they are a comeback kind of team. So even when they do go to the play-offs after an 18-year hiatus, and they lose in the first round, the fans never really desert them. Perhaps, it is because they figure there is always next year and you can never give up.

Note to self: Show some Moxy. Be like those "Bills." You are never out of the game if you keep on playing to win.

90. The Economics of the Fish Fry

Before we get into the economics, regardless of the alliteration of this popular dish, we have to consider the event. The average reader, who doesn't hail from Buffalo and its environs, would think that a *fish fry* is a seafood specialty whereby one expects to be served fried fish. That isn't 100% incorrect. For those that live in and around what many simply refer to as WNY (Western New York), a *fish fry* is more than that. It is an event where working-class families get to take mom and or the Mrs. and the sundry tribe of swinish children out for a relatively inexpensive meal on a Friday night; Guess what's on the menu? It's a practice that started way back during the frugal years of the Great Depression where many of the local bars would attempt to get folks to come in and spend a few extra dollars on a few extra brews. Since there was a strong Catholic population, everyone knew they had to eat fish of Fridays. Fish was still relatively cheap so the saloon keepers got together and they brought fresh fish in from the Atlantic Ocean, and they got it trucked in to the Queen city which was about 400 miles west of NYC.

Virtually all of the fish that was served in the bars was Haddock which appealed to just about everyone (even the non-fish-eating aficionados) since it offered a great source of protein and an extremely mild non-fishy taste. Since capitalism reigns supreme, eventually the various saloon keepers started to try to outdo their competitors and they would include a myriad of extras to entice you into their place instead of yours. They might provide their own specially prepared German potato salad, or French Fries, or Cole slaw, or maybe even some macaroni salad. Throw in a few slices of homemade bread and butter, and a family could really go to town and have a virtual feast. The *Friday Night Fish Fry* became a beautiful thing. After not too long a time, however, high end restaurants wanted to distinguish themselves by not being thought of as "your typical fish fry" place. They might still offer a relatively inexpensive meal on their swanky menus that consisted of fried fish. They might call it their popular *special fish fry*. Just don't think that this was a fish fry joint, that's all, brother.

I am one of those guys who doesn't want all the extras. I just want the fish and the potatoes. Then, it is more like fish and chips for me.

211

Now many will argue with me that I'm missing the best part of the meal. In some of the fish fry places I have visited that is absolutely true. I still don't want all that other stuff. I feel super guilty if they bring the stuff out to me after I have asked them not to include it but many times the chef is on automatic pilot and they can't help themselves. They seemed obsessed sometimes. They just have to throw it on the plate. So here comes the big economic question. Should I pay less for my fish fry because I am letting the restaurant off the hook and they don't have to give me all that stuff that everyone else loves? The answer shouldn't surprise you because it is simple; the answer is NO. If you don't want what we were giving you for free, that's too bad for you. We will not discount the price just for YOU. Many people would presume that that is unfair. To those people I would simply say that is the way it is, and that is the basic economics of the fish fry. This is true about many of the other aspects of life too. The price is the price. If I want to sweeten the deal and you don't want to take advantage of it, well, that's on you too. I don't think it is a difficult concept but I never cease to be amazed at how many people will question the logic of it.

Note to Self: Consider the economics of the Fish Fry.

91. Bring Me the Head of Martin Luther King, Jr.

By most people's reckoning, Martin Luther King, Jr. was a great man. He was a man of vision, and passion, and guts. He was a leader who literally died for his convictions. It is right that he is honored not just by setting aside a special day in his remembrance but by understanding what he said. We would all be better served if we read his sermons more closely and acknowledged the truth he spoke to all of us that cost him so dearly. We might even erect monuments to him. We have done just that in our nation's capital and it has become a place that is visited by many.

In the city of Buffalo, however, there is a monument to him that is an absolute affront to the man himself. If you go there, you will find a park called MLK, Jr. Park. In the middle of it, there stands an 8-foot-tall statue that is little more than a giant head of someone that bears virtually no likeness to either the real Dr. King or the remotest possibility to the man, the myth, or the legend of him. I don't know who it is supposed to be. It is hard to find anyone else who can figure it out either. Even the locals who live there, many of whom are persons of color, simply refer to it as "the Big Black Head." It finally has irked enough people in the neighborhood, so they have started a petition to get the monument replaced. I am not sure how they stood it for so long as they did since the artist originally placed it there, way back in 1983.

Some of the supporters to the work claim that it is an example of artistic expression. "They feel that it was designed to abstractly convey the dignity, strength and power of Martin Luther King and the whole civil rights movement." (*Buffalo News,* 1/16/18) I tend to stand with one of the petitioners who uttered in frustration that, "it could have been anybody and that's not what we are celebrating: anybody." I may not be an art critic, but I looked at this thing and I have to tell you, its bad art. The city of Jamestown, NY recently had to deal with a similar issue. In their case, they hired a sculptor to make a statue commemorating that city's most famous hometown hero, Lucille Ball. It was kind of a monstrosity when it was completed. It bore a closer resemblance to me than it did to the famous comedienne. They noted it immediately and complained about it. 7 years later *Ugly Lucy,* as it became to be known, was replaced. Now, there is a nice new statue of that famous, artificial, redhead (that looks less like a gargoyle.) The folks up in Buffalo, frankly, are just too darned patient. Even if we consider the abstract premise of the original artist, most people who look at the finished product agree, it's a major fail. Let's get it fixed. Now I suspect that Dr. King was probably a pretty humble guy and I don' think he would be rolling over in his grave if he actually saw the current monument. I also think that if he was alive and considered this terrible likeness of himself, he would have to ask. *Is that supposed to be me?*

Come on guys, down with bad art and let's do a better job and get it right the first time. Dr. King deserves to get ahead. Or should I say that Martin Luther King, Jr. deserves to get *a head* that at least looks like him.

Note to self: Let's demand better art.

92. The Obsession with Weather

In most social settings, if you have nothing to discuss, you can always go to the default conversation and talk about the weather. If you are in Buffalo, you can probably get a 20-minute conversation going just about any time on this ridiculously tedious subject. What's that all about? It isn't like it is going to change anything, is it? Here's the screwiest part about this conversation in Buffalo. There are two distinct camps, those who will tell you that that they like the weather in this city and to them, it is great, and those that complain about it all the time.

Let's consider the first group of optimists. They will tell you that there are few places on the planet that can boast a better summer. On this one, I have to whole heartedly agree. The downside is that it's short, but rest assured, you will experience delightful, balmy breezes, with low humidity and they never have had a day that went to 100 degrees. In fact, even with the so-called global warming threat, they might only have a few days there where it actually goes into the 90s. Not surprisingly, the vast majority of homes do not have central air conditioning. Many of the newer houses do, but that is more of a marketing thing than a necessity. Most of the historical homes feature wonderful open porches that are great for catching the breezes that come off Lake Eire and the Niagara River. During the summer there, with rare exception, cross ventilation is more than enough to handle even the dog days.

With regards to the other seasons of the year, those that are in this same camp will tell you that the springs there are fabulous, as well. All will agree that the best season has got to be autumn. Everyone knows that if you want to see the fall foliage you have to hop in your car and go to Vermont, right? To that noteworthy factoid, let's just say: not so fast, buckaroo. Buffalo and a day trip, anywhere for up to 3 hours away, will rival the familiar New England state anytime. Less than one hour from the center of downtown, you can actually be into Amish country and really have a delightful fall drive on a Sunday afternoon.

But then there is winter. The winters in Buffalo are, without exaggeration, legendary. In spite of that, I know a lot of people who like the winters. I happen to be one of them. But I would be seriously remiss if I didn't mention that it snows. It snows a lot. But the amazing thing is that everyone there deals with it. The plows can handle it easily and 6 inches or even a foot of snow in Buffalo is simply considered *a dusting*. Anywhere else it would be time to call out the National Guard.

I would be less than truthful if I didn't share one peculiar thing about the snow, however. Even if you love it, and many do not, everyone at some point will complain about it. Sometimes, I think they whine not so much because of the snow itself; it is just that it seems to get to people after a while, because winter seems to last about 6 months. It actually doesn't, but there are so many overcast days that it leads one to believe that the cold months are going to go on forever. They truly don't. I always figure that once you get to St. Patrick's Day, unless you are in ski country or the higher elevations, winter is pretty much done.

Then there is another thing that makes the weather a major topic of conversation in this part of WNY; the entire area is surrounded by a series of micro-climates. You will hear everyone quoting the same maxim: "If you don't like the weather, wait 20 minutes or drive 20 miles."

It is absolutely true. When I lived just outside of Buffalo in East Aurora, I was on top of a hill. It could be a blizzard there with white-out conditions, and yet, down in the village, just three and half miles away, the sun would be shining and people would be going in and out of the crafty little shops, wearing little more than sweaters. When we had what became known as the *November Storm* in 2014, South Buffalo was buried under seven feet of snow. There was a travel ban for a week. A half mile away on the other side of the expressway (locally referred to as the 190), there wasn't a single flake of snow to be seen, and it was mild weather in the 30 to 40-degree range. There was literally a wall of snow that appeared. On one side, it was the twilight zone, the Siberian tundra, and on the other side, nothing.

Here's the thing that gets me the most. There are people who complain about the winters in Buffalo all the time. They never stop complaining about it. They're angry about it. They hate it. Every time they go off on their relentless tirades about how awful it is, I always stop them and simply ask, "Why don't you move then? If you hate it that much, there are lots of other places you could go to, couldn't you?"

Most of the time, they just stare at me blankly. Once in a while, they will mumble something about their families being there, and well, they just couldn't move; it would be too difficult, and blah, blah, blah. It really frosts me. (OK, I guess that pun was intended.) SHUT UP, already.

Note to self: I just like getting up every day and having weather, any kind of weather.

93. St. Patrick's Day

I'm not sure if it is still there anymore. But on Sixth Avenue, (the Avenue of the Americas) in Manhattan, there was a familiar countdown clock. It digitally counted the ever-growing massive number which is in the trillions now and is known as the National Debt. It moved so fast that the numbers were a blur to most onlookers. Similarly, in many Irish Bars in the Big Apple, you will more than likely see an electronic digital clock counting down the days till St. Patrick's Day. These particular countdown clocks are not isolated to the bars in NYC. They can be found in virtually any Irish bar in America. One such clock decorates the walls of one of my favorite watering holes and it happens to be in South Buffalo.

I am talking about Conlon's in the heart of the Irish Heritage District, just down from the Irish Center. I recently had to explain the concept of St. Patrick's Day to my beloved Marilynn, and how it was kind of a big deal to the Irish, particularly in America. What did a nice Italian girl know about St. Patrick's Day? She probably thought it was about a lot of people *wearing green* and that's about it. No, quite to the contrary, St. Patrick's Day has taken on, for better or for worse, a certain mystique that seems to require an excessive amount of drinking (especially for the younger generations.) Fortunately for me, I'm a little older and this old body cannot quite handle that amount of alcohol consumption. Either way, regrettably, the young folks really like to *pound them*, especially as this very special day.

Now in South Buffalo, this special place I live in right now, right around March the first, the locals think of the approach of what many refer to as *the high holy days*. This has nothing to do with the ending of Lent or the approach of either Easter or Passover. It has to do with getting ready for some serious power drinking on St. Patrick's Day. It is just expected that especially on the day itself, you will get annihilated. Nobody is stopping at the neighborhood saloon for just one Guinness. If they are, it is only because they are stopping there on their way to the next bar which is probably less than a block away. This is the essence of what has become known as the pub crawl. By the time you hit your 6th or 7th tavern, you are pretty much crawling on your hands and knees. Recently, in an effort to keep people safer, there are actually busses that are chartered on the big day. They will make stops at a series of joints for about 20 minutes and allow you to go in and belly up to the bar. This way you can down your drink with just enough time to race back to the bus and you can be ready for the next stop. Would I shock you if I told you there will most definitely be beer and whiskey on the bus as well? This is provided for emergency purposes only, just in case you start to run a little dry. I suppose it is a good thing because at least they are keeping you from being tempted to get behind the wheel of your car and drive off into the night and kill either yourself or some other poor unsuspecting Irishman. Somehow, I think St. Patrick would not be proud to see what has happened to this simple Christian holiday that bears his name.

Note to self: Come on; it's St. Patrick's Day. Let me buy you a drink.

94. The Three Minute Egg Timer

When was the last time you ate a soft-boiled egg? I'm not sure, but I am willing to wager that it has been quite some time. The soft-boiled egg has gone the way of the smoking jacket and the morning newspaper. Who reads a newspaper anymore? Remember those halcyon days when that young lad tossed one at your front door on his paper route. Good luck trying to get a junior high school kid or any kid that age to work today.

We're talking about a time, not that long ago, when the man of the house would sit at the head of the breakfast table and make a big production out of tapping into his perfectly cooked 2 minute and forty-five second egg. There was so much ritual surrounding the whole thing. Back then, there was a reasonably good possibility that the lady of the house or the other erstwhile domestic help would have used the device called the 3-minute egg timer to accomplish the perfectly delivered egg. For those modern master chefs that have become accustomed to using electric timers and meat thermometers, the egg timer was nothing more than an old hour glass timer that had just enough sand in it to measure out 3 minutes. These little *sands of time* devices were amazing in their accuracy, but you will rarely find them being used anywhere today.

A guy I work with has rediscovered an even better use for the tiny forgotten device and it has nothing to do with eggs. He uses it as the ultimate time management system. He keeps one on his desk. Whenever he receives a call, he turns the egg timer upside down. The conversation is going to last no more than three minutes. There is nothing that you can say to him that should last more than three minutes. How many of us find ourselves literally blowing through an entire day and somehow, we would be hard pressed to tell you what we got accomplished. Frequently, we get ourselves embroiled in conversations that deteriorate into the most ridiculous small talk imaginable. Before we have a chance to look at our watches, we discover 25 minutes have gone by, and whatever the problem was, it still isn't resolved. If you do that all the time, you are being extremely inefficient with your very valuable time.

With this guy, when the phone rings or if you walk into the office, the egg timer gets inverted. You have his utmost attention. Once you get to the 2-minute mark, however, he starts to do a wrap up so that he can either answer the question or get enough information so that he can constructively tell you when he expects to get back to you. He might conclude with a thank you or some other closing comment, but that's it, and he is on to the next task or the next call. It may sound cold, but I can assure you it is not. It keeps him focused and on point and forces him to steer clear of small talk as much as possible. Most guys could easily spend 20 minutes discussing how they would armchair quarterback the Sunday game, and it's a lot of fun when one does that. Unfortunately, it takes a toll on your overall effectiveness, and if time is money and you tend to be a bit of a *jabberjock*; man, you could be seriously hampering your value to the team or the organization.

Now in the case in which someone walks into the office to speak to him, he doesn't grand stand and make a big production out of turning the hour glass upside down right in front of them. He has it in a place where they wouldn't necessarily see it and he makes a very subtle move. Come on, dude; he's not a totally barbarian. He is just trying to maximize his time, and yours, for that matter, and the system works. The 3-minute egg timer: who knew?

Note to self: this is something worth trying.

95. Continuing Education

Many businesses and professions require their practitioners to take some sort of continuing education. In some instances, it might not be an official requirement (i.e. to maintain licensure, etc.). In other cases, it might be just something that is recommended for good sound business practice or to simply keep one current on changes within an industry. Either way, to my way of thinking, it's all good. I am a firm adherent to the Confusion maxim that states, "Education is like water running up hill; once it stops, it goes backwards." I do a lot of things and I am constantly learning.

One of the things I have been doing for what seems to be nearly forever (actually 39 years) is Real Estate. As a licensed Realtor in New York State, there is a requirement at this time that every agent take a minimum of 22 ½ hours of additional training every 2 years. In my case, because I have been doing it for so long, I'm considered grandfathered and the requirement has been waved. This doesn't stop me from taking classes. I am constantly taking classes and I go well beyond the minimum requirement that has been waved for me. Since I am a State Certified member of the faculty, I think it keeps me sharp. Not only do I think that continuing my industry specific studies makes me a better teacher, I am convinced that it adds to my value and makes me more knowledgeable in the field. I once read a statistic that asserted that most people wouldn't read another book after they got out of high school. I'm not sure how accurate that is, but I suspect it isn't all that far from being the truth. How tragic is that?

Is it any wonder why conditions in Washington are what they are? We have essentially become a population of morons, most of whom don't vote, and those who do, are watching *the Bachelor* or playing video games. We have become a nation of dolts who have nothing intelligent to say because, as Confucius was implying, the *water is running backwards.*

I'm not suggesting that we become a nation of professional students. I'm not saying we should mandate that people read a minimum number of books every year. That's not the solution. But just because there is so much garbage on TV with the 500 plus channels you can get from your local cable provider, it doesn't mean we must acquiesce and watch the worst of it. There are so many great stations on the boob tube that are not only worth watching, but could actually make us smarter. Take a look at the *History Channel*. Even if you hated history in high school, even if your teacher was an imbecile who thought that *Henry VIII* was just a song by Herman's Hermits, the most boring show on that channel is absolutely, positively, nothing short of fascinating.

If you hated science way back when, during your adolescent years, you need to watch the *Discovery Channel* or the *Science Channel*. You will learn and be thoroughly entertained at the same time. Have you seen the *Smithsonian Channel*? What a wonderful educational resource it is, and you can sit back and wolf down your *Potato Chips* (or read this book) and get smart at the same time.

And all of that being said, it wouldn't kill you to open a book. God Damn it! Too lazy to do that, you can get *books on tape*. I have trouble with this last suggestion only because I would tend to want to use them while I was driving. They're just too good and I would just get too absorbed in what is being read to me. Talk about distracting, I might as well just be texting the *Gettysburg Address* to someone and be done with it.

Oddly enough, I find that when I listen to language tapes, I learn the language and I don't have to worry about driving off the road. The best part about that is that it makes me kind of a cool dude, too. You should see people's faces when I whip out a little Arabic on a person in line at the store. I always get a smile when I throw out a word or two of Russian to someone. Most people don't realize that I am just picking it up in the car. It makes me a lot smarter than listening to old *Beatles* songs. The point is, if we are not constantly learning, something, anything, we are taking a one-way trip to stupid. If that's where you want to go, God Bless You. Please take that trip without me.

Note to self: What am I going to learn today?

96. The Major Benefits of Getting Older

Suffice it to say, that no matter who we are, no matter where you are, we are all going to get older. With the passage of each age, come some good things and some bad things. But ultimately, if we are lucky enough, some of us will actually live long enough and get what is euphemistically called, *older.* Now here's the good news for you senior citizens out there. If you have been smart enough to keep your weight down and exercise regularly, if you have been prudent enough to pay attention to your diet and keep your alcohol intact to a minimum, and have gotten regular checkups with your respective doctors, and of course, if you have a few half-way decent genes, you might be in pretty good condition. You might even be what I might call one of the beautiful people. Take a look a Susan Sarandon, or Sophia Loren. Now I know they have had more than their shares of *nips and tucks,* but these two women are at the time of this writing in their 70s and 80s and they look magnificent. Most of us can't be that lucky. We don't, on the other hand, have to become a bunch of *schlumps and fatsos,* either.

So, let's presume that we have stayed in at least semi-decent condition. We might not be able to run the hundred-yard dash in 10 seconds flat any more, but chances are most of couldn't do that when we were in our prime. Don't sweat the *small stuff,* and let me salute all you baby boomers out there and tell you: here's the greatest part about getting older. Most of us truly get to finally accept the fact that it is all *small stuff.* We become blessed with the gift of *perspective.* That fire in the belly that manifested itself as a lot of *piss and vinegar* when we were young gets to be replaced by wisdom. We get to put things in a better context. We don't have to become like George Costanza's father who kept fruitlessly yelling, "Serenity Now, Serenity Now."

Nor should we want to do that, either. Perhaps we all have to reconcile that we are concerned about this and that, and we will all suffer from a certain amount of daily anxieties. There are a minimum of 30 references to *worry* in the Bible alone. Maybe there is no escape from all of it. The gift of perspective, however, should go a long way to eliminating most of it. In my most jaded like New York manner, I am constantly reminding people that "None of us are going to get out of this alive anyway."

You know what else is kind of cool about getting older? I really have noticed that people are a helluva lot nicer to me. They cut me a good bit of slack just because, I guess, they figure, I am not quite as sharp as I used to be. They foolishly feel almost sorry for me (little do those young *whipper snappers* know.) I chuckle to myself often and continue to take deep solace in the axiom that reminds us that "youth and enthusiasm is no match for old age and treachery."

If you're older, remember to enjoy the ride. Hopefully, you have someone special beside you. At this stage you are not built for speed. You are designed for comfort.

Note to self: Thank God for the gift of perspective.

97. Valentine's Day

Why do I like Valentine's Day? A lot of people, who are less romantic than I am, will argue that it is a goofy made-up commercial holiday that card manufacturers have capitalized on over the years. It doesn't have a lot to do with anything other than making money. Make no mistake about it. An awful lot of cards get purchased to celebrate this made-up holiday. It is second only to Christmas, and nearly 85% of all of the billions of cards sent out each year will be done so by women. It is also a big day for buying chocolate. If you are a florist, don't even think of taking that week off. Well, don't, if you want to stay in business. If you are a restaurateur, expect to have a busy week and make sure you have some sort of Valentines Special on the menu. Jewelers will do well during the two weeks prior to February 14th, too. OK, already, it's a big money maker, I get it. But it is not all about the money.

We could say the same thing then for Christmas and bag that too, couldn't we? Just as Christmas should be a season for bringing family and friends together and thinking about spreading *Peace on Earth,* Valentine's Day should be a special day to acknowledge our sweetheart or someone who is very special to us. I suppose if you didn't have anyone in your life that fit that bill, this particular winter holiday would lose a lot of its impact with you. It is for a similar reason the many people find Christmas depressing. If, on the other hand, you're blessed (and I do mean blessed) and you do have a wife, or a husband or a sweetheart, then bro, have at it. Celebrate it in a big way.

Go to dinner. Buy some flowers. Get a mushy assed card (the mushier the better). Throw in a box or two of chocolates. Here's the deal. We all get busy and it is easy to forget the little things that go a long way to making a special relationship special. I'm not an expert in the subject and I don't know a lot about this *relationship business,* but I have some suspicions. One of them is that if you want to have a wonderful and healthy, deeply committed loving relationship, you can never stop treating it like it's a courtship. When couples first start going out, they tend to be on their best behavior and after a while they get super comfortable and they start farting in front of one another and not keeping up with their regular dating grooming habits. Women tend to start living in sweatpants and men start burping out the national anthem.

Putting it simply: they get sloppy. It's a natural process but a dangerous one.

Valentine's Day gives us a chance to get our acts back together again. Now, God forbid, you're thinking you should wait to do this and you decide to get ship shape only once a year. If that is the case, all the cards at the Hallmark warehouse are not going to help you. Ten thousand pounds of Godiva chocolates are not going to save you either. Valentine's Day should be more like getting a tune up and an oil change for your car. We presume you take care of your car all the time. If you only take it to the garage when it is broken, you are probably not going to have the most satisfying driving experience.

So do the right thing. You should look for opportunities to tell your sweetheart how you feel all the time. We all have heard that it isn't what we know that is important. It is how we make people feel. It is the ultimate truth. On Valentine's Day, you should kick it up a notch and show them (your special someone) how you feel.

Note to self: Hey lovey, pass me one of *dem dere* chocolates.

98. Eat a Snickers Bar

Every once in a while, our friends on Madison Avenue come up with an advertising program that really hits the mark. Over the years, we have seen them deliver characters and slogans that have become iconic in our culture. Some of us remember the *Jolly Green Giant* laughing (HO, HO, HO), and *Speedy Alka Selzer, Mr. Clean* and *Mr. Whipple* and more. Recently our friends over at *Mars Candies* have come up with one of my favorite campaigns based on the premise that from time to time everyone needs to "Eat a *Snickers* Bar." We see almost *Jekyll and Hyde* transformations in people when they eat one of these delightfully, chocolate, little morsels. It's so good. It is like magic.

I have to tell you, I like those *Snickers* bars, but I absolutely love these commercials. This ad campaign truly hits it out of the park for me. Imagine if all we needed to do, if we were having one of those really bad days when we wanted to kill just about everybody around us, was to just eat a S*nickers* bar. How awesome would that be? Unfortunately, I think as good as they are, and believe me I am salivating over the thought of eating one right now, but it might take a little more than that, for most of us, most of the time.

Passing moods are tricky things. I marvel at how we hear some people actually justify extraordinarily bad behaviors because as they go on to explain that they *were in a bad mood.* Making the statement more comical is when you hear them preface it with the phrase:

"You don't understand."

Guess what, you're right, I don't understand. I suppose what you are telling us is that because you are a slave to your moods, and you have no control over your current emotional state, we are simply supposed to not only understand, but are expected to submit to your boorish or otherwise offensive behavior. Sure, I guess that makes sense. NOT.

Listen, schmuck head, if you are having a bad day, I don't care how bad it is, your lack of control over your current emotional state ends as soon as it moves into my circle of influence. If it doesn't, then you are telling me that I too have license to inflict my overzealous wrath on you because (fill in the blanks): My spouse is cheating on me, my dog ate my homework, I lost my job, my house burned down, etc. All of these occurrences are serious issues, and I would expect that I would have compassion for you if you are on the receiving end of any one of them. All of that being said; it still doesn't give you a pass to be a douchebag. You don't get to take it out on me. This is true for you, too, in that I don't deserve a pass either. Bad things happen. I really resent when people try to get a pass for truly outrageous behaviors by trying to explain, "Well, I was drunk at the time."

OK, so you killed a family of 4, you cheated on your wife, you said rude and hurtful things; it's all good. You see if I had known you were drunk, that would have made it all better. It would have been totally acceptable. Do you see how ludicrous that is? Nobody wants to be accountable for their behaviors anymore and we have simply come to accept whatever lamebrain excuse one can come up with today. I think this is, simply put, incredibly unacceptable. Believe me, as much as I love those *Snickers* bars (and I am going to keep on eating them regardless of what anyone says), I'm not sure I can get away with the kinds of nonsense I have described here, just by eating one.

Note to self: You can eat the Snickers bar but, in the meantime, you need to manage your behaviors.

99. Say your Prayers

The vast majority of the people who take up residence on this Big Blue Marble claim to profess some sort of a belief in God or what *12 Steppers* describe as a *higher power*. Whether they are correct in their beliefs is neither here nor there, and everyone gets to find out after they die. That is presuming, of course, that there is that thing called the afterlife. For those that espouse a belief system that extends to a personal relationship with the entity known as God, the next idea that falls into the mix is the concept of communication with Him or Her or dare I say, it? For lack of a better term, we call that prayer. Now here's where it gets complicated.

There are three primary groups that worship or pay homage to a God. There is a fairly large group that directs their prayers to a series of Gods. We refer to this as a Polytheistic system with many gods and with no single god monopolizing his or her power over the others. Then we have a Pantheistic approach. This is a belief system in which God is equated with the forces of the universe. Finally, we have those who believe in a monotheistic, all powerful God. This latter camp takes in all of those that descend from the *Abrahamic* traditions. The first group prays to select gods for this and that and prayers of petition are common. The second group does less in the way of petitioning and more in the way of simply paying reverence to the elements of the universe, and accepting, as they do in the Taoist traditions, and follow "The Way." They show a certain homage to those things that lead to the natural order of things. The third group prays and speaks to their God, directly for the most part, and in doing so, if they are truly discerning, they understand the concept of "all powerful" and accepts it as truth.

Most of the people that I know fall into this latter category. Most of those in this category, however, vary greatly and one hears them petitioning for things all the time. I am reminded of the song called *Soft Parade* by Jim Morrison from *the Doors*. The famous quote, shouted out in this song's preamble says that we can't petition the Lord with a prayer.

This is based on the premise that if God is all powerful, he knows what we need before we even think of it. One of my favorite passages in scripture comes from Matthew 6: 26-34, New King James Version (NKJV).

> 26 Look at the birds of the air, for they neither sow nor reap nor gather into barns; yet your heavenly Father feeds them. Are you not of more value than they? 27 Which of you by worrying can add one cubit to his stature?

> 28 "So why do you worry about clothing? Consider the lilies of the field, how they grow: they neither toil nor spin; 29 and yet I say to you that even Solomon in all his glory was not arrayed like one of these. 30 Now if God so clothes the grass of the field, which today is, and tomorrow is thrown into the oven, *will He* not much more *clothe* you, O you of little faith?

Our Muslim brethren have a more concise way of saying the above with their simple prayer: "Allahu akbar!" or "God is great!" I have indicated earlier in these chapters that I am a truly, died in the wool, Roman Catholic, and, as such, I have been reared on what many consider to be the greatest prayer of them all: (the Lord's Prayer). It reminds us that we should only ask God "to give us *this* day, our daily bread and forgive us our trespasses…" If we get that, we are way ahead of the curve. Many of my recovering alcoholic friends will say it differently: "let go and let God." Christianity is often times thought of as the religion in which you ask for things and magically your God responds almost like a puppet and delivers them for you. Like many, I was raised to ask for this and that. I recall hearing a story when I was a struggling actor. An actor prays and prays.

"Please God; all I want is a *Sanka* commercial, just one measly *Sanka* Commercial."

He prays for this all the time and one day he dies and when he gets to heaven, he somewhat impatiently asks God, "God, I don't mean any disrespect; I mean I was always told you answer all of our prayers. I prayed and prayed and I didn't think I was asking for all that much. All I ever asked for was one crummy Sanka spot. What's the story?"

And God answered him in His all too familiar thunderous sounding voice. "I heard your prayer. I answered you many times. The answer was NO."

Note to self: God knows what we need; He just likes to hear from us from time to time.

100. Hand Sanitizer

Howie Mandel is a famous for a number of things. He is famous for making the following four words, "Deal or no Deal," more than just a household term. They are now part of our everyday vocabulary when it comes to a negotiating strategy. He is also famous for making *baldness* so fashionable that *bald* has become truly beautiful. Because of this, toupee manufacturers everywhere can be heard screaming for his blood as they watch their sales plummet. He has made it much more challenging for them to stay in business. He is additionally world famous for being a self-admitted germophobe. Those that know him can assure you that this is one dude who you are not likely to shake hands with anytime soon. If you are truly one of the fortunate, you might get an extremely reluctant fist pump from him, but that's about the only physical contact you should ever expect from this seriously funny and talented guy. Let's talk about this last peculiarity of his.

Ever since Louis Pasteur came up with his "Germ Theory," people have become increasingly aware of how sicknesses and diseases are spread and many have become obsessed with hygiene and overall cleanliness. Every grade school kid knows that you need to wash your hands before meals. Even if they only do it as a matter of rote or because their mothers have admonished them all too frequently, most of them realize they are washing their hands not just to get them clean. They are trying to reduce the number of germs that will get passed along on to their food, and subsequently then, into their bodies. If everyone washed their hands on a regular basis, we would greatly reduce all kinds of sickness. It is the number one thing we can do to ensure good health.

It is amazing when you think back to surgical practices in the 1800s. People scoffed at Pasteur, who insisted that doctors should wash their hands *before* they attended to their patients. How ridiculous? Everyone knew back then that it only made sense to wash your hands *after* you handled patients, so you could wash *all* of the blood and guts off your hands. In those idyllic times, few things contributed more to the mortality rate in hospitals than the lack of hygiene and the nonexistence of disinfectants. It was standard procedure for a doctor to work on one patient who might have required an amputation (even for infectious gangrene) and then to go on to deliver a baby in the next room. Why would you wash your hands between patients? They were only going to get dirty again. Who knew from germs? Now, more and more people are obsessed with the idea of "picking something up" and have become almost like *Lady Macbeth*. For those non-Shakespeare fans out there, she is the one who became obsessed with washing her hands over and over again, but in her case, she was trying to wash away her crimes, not surplus bacteria.

Today it's not unusual to find anti-bacterial soaps even in public washrooms. We see waterless, hand sanitizers in every supermarket so we can instantly freshen up after handling those germ laden shopping carts. (Make no mistake here; they really are unbelievably germ laden, too.) Have you ever looked around at the people in a typical supermarket? I sometimes think that I should plunge myself into a 50-gallon vat of that stuff after I come out of there. Suffice it say, we have now seen the pendulum of cleanliness swing to the opposite extreme. We have gone from living in actual filth and accepting that as a normal consequence of life, to being obsessed with even a fractional part of the presence of a germ. Those sanitizers, which are predominantly made up of alcohol, are repudiated to kill up to 99.99% of all household germs. That should be good enough for most of us but even with those statistical odds in your favor, Howie Mandel and those like him are not buying it.

I am not sure who is right, but I know one thing: I am using hand sanitizer a lot more than I used to and I even keep the large economy sized bottle on my desk.

Note to self: Maybe Howie Mandel is on to something here.

101. An Incomplete Inventory

I am blessed. Each of us is, and some of us are aware of just how much we are blessed.

I am blessed for the gift of good health.

I am blessed for being born an American.

I am blessed for having wonderful parents who taught me important life goals.

I am blessed for the gift of having the faith of a child.

I am blessed with my devotion to God and know that He loves me.

I am blessed because I want to keep Christmas in my heart 365 days of the year.

I am blessed because I have been afforded a series of talents that I can share with you.

I am blessed with the gift of confidence as well as the gift of whimsy.

I am blessed with a roof over my head and that I get to sleep at night with a full stomach.

I am blessed for being a part of a mildly dysfunctional family that loves me.

I am blessed in that I have a sense of fulfillment in my work.

I am blessed because I have respect for the natural order of things.

I am blessed because I love broccoli. It is good for you.

I am blessed because I am unafraid. The dark still scares me a little.

I am blessed that I have a decent car. It wasn't always that way.

I am blessed for having the advantage of a higher education.

I am blessed for knowing that this education never ends.

I am blessed because I have a daughter who makes me proud.

I am blessed with the special gift of having *le joie de vivre.*

I am blessed because I am *a willing participant.* I never want to simply sit on the sidelines.

I am blessed in that I have done more traveling than the average person and been to many places that most would describe as magical.

I am blessed with the gift of a solid work ethic and doubly blessed in that I have been able to pass that gift on to my child.

I am blessed with my dog Louie. He's the best dog ever and a great ambassador for all rescue dogs. He gets to go to work with me every day and spread a little sunshine when he arrives. How could anyone not love a dog, named Louie?

I am blessed because I have accomplished much and feel like I am just getting started even in my late sixties.

I am blessed for receiving the ultimate backhanded compliment. Somebody once described me as, "you don't have to throw up to look at you."

I am blessed with the love of a special woman who thinks that I am pretty cool and whose face lights up when she sees me. What an incredible blessing that is.

This is such an incomplete inventory and I could fill 10 volumes with all of the blessings I have received. Even if all of those blessings went away tomorrow, I would still have been blessed for experiencing each of them, if only once.

There is a credit card commercial that asks the question, "What's in your wallet?"

Ask yourself, how are you blessed? Your list will probably be as incomplete as mine is and perhaps that's the message here. You might even have gotten to experience some of my same blessings as well. Even if you don't have the gift of good health, it could always be worse and maybe it is OK to say thank God for small blessings. We are all so incredibly blessed. Some of us simply know that we are. Each of us needs to take the time to acknowledge just how much we are blessed. Perhaps my greatest blessing of all is that I am grateful for each one of those blessings.

Note to self: Take the time to admit how much we are blessed.

102. The Profile Picture

With the emergence of Facebook, users have been met with the challenge of establishing what is known as the *profile picture*. This should be a simple enough decision, right? So based on the requirement, one simply needs to get a picture that looks like them and *voila*, you got yourself a *profile picture*. Nothing could be further from the truth. Compounding the surprising complexity of this task, most users seek to change their profile pictures often and some seem to be obsessed with doing it almost daily. Some of my Facebook friends remind me of Lon Chaney Senior. For those non-silent movie buffs out there, he was the guy that earned the appropriate moniker, *The Man of a Thousand Faces*. By the way, they made a bio pic about him with James Cagney in the starring role back in the early 50s. I liked it. It was a good movie and you might want to catch it on *Turner Movie Classics*.

But let's get back to Facebook. Most users seem to think that they should have a picture that doesn't necessarily provide a photographic likeness of themselves. For some, it is more important that the picture used is something that describes how they feel at the moment, or what their hobbies might be. The picture might even show an event that they really enjoyed. The key is here is it doesn't have to look anything like you at all. There is no obligation to do so and some users think that simply putting a picture of them smiling is just boring.

For a while, I was using a profile picture that clearly showed me in a business suit. OK, there was more to the photo than just that. Let me give you the story behind the photo. I happened to go to lunch one day with one of my associates and we went to a nearby Thai restaurant. I was really hankering for a good plate of *Pad Thai* that day, extra hot. I was truly in glee consciousness when not only did I see that the place was filled to capacity with Asians (that's how you know the food must be pretty authentic) but more specifically, they were serving a minimum of fifty Buddhist monks, fully decked out in their official saffron robes. They must have been enjoying the lunch because their chopsticks were flailing at lightning like speed. I reasoned that this had to be an unusually auspicious event. If one visits the Pope, you get a plenary indulgence. I figured that if I was surrounded by all these Buddhist monks it would probably be good for a serious karma cleaning for me and I would have to be good for at least the next 12 incarnations. I became obsessed. I had to have my picture taken amidst them. I was very polite and asked for permission first. Just because I am an American, it doesn't mean that I have to be an *ugly* one, does it? They were quite happy to have me included with them. I immediately went to my computer and made this my Facebook profile picture. The comments were amazing. Most people thought I was in Thailand. In any event, I got a good kick out it and many of my friends seemed to LOL.

After a while I grew tired of that photo. There were a number of reasons that made me think it might be time for a change. As it turns out, I grew a beard for a part in a play. Add to this the fact that it was winter and I also picked up an Ushanka (Russian policeman's hat) complete with the communist sickle and hammer pin on the front of it; suffice it to say, it gave me a whole new style. I looked like a fugitive from the gulag.

I have one Facebook friend who uses a picture of Teddy Roosevelt. I think that's kind of cool, especially since Teddy was one of my favorite presidents. Perhaps he uses it because they share that same "walk softly and carry a big stick" philosophy. Another friend of mine has a picture of him walking along the banks of Lake Erie with a beautiful sunset over his shoulder. Still another has a photo of an eagle with an American Flag clinging from its talons. That sure makes a statement doesn't it? The Facebook photo is more about you than just what you look like. It's kind of like when someone asks about you and you tell him what your job is. Aren't you a whole lot more than just what you do for a living? I would say so and maybe that's the point here. There's more to you than your simple reflection in the glass.

Note to self: Is it time to change my Facebook photo?

103. The Trilogy Minus One

This is the end. The previous book, entitled *Potato Chips for the Soul,* brought you 102 little nuggets of what one might do in difficult situations, and offered some insights into who I am and how I think. In some cases, I simply provided you with some richly deserved whimsy and a chance to get you away from your day to day grinds. As I indicated in the introduction, this *Second Bag* was not so much intended to be the sequel but a continuation and perhaps, simply a bit of more of the same, since many people told me how much they liked what I wrote in my initial foray. I hope you noticed that in this *Second Bag,* I gave you one extra chip to grow on here too. I was careful not to make it a sequel. Growing up near the ocean I have always found those dirty white disease carrying birds both annoying and filthy. Oh, I'm sorry, those are *sea gulls*, no matter, but let me expand on my caution. Sequels are tricky. They almost always fall flat and rarely can they stand alone.

There are, of course, some exceptions to this. Most noteworthy is probably the film, *Godfather II.* Francis Ford Coppola managed to produce a much better story the second time around by skillfully adding flashbacks and following up where the original left off and it did so much better come Oscar time than the original. Then he decided about 15 years later to take one more bite at the apple. I'm one of the very few who liked the last one and thought that it was an appropriate capstone for the trilogy. For me, it completed the perfect tragedy and provided a tale that was not just a story of the rise and fall of an American family. It was a morality play. Most of the critics disagreed with me and said, "Nuts to that."

So, consider this book, a trilogy minus one. I hope you enjoyed some of my tales of woe, and my otherwise ravings and ramblings this time around. After I wrote the first book, I had several fans come to me and they said they liked this story and others said they liked that one, but there was one that seemed to stand out the most. It was the chip that I called *Use the Good China.* If you didn't read it, and you should be drawn and quartered if you didn't, it explained how I like to use my mother's good china every day. It was based on my belief that it doesn't make a lot of sense to save it for special occasions. Every day is a special occasion. Isn't it? Who's better than me? If you are sitting down with me for a quick meal, it is you that makes the event that much more special. We may never get the chance to do this again. A safe could fall on my head tomorrow and what happens then, the good china gets stuck in a box and maybe it never gets used ever again, or worse, it winds up at a garage sale. I remembered serving my mother a sandwich and she gurgled with delight when I served it on the good china that she gave me just before I left home. It made her feel special. She even said, "Wow, you took out the good china just for me."

I winked at her. "Come on Mom, who's better than us?" It made her extra happy and added to that ever present, impish, twinkle in her eye. Those of you who are more frugal might criticize me and warn that I should be particularly careful because I might break a piece (of the good china) and then where would I be. I hear you, but I want you to know on this count you are almost too late. I have very few pieces left because I am a klutz. But every time I use one of those adorable little plates, it makes me think of my mother. It brings an inner smile to my soul. When the last piece is gone, it will be gone, but I will still have the warmest of memories and the kindest of thoughts for my mother because of them.

My daughter Alice has now left the house and gone out to seek her fortune as a young attorney freshly admitted to the bar, and I could not be happier or prouder of her. I gave her something special just before she left, her own set of good china. It is really a pretty pattern and looks terrific in her new house. I hope that she uses those plates often (even every day) and that it makes her meals look better when they are served on them. Maybe she will think of me when I am gone and how much we enjoyed cooking together. Perhaps eating off of them will remind her how we two relentless foodies would blow up my kitchen making those sundry delectables together.

Each of us goes around once in this life. It is only prudent to save in general. It makes sense to be careful with those things to which we assign a special intrinsic value. But as much as all of that might be true, perhaps you too need to look in the mirror sometime and ask yourself the same question that I was forced to ask myself. "Who's better than me?"

I hope you have enjoyed these 103 essays revolving around life, liberty, and the pursuit of your personal happiness. Don't look for a third bag of chips because as Porky Pig told us:

"...that's all folks."

Note to self: Now what I am going to write about?

CPSIA information can be obtained
at www.ICGtesting.com
Printed in the USA
BVHW082015070519
547681BV00002B/3/P

9 781945 181580